THE DEVIL'S BIRTHDAY

The Bridges to Arnhem, 1944

Geoffrey Powell

Foreword by
General Sir John Hackett,
GCB, CBE, DSO, MC, MA, BLitt., LLD, DL

FRANKLIN WATTS   NEW YORK   1985

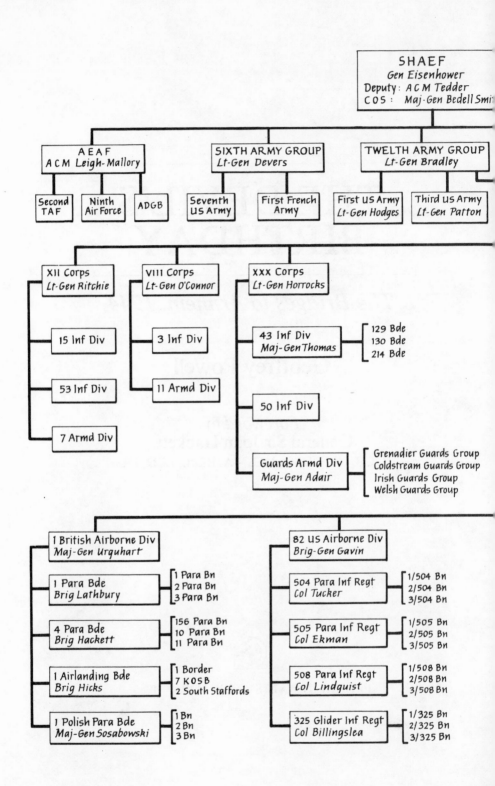

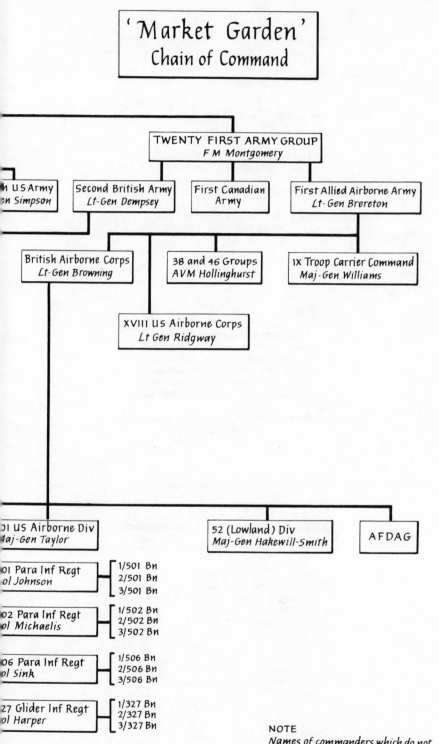

'Market Garden'
Chain of Command

TWENTY FIRST ARMY GROUP
F M Montgomery

h US Army
en Simpson

Second British Army
Lt-Gen Dempsey

First Canadian Army

First Allied Airborne Army
Lt-Gen Brereton

British Airborne Corps
Lt-Gen Browning

38 and 46 Groups
AVM Hollinghurst

IX Troop Carrier Command
Maj-Gen Williams

XVIII US Airborne Corps
Lt Gen Ridgway

01 US Airborne Div
Aaj-Gen Taylor

52 (Lowland) Div
Maj-Gen Hakewill-Smith

AFDAG

01 Para Inf Regt
ol Johnson
- 1/501 Bn
- 2/501 Bn
- 3/501 Bn

02 Para Inf Regt
ol Michaelis
- 1/502 Bn
- 2/502 Bn
- 3/502 Bn

06 Para Inf Regt
ol Sink
- 1/506 Bn
- 2/506 Bn
- 3/506 Bn

27 Glider Inf Regt
ol Harper
- 1/327 Bn
- 2/327 Bn
- 3/327 Bn

NOTE
Names of commanders which do not appear in the text are not shown

Copyright © 1984 by Geoffrey Powell
Foreword copyright © 1984 by General Sir John Hackett

First published in 1984 by Buchan & Enright, Publishers, Limited

First published in the United States in 1985 by Franklin Watts, Inc.,
387 Park Avenue South, New York NY 11016

Printed in the United States of America
6 5 4 3 2 1

Library of Congress Cataloging in Publication Data

Powell, Geoffrey.
The devil's birthday.

Bibliography: p.
Includes index.
1. Arnhem, Battle of, 1944. I. Title.
D763.N42A7375 1985   940.54'21   84-29128
ISBN 0-531-09791-9

CONTENTS

ILLUSTRATIONS

Nijmegen road bridge, the day after its capture (*IWM*)
A badly wounded 82nd Division soldier in Nijmegen (*US DoA**)
Browning and Dempsey visit Gavin (*IWM**)
XXX Corps transport in Valkenswaard (*IWM*)

Following page 212

Maj-Gen Stanislaw Sosabowski (*AP*)
1 Polish Independent Parachute Brigade parades its colours (*Sikorski Institute*)
British armour on a Dutch road (*IWM*)
Air re-supply to 1st Airborne (*IWM*)
Soldiers try to attract pilots' attention (*IWM**)
Supplies that did reach the perimeter (*IWM*)
One of the 75mm air-transportable howitzers (*IWM*)
British troops at the Hartenstein, 23 September (*IWM*)
A wounded paratroop in the perimeter (*IWM*)
German soldiers attacking towards Oosterbeek (*AG**)
Captured British soldiers at the MDS crossroads (*AG**)
British prisoners are marched off (*AG**)
Men of 1st Airborne who escaped (*IWM*)
The unofficial monument near Oosterbeek (*IWM*)
The commemorative ceremony in Oosterbeek, September 1946 (*AG**)
'We have no regrets' – Urquhart returns (*AP*)

* Illustrations marked with an asterisk were kindly supplied by Drs Adrian Groeneweg, the Director of the Arnhem Library.

MAPS

Drawn by Neil Hyslop

'We have no regrets'

Major-General R.E. Urquhart, CB, DSO
*The concluding words of his official
report on Operation 'Market'*

FOREWORD

by General Sir John Hackett, GCB, CBE, DSO, MC, DL

A striking phenomenon in military commentary in our time upon World War II, high in volume and still rising, has been the attention given to Operation 'Market Garden'. What we loosely call in Britain the battle of Arnhem and in the Netherlands they refer to as the battle of Arnhem-Oosterbeek was a major part of this. The reasons are not hard to find. 'Market Garden' was a bold attempt to bring the 1939-45 war to an early conclusion. It embodied the first, which may well be the last, use of large formations of airborne troops in a role uniquely their own. It offered the first real glimpse of a hope of liberation for a brave and peaceful nation from Nazi rule. It was carried out by airborne soldiers and, as these were a true élite in every proper sense of that much misused word, it brought forth a display of fighting skills, fortitude, courage, endurance and compassion not easily matched elsewhere. It was acted out on a stage set apart in some detachment from the main theatres of continuous action in World War II, as the Dardanelles operations were in World War I, and like them has invited study as a complete whole, in its own right. It was, moreover, so fully packed with action, drama, miscalculation and mischance as to offer an absorbing field of study which is by no means yet fully exhausted.

Here is another book about these events, worth careful attention for several reasons. The first is that the author was a fighting infantryman, a company commander in a battalion as good as any

1

in the whole action. Geoffrey Powell had a company in 156 Battalion in my own parachute brigade and brought the remnants of the whole battalion out from the long agony of Oosterbeek with high panache. We shall come back to that.

The second reason for looking seriously at this book is the rarity of lucid and informed comment on the whole untidy business of war, and above all on these operations in particular. Were they justified? Were they successful, and if so in what degree? If they were not successful why not? Could the use of British airborne troops, at this stage in the war, have been avoided? Can you lock up some of a nation's finest fighting men in wartime in a chest you cannot broach, except in dire emergency? Was this a dire emergency? Is it sensible, when good fighting men after years of war are scarce, to do this anyway? These are some of the questions to which answers are still sought. To those who ask them this book will be of help.

Thirdly, I do not myself know of any book written on our side of the Atlantic which has yet done anything like justice to the performance of those two magnificent formations, the 82nd and 101st US Airborne Divisions. We in Britain talk about Arnhem and sometimes forget that the hardest and the longest pounding, with the worst casualties, took place not around the Arnhem bridge, vital though that was, but in Oosterbeek a few miles away. We talk about the splendid performance of the men in our 1st British Airborne Division, which was indeed beyond all praise, and forget the Americans. What was left of us came out. The Americans stayed on, when the drama of the airborne carpet to end the war had been played out. They had already done magnificently but were kept in the line for a long time yet. Geoffrey Powell's book does a measure of justice here which is long, in British writing, overdue.

I come back to the author. This was a great fighting man in a great tradition, that of the company officer in a British county battalion of the line, competent, courageous and self-effacing. I saw a good deal of Geoffrey Powell in the last stages of that grim battle in the battered houses and sad groves of Oosterbeek, when he was commanding a little mixed force which included the few men still in action of his own battalion. I rather think I irritated him a little once, though he was too courteous to suggest it at the time, when I protracted a conversation conducted in the open rather longer than the enemy's fire made healthy. But we had each other's confidence and that is what makes battle fighting possible. His was a splendid performance which I shall always admire. It did not end when the remnants of my own parachute brigade, of which this was pretty well the last company commander in action, was withdrawn across the Rhine on the night of 25 September. You will read in these pages that after the rain-soaked, shell-stricken crossing over the swirling Lower Rhine that night, when the men who came through were being brought together, one company, all of fifteen strong, formed up in style and marched off with sloped arms. They were withdrawn but undefeated. What the author does not tell you is that this 'company', with pretty well all that was left of the whole battalion in it, was his own. It was Geoffrey Powell, the author of this book who brought it out like that.

PREFACE

It is all but impossible for a writer to eradicate personal bias completely, however hard he or she may try to do so, and however closely the available sources have been studied. It is, therefore, important that I should make clear the influences which may possibly have produced bias in this book. Without doubt, the most important is that I served in Operation 'Market' as a company commander. It was a battle in which I lost many close friends, one of whom was especially dear to me. Secondly, I have always profoundly admired the achievements of the late Field-Marshal Lord Montgomery, even though I saw and listened to him only from afar: he was the man who conceived the operation. Last, I have worked and studied with officers of the United States Army over the years. My respect and liking for them is considerable.

I have received unqualified help from nearly everyone who I approached. That they did assist me does not mean that they will all concur with everything I have written. Some will disagree, possibly vehemently, about some of the conclusions I have reached. This is inevitable if I were to try to tell an honest story, but I hope that I will not have caused anyone needless pain. It has been impossible to avoid dwelling upon what went wrong in the battle, and I have certainly laid myself open to the accusation of being wise after the event. To defend myself, I can only quote the author of the report of the part played by 38 Group, Royal Air Force, in the operation. 'Wisdom after the event', he wrote, 'is the precise aim of any record of lessons learned.' The lessons were learned forty years ago, but

4

they concern the way people behave under stress, both physical and mental. Perhaps some may still be relevant today.

Outstanding among the many people who have helped me in the writing of this book has been my friend, Drs Adrian Groeneweg, the Direct of the Arnhem Library. As well as spending long hours extracting information from both his personal and his official archives, he has provided me with the benefit of his encyclopedic knowledge of the events of the autumn and winter of 1944. His advice, so wittily and modestly offered, has always been sound, and he has been especially generous in letting me have prints from his extensive collection of photographs. As well as discussing the battle with me, Major-General R.E. Urquhart has been kind and trusting in lending me his personal papers for over eighteen months; Sir Edgar Williams, Major-General J.D. Frost, Brigadier G. Taylor and Colonel John Waddy have also loaned me papers as well as providing advice and information. Among others to whom I am grateful for helping me in a variety of ways are Mrs Ellen Belchem, Colonel R.G. Collins, Mr Leo Cooper, Lieutenant-Colonel D.E. Crawley, Mr John Fairley, General James A. Gavin, Major-General R.F.K. Goldsmith, Mr Nigel Hamilton, M. Stephen de Prémorel Higgons, Mr Richard Lamb, the late Mr Ronald Lewin, Brigadier C.B. Mackenzie, Mevrouw Jeanne M. Melcheks, Mr J.H. Money, Brigadier E.C.W. Myers, Dr D.E. Olliff, the late Professor John Pringle, General Sir Charles Richardson, Mr Peter Robinson, Mijnheer Joop Sieperman, Brigadier J.O.E. Vandeleur, Mijnheer Robert Voskuil, Mevrouw Kate ter Horst, Brigadier A.G. Walch, Colonel Graeme Warrack, Mr Philip Warner and Colonel Carel Wilhelm.

As always, libraries and other institutions have provided me with unstinting help. My thanks are due to the Regimental Museum of the Border Regiment and the King's Own Royal Border Regiment, the Chipping Campden Branch of the Gloucestershire County Library, the London Library, the Air Historical Branch (RAF) of the Ministry of Defence, the Doctrine Retrieval Cell of the Ministry of Defence, the Liddell Hart Centre for Military Archieves, King's College, London (for the use of the Alanbrooke Papers), the Institution of the Royal Engineers, the Regimental Headquarters of the Royal Green Jackets, the Sikorski Institute and the Robert F. Simpson Research Memorial Centre. Particular mention must be

5

made of the Airborne Museum at Oosterbeek (especially for the loan of photographs), and of the Royal United Services Institute for Defence Studies for allowing me access to material from their 1978 seminar on the Battle of Arnhem and for help generally. Mrs Tineke Pugh and Mrs Rosanna Viita were kind enough to help me in the translation of documents, as was Major Lorys of the Sikorski Institute.

Four other persons deserve special mention. My old brigade commander, General Sir John Hackett, was generous in finding the time in an over-busy life to read the typescript, to criticise it incisively, and to write the Foreword. Mr Charles Boydell was all that an able research assistant should be – assiduous, imaginative and cheerful. Mr Toby Buchan, my publisher and editor, provided far more encouragement and detailed assistance than any author could reasonably expect. And lastly, my wife shored me up in her usual unselfish way, as well as reading and amending two of the many drafts.

Never to be forgotten are the words on the memorial to the dead of 21st Independent Parachute Company. It stands in Oosterbeek, at what was to be known as the 'MDS crossroads', and the words read: 'To the people of Oosterbeek who suffered so much to give their support'.

The author and publishers are grateful to the following for permission to quote from material which is copyright:

Mrs Ellen Belchem for extracts from the correspondence of the late Major-General R.F.K. Belchem; General James A. Gavin; Major-General A.G.C. Jones for the extract from his letter to the Royal Engineers *Journal*; Major-General R.E. Urquhart; Messrs Leo Cooper Ltd and Messrs Sidgwick & Jackson Ltd for material, respectively, from *A Full Life* and *Corps Commander* by Lieutenant-General Sir Brian Horrocks; The United States Department of the Army for extracts from *The Siegfried Line Campaign* by Charles B. MacDonald. Other valuable works have been *The 43rd Wessex Division at War* by Major-General Hubert Essame (William Clowes, 1952); *The Brereton Diaries* (William Morrow, New York, 1946); *The Grenadier Guards in the War of 1939-1945*, Volume I, by Nigel Nicolson and Patrick Forbes (Gale & Polden, 1949). Transcripts of Crown Copyright material in the Public Record Office appear by permission of the Controller, Her Majesty's Stationery Office; material from the Alanbrooke Papers by permission of the Liddell Hart Centre for Military Studies, King's College, University of London; material from the 1978 Seminar on the Battle of Arnhem by permission of the Director, Royal United Services Institute for Defence Studies. Details of books and documents listed in these acknowledgements will be found in the Notes and Sources, as will details of other works consulted.

6

INTRODUCTION

Overhead, two parallel lines of Bofors shells scored the sky. Fired from the far side of the river, the red tracer gave direction to the long lines of soldiers stumbling down through the woods, past the broken houses to the water. There boats should be waiting for them.

In one hand each man held the loosened tail of the airborne smock of the soldier ahead of him, in the other he gripped his weapon – rifle, Sten or Bren, or a German Mauser picked up during the battle. Filthy, haggard faces had been further blackened with soot, nailed boots muffled with strips torn from curtains or blankets, loose equipment tied down to avoid it rattling. When the news had come through that they were to withdraw south of the river that night, a few had found razors to scrape away a week's stubble. It was a final gesture of defiance, futile but proud.

For days these soldiers had fought within an ever dwindling perimeter, cursing the troops who had failed to arrive to relieve them. They had been told that the link-up would occur about two days after they had first landed, but except for a few Polish paratroops and infantrymen of the Dorsetshire Regiment, no one had come. As hope had drained away, annihilation had seemed even more certain. At no time, however, had the exhausted and starving men, fighting from their slit trenches in the woods and once-trim suburban gardens, expected an order to pull out. So, when the news arrived, many had responded with rage. For the few bemused survivors of the units which had landed west of the Dutch city of Arnhem more than a week before, to leave in this manner was to

7

abandon all they had fought for. The loss of their friends had been pointless. The battle had been just purposeless waste. But relief had quickly replaced the rage, relief at the unexpected chance of survival if they could succeed in getting away. Many judged the odds to be poor. With Germans shooting at them from the next-door house, or waiting for them in the woods, the chances of reaching the river unheard and unseen seemed to be meagre.

The rain helped them. No more than a thin drizzle when the first troops left their positions, it quickly developed into a harsh downpour, trapped by thirsty men in open mouths as they stumbled along. To the noise of the storm was added the din of the bombardment from the British guns across the river, hammering the Germans around the perimeter, and forcing them to crouch for shelter. Then the German guns and mortars opened up as well.

Glider pilots directed each small party along one of the two routes that they had reconnoitred during the afternoon. In order to help keep direction, difficult sections had been marked with parachute cord or tapes tied to the trees, while overhead the tracery of the Bofors shells bisected the sky. Soon after the withdrawal began, the Germans heard the noise of the outboard engines, but it was midnight before they realized that the British were abandoning their positions, and not staging a fresh assault across the river. Blazing houses and flares fitfully lit the dark woods and streets; streams of red tracer bullets appeared to float lazily across the sky. Away to the west, the glare from a burning factory outlined the high ground of the Westerbouwing ridge.

Whenever one of the guides stopped to check his route or clamber over an obstruction, the line of men behind him jerked to a juddering halt. Columns split, small parties became detached and veered away towards the encircling Germans. Men came face to face with grey-clad figures. Spandaus rasped, and soldiers fell, some to be left where they lay, others to be dragged on towards the river by their comrades. But there was little panic, and the spent men trudged on past the debris of war, the shattered church, the body of a Dutch girl sprawled across the path.

As the troops neared the river bank, their way lay across flat meadows, cut by steep-sided ditches through which they floundered waist-deep, until suddenly the river was ahead of them, the Neder Rijn, seen now by many for the first time. Its width shocked them.

8

The far bank, glimpsed for a moment in the light of a flare, was a long way off across the dark, rushing water. Enemy shells and mortar bombs raised spouts of spray, and tracer indicated the machine-guns enfilading, from both flanks, the 600-yard stretch of river bank from which they were to embark.

Boats were scarce and became scarcer as the night dragged on. The flat, punt-like storm boats, with their outboard engines, were robust enough, but the canvas assault boats, propelled by paddles, were too often carried downstream. Some were hit and sank, their passengers struggling in the grey water for a short time until they too went under. On the north bank, the queues lengthened. Once, panic erupted, and men rushed the boats, but officers quickly restored order. The patient waiting continued.

When the German realised that the defenders were withdrawing, they sent out fighting patrols to harry the retreat. The plumes of spray and spattering of bullets on the water grew more dense, while mortar bombs, dropping along the river banks, threw up blankets of mud from the soggy polder.* The current quickened with the heavy rain, and the crews of the assault boats had to be increased, first to six and then to eight men.

When one of the boats reached the far bank, its passengers heaved themselves out of it into the water, and then pushed it back into the stream to start yet another journey. It was no place to linger, but often the men paused to shout a word of thanks to the crew before making for the high dyke they could see ahead of them, 200 yards away. Scrambling up its steep face, they tumbled down to the comparative safety of the far side. It was as though a curtain had dropped behind them. They were alive.

Guides were waiting to direct them to Driel. Short though the distance was, it was hard to summon up the strength and willpower for this final challenge. Some men shambled off down the path in twos and threes. Others collapsed after a mile or so by the side of the track. But most, clinging to the life-line of their discipline, kept together in their groups, some even marching in step. One fifteen-man strong remnant of a parachute battalion arrived at Driel marching to attention in threes, with their rifles at the slope, just as if they were returning to their barracks in England: it was disciplined

* Low-lying, flat reclaimed land.

9

pride of this calibre that had kept them together through the eight-day battle.

In the hot and crowded schoolroom at Driel the stench of wet, filthy clothing and bodies was overpowering. Mugs of tea, well laced with rum, were thrust into outstretched hands, but the plates held no more than minute quantities of the hot stew; it was not that there was any shortage of food, just that the doctors had advised of the danger of overburdening starving stomachs.

On the next day the roll-call was taken. Of some 10,000 officers and men who had been dropped by parachute or had landed by glider north of the river, less than a quarter answered their names. The two parachute brigades had brought back little more than 100 men each. Among those who had returned there was a deep sadness, but few regrets. They had been given a job to do and they had done it: their 1st Airborne Division had been ordered to hold the Arnhem road bridge for forty-eight hours, and this they had accomplished.

But, over the years, many have wondered how it all happened as it did, and why it had to happen at all.

CHAPTER ONE

'COINS BURNING HOLES IN SHAEF'S POCKET'

Before the invasion of Normandy in June 1944, General Dwight D. Eisenhower, the Supreme Commander of the Allied Expeditionary Forces in North-West Europe, had been badgered by his superiors in Washington about the way he should use his American and British airborne divisions. The concern was perhaps understandable. The resources, both in men and in hardware, that the two Allies had committed to this radical form of warfare had been vast. By the end of August that summer, Eisenhower had under his command in Europe twenty-five infantry and thirteen armoured divisions, more than half of them American – two million men in all. In addition, he had five airborne divisions, three American and two British, together with an independent Polish parachute brigade and a British air-transportable division; organised as the First Allied Airborne Army, these formations were the only strategic reserve the Supreme Commander had at his disposal, about one-sixth of his total fighting strength. And, so far as the British were concerned, their three divisions were all they still had available to commit to the battle. The flow of fresh American formations across the Atlantic was still in spate, but Britain's reserves of manpower had been exhausted after five years of war.

During the late 1930s, Russia and Germany had developed the concept of landing troops by glider and parachute in the rear of an enemy, but Germany had demonstrated its feasibility during the invasion of the Low Countries in 1940, and again at Corinth, during the Greek campaign, and in the invasion of Crete in 1941. But to some American officers it had been a matter of pride that their army had first conceived this novel form of warfare: in October 1918, Brigadier-General 'Billy' Mitchell had gained acceptance of a plan to drop the larger part of an infantry division behind the German lines at Metz, and he had given the task of working out the details to a young staff officer by the name of Lewis H. Brereton. The Armistice of November 1918 had overtaken events, and post-war financial stringency had limited the development of the idea to a single small experiment in 1929, even though it possessed just the novelty to appeal to the American imagination. So it was that the successful use of this new weapon in Belgium and Holland by the Germans stimulated not only Winston Churchill, but also the United States War Department into raising and training airborne formations. General George C. Marshall, the US Chief of Staff, believed that airborne forces offered a simple method of breaking the tactical deadlock in the ground battle, the hallmark of twentieth-century warfare until 1940. Equally enthusiastic was General 'Hap' Arnold, the commanding general of the United States Army Air Force, his attitude being in marked contrast to that of most of the British air marshals, faced as they were with the problems of defending the United Kingdom from attack, carrying the bomber offensive into Germany, and providing tactical and strategic support for the ground forces in all theatres.

Brigadier Orde Wingate's first and brigade-sized long range penetration into Burma in February-March 1943, when the Chindit columns had been fully supplied from the air, had especially impressed Arnold, although the boldness and imagination of the operation had concealed the fact that it had been a costly failure, lacking any tangible return except for the boost to morale produced by the discovery that the Japanese could be tackled in the jungle. Churchill, however decided that Wingate would accompany him to Quebec in August of the same year for the planning conference with President Roosevelt, and there the young brigadier was provided with the opportunity to propound his plans for a second and glider-borne incursion at division strength, and to obtain the unique luxury of his own private and self-contained American air force, not only to carry his force into battle, but also to protect and supply it.

Although some purists have refused to acknowledge the Chindits as airborne troops, it was this so-called 'strategic' use of the new arm, the 'vertical envelopment' of the enemy, to use the jargon of the time, that had impressed Arnold, and Marshall as well. During the planning for the Normandy invasion early in 1944, both men had become concerned because Eisenhower's staff officers limited their plans to using the available airborne divisions to protect the flanks of the bridgehead from counter-attack. Arnold visualised something much bolder, the use of the airborne troops to strike well behind the German lines, aiming for the enemy's reinforcements and supplies. Marshall was of the same mind. When, in February 1944, he sent staff officers to London to suggest a plan for forming an airhead of three airborne divisions south of Evreux, some ninety miles from the invasion beaches, Eisenhower refused, understanding full well the vulnerability of lightly armed airborne forces to armour, and their all but complete lack of mobility once on the ground. Insisting that the first task of the Allies was to establish themselves on the Continent and seize a port, the Supreme Commander had countered with sound argument Marshall's emotive contention that 'The trouble with this plan [to land airborne forces near Evreux] is that we have never done anything like this before, and frankly, that reaction makes me tired'. Eisenhower, diplomatic as ever, assured his senior that 'I instinctively dislike ever to uphold the conservative as opposed to the bold'. Needless to say, the commanders of both British Twenty-First Army Group and US First Army (the forces that would bear the brunt of the invasion), General Sir Bernard Montgomery and Lieutenant-General Omar N. Bradley, stood firm in support of their Supreme Commander.

Eisenhower's position was none too strong, for he had in the past shown little enthusiasm for the new airborne arm. After the invasion of Sicily in July 1943, when most of the British and American airborne troops had been put down by raw transport pilots wide of their targets, some of them in the sea, he had declared to Marshall that he 'did not believe in the airborne division'. It was easy, therefore, to see why Arnold should have pressed Eisenhower so hard to make good use of the vast resources the US Army Air Force had invested in transport aircraft, men and material that might otherwise have augmented the strategic bomber force, the arm that many of its supporters still believed could win the war on its own.

The formation of the First Allied Airborne Army on 8 August 1944 owed much to this pressure from Washington. In any case, there was a clear need for a single commander to control the airborne divisions, both American and British, and the transport aircraft which would carry them into battle, as well as to plan operations and attend to co-ordination with the ground force commander under whom the airborne divisions would be placed for any particular operation. But, by early August 1944, the affairs of airborne forces were somewhat in the doldrums. US 82nd and 101st and British 6th Airborne Divisions had been used in the invasion of Normandy, and had been kept in France to fight on as ordinary infantry while British 1st Airborne Division had remained in the United Kingdom, suffering the frustration of being briefed for one operation after another, each one of which was in its turn cancelled. The feeling was growing among some of the planning staffs concerned that the game was hardly worth the candle. The unpredictability of the weather in North-West Europe, when matched with the diversionary effect that each planned airborne operation had upon other air operations, made it necessary to have contingency plans available in case the airborne side of an operation could not be launched. The effect was to turn each airborne plan into a 'bonus', rather than its being the keystone of an operation. In many respects, First Allied Airborne Army had been born of military and political expediency rather than of real operational need – the need for a formation of sufficient status to ensure that airborne operations were given their full weight. Unfortunately, the headquarters itself was, in the nature of things, a large military bureaucracy, and one that had been thrown together at short notice in the middle of a major campaign.

Eisenhower had given command of this new formation to Brereton, now a war-experienced lieutenant-general who had served in turn as commanding general of the US Far East Air Force in the Pacific and of the US Middle East Air Force, before moving to Europe to take charge of the US Ninth Air Force both before and during the invasion of Europe. As well as the four airborne divisions already mentioned (all of them now in the United Kingdom, the three which had been fighting in Normandy having recently returned), Brereton had under his command US 17th Airborne

Division, newly arrived from the United States, 52nd (Lowland) Division, trained for mountain warfare and now adapated to be air-transportable, and Polish 1 Independent Parachute Brigade Group. To fly these formations into battle were some 1,300 C-47 transport aircraft,* most of them belonging to US IX Troop Carrier Command. On the British side, 38 and 46 Groups, RAF, possessed between them some 250 aged bombers for use as glider-tugs, together with enough Dakotas to lift a single brigade group.

Under Brereton were two airborne corps headquarters: Major-General Matthew B. Ridgway, undoubtedly the most experienced senior airborne commander at the time, was in charge of the US XVIII Airborne Corps; wearing two hats, Lieutenant-General F.A.M. Browning, known throughout the British Army as 'Boy', was both deputy to Brereton and in command of the British Airborne Corps.

When discussing the formation of this new airborne army with Brereton in mid-July, Eisenhower had demanded from his subordinate a plan which would 'have as its purpose a maximum contribution to the destruction of the German armies in western Europe'. As Brereton was to write in his diary, 'He wants imagination and daring', and when he left the meeting he recorded that he told Eisenhower that if he wanted plans with daring and imagination he would get them, but that he did not think that the Supreme Commander's staff or ground commanders would like it. A bold use of airborne forces appealed to the commander of First Allied Airborne Army, and was, of course, precisely the sort of thing envisaged by Arnold and Marshall. On the wall of his office in his HQ at Ascot, Brereton was to hang the words of another visionary American, Benjamin Franklin, written in 1784:

> Where is the Prince who can afford so to cover his country with troops for its defence, as that ten thousand men descending from the clouds, might not, in many places, do an infinite deal of mischief before a force could be brought to repel them?

During the first forty days of the life of Brereton's army, his staff was to prepare plans for eighteen separate operations; the aim of

---

* The military version of the pre-war Douglas DC-3 air-liner. The C-47 was designated the 'Skytrain' by the Americans, and the 'Dakota' by the British.

several was to cut off the German forces, now retreating across France from the Normandy battle after their collapse when the 'Mortain Pocket' had been sealed off by the closing of the 'Falaise Gap'. Some of these plans were sound, others less so. Second thoughts killed off several of the more fanciful, while others were cancelled because the Allied armour swept forward so quickly, but, by the second week in September, plans for ten separate operations were still in being, ranging from a landing on Walcheren Island in the Scheldt estuary to open Antwerp to sea traffic,* through the capture of various bridgeheads across the Rhine, to the seizure of airfields around Berlin in the event of an unexpected German surrender. The newly formed and largely untried staff was kept busy, if not over-stretched, and the search to find a worthwhile use for the airborne divisions was becoming a little desperate. The airborne forces were, as the official historian of the United States Army so aptly put it, 'coins burning holes in SHAEF's pocket'.

By the end of August the retreating German forces, which Eisenhower had hoped the airborne army might help to destroy, were 'no longer a cohesive force but a number of fugitive battle groups, disorganised and even demoralised, short of equipment and arms'. Thus, in their intelligence summary covering the week ending 4 September, did Eisenhower's staff describe the state of the defeated German army. The authors were by no means alone in their optimism. Major-General J.N. Kennedy, the usually cautious Assistant Chief of the Imperial General Staff at the War Office, noted in his diary four days later that the Allied forces should be in Berlin by the end of the month. Other Allied commanders expressed, at various times and in different degrees, similarly optimistic sentiments.

This euphoria, mirrored in the press on both sides of the Atlantic, was not hard to understand. On 25 August, French and American armoured columns had swept into Paris amid scenes of wild excitement, the flowers, the embraces and the flowing wine caught by the newsreel cameras for the cinemas of Newcastle-upon-Tyne and Pittsburgh. Since D-Day – 6 June – the Allies had killed,

* The speed of the Allied advance through Normandy made it vital that another port should be captured to supply the swift-moving armies. At that time all supplies were brought in through Cherbourg or the improvised harbours at the invasion beaches, now many miles behind the advancing Allied formations.

wounded or taken prisoner half a million German soldiers. On the eastern front, the Russians had, by the end of August, forced the Germans back to the outskirts of Warsaw and had captured the Ploesti oilfields in Rumania, although they still had 300 miles to travel to reach Berlin. There seemed to be little question that the end of the war was in sight. By an odd quirk, the excellence of the Allied intelligence added to the general optimism among the higher command. The select few privy to Ultra, the code-name for the material produced by the highly secret interception and deciphering of enemy radio traffic, received possibly too clear a picture of the German confusion and the paucity of their resources as their troops flooded back towards the Fatherland. In 1918, the German army had surrendered while still in far better heart.

As Montgomery's Twenty-First Army Group rolled forward from the Seine, the German garrisons of the Channel Ports, each held by about one weak division, had been by-passed for attention later, a task which, with the clearing of the Scheldt estuary, Montgomery gave to the six divisions of Canadian First Army. During the month of September, this army was to be busy assaulting and capturing what Hitler had vaingloriously dubbed the 'fortresses' of Le Havre, Boulogne, Calais and Dunkirk; Dieppe and Ostend both surrendered without a fight, but the others were to hold out staunchly.

British Second Army, commanded by Lieutenant-General Miles Dempsey, had been made responsible for the main thrust through Belgium and Holland, but, because of the over-extended lines of communication from the Normandy beach-head, supplies were short, with the consequence that Dempsey had to leave his VIII Corps, together with most of his heavy and medium artillery, behind on the Seine. With XII Corps on the east of the advance keeping in touch with the Canadians, the principal effort was in the hands of Lieutenant-General Brian Horrocks's XXX Corps. Advancing on a fifty-mile front towards Antwerp and Brussels, Horrocks had succeeded in averaging fifty miles daily against only sporadic resistance during the last days of August and the first of September. After the bitter slogging-match of Normandy, it was a time of hope and elation for all, not least the people of occupied Belgium and Holland, who now experienced the joy of watching and hearing the defeated Germans retreating from their countries towards the Reich, some of them on foot, others in every shape of vehicle – truck,

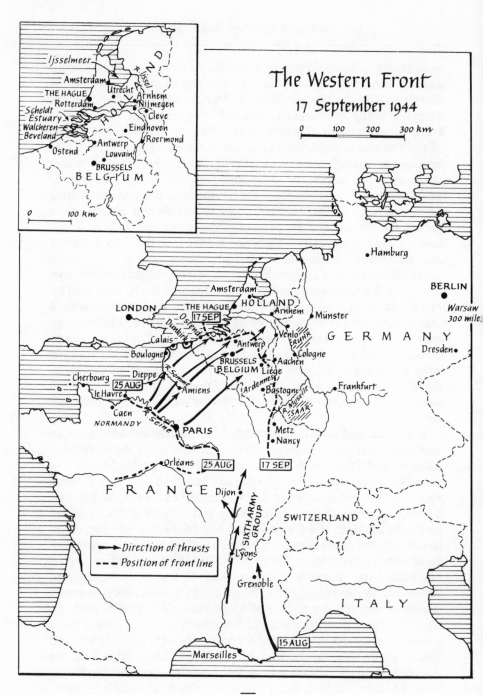

The Western Front
17 September 1944

0   100   200   300 km

Inset map:

Ijsselmeer
Amsterdam
THE HAGUE
Rotterdam
Utrecht
Arnhem
Nijmegen
Cleve
Scheldt
Estuary
Walcheren
Beveland
Eindhoven
Roermond
Ostend
Antwerp
Louvain
BRUSSELS
BELGIUM
HOLLAND

0   100 km

Main map:

Hamburg

BERLIN

Warsaw
300 mile

Amsterdam
LONDON
THE HAGUE
HOLLAND
Arnhem
Münster
17 SEP
Ostend
GERMANY
Calais
Dunkirk
Venlo
RUHR
Boulogne
Antwerp
Cologne
Dresden
BRUSSELS
BELGIUM
Liège
Aachen
Cherbourg
Dieppe
R. Somme
25 AUG
Ardennes
Bastogne
Frankfurt
le Havre
Amiens
R. Moselle
Caen
SAAR
NORMANDY
R. Seine
PARIS
Metz
Nancy
Orléans
25 AUG
17 SEP
F R A N C E
Dijon
SWITZERLAND
SIXTH ARMY GROUP
Lyons
→ Direction of thrusts
--- Position of front line
Grenoble
I T A L Y
15 AUG
Marseilles

18

horse-drawn wagon, car, bicycle, even the odd armoured car or tank. Then a few hours – sometimes only minutes – later, their khaki-clad liberators would appear. On 3 September, Guards Armoured Division, the spearhead of XXX Corps, captured Brussels to scenes of even wilder jubilation than those experienced by the French and American troops in Paris. On the next day, 11th Armoured Division entered Antwerp and seized the city's port installations intact, yet another measure of the demoralisation of the German forces. But here, on the same day, XXX Corps was ordered to halt for the time being, the reasons given being that the advance had outrun administrative resources; it was an instruction that did not please Horrocks, whose vehicles had just been topped up with petrol and who had a further day's supply within reach.

Among those who had not succumbed to the general euphoria had been the British Prime Minister. At sea on 8 September, travelling again to a meeting with President Roosevelt in Quebec, Churchill had read a report by the Joint Intelligence Committee which concluded that the continuation of any organised resistance in Germany beyond 1 December was improbable. The Prime Minister criticised the report because, as he wrote, 'It errs on the side of optimism', and he went on remind his military advisers of the absence of any large harbour in Allied hands, and warned them of the stubborn resistance that might be met in clearing the heavily mined and defended Scheldt estuary in order to open Antwerp to shipping. He concluded that any collapse in 1944 would stem from political rather than military causes.

Antwerp was the nub. To the senior soldiers on the spot, there seemed to be no reason why the Canadians should not overrun the German coastal defences along the banks of the Scheldt, thus allowing the estuary to be cleared of mines, as easily as the defenders of Brussels and of Antwerp itself had themselves been overwhelmed. Others saw the problem in a different light. On 3 September, Admiral Sir Bertram Ramsay, Eisenhower's Naval Commander-in-Chief, had signalled SHAEF, with a copy to Twenty-First Army Group, warning of the vulnerability of Antwerp and Rotterdam to mining and blocking, and of the time it would take to open the ports if this was allowed to happen. On the following day Hitler issued a directive emphasising the importance of denying the Scheldt area to the Allies: the Germans clearly understood that the estuary was

19

not only an eventual way of escape for their Fifteenth Army defending the Channel Ports and the Scheldt estuary, but also an obstacle to the Allies making use of Antwerp. A measure of the lack of thought which the army had given to the geographical importance of the surroundings of Antwerp was the failure to block the exit from the Beveland isthmus, only a few hundred yards wide, the narrow bottleneck on the only withdrawal route of German Fifteenth Army towards the east. By itself, 11th Armoured Division had hardly been strong enough to seize Antwerp and exploit fifteen miles northwards to seal this escape route, but somehow troops could have been found. Despite the order to halt that he had been given on 4 September, Horrocks was to accept the blame for this undoubted error, admitting that he had failed to appreciate the full scope of the problem, even though no one senior to him had done so either. Such honesty and generosity are all too rare in a general's memoirs, but are not untypical of Horrocks, an honest man.

On 6 September, XXX Corps was permitted to move forward once again, but the two-day delay had proved costly. In an operation designed to seize bridges over the Rhine between Wesel and Arnhem, Guards Armoured Division, advancing on the axis Louvain-Eindhoven-Nijmegen, immediately started to meet resistance of a calibre quite different from that encountered during the previous week. It took the division four days of hard fighting to reach the Meuse-Escaut Canal and for the Irish Guards to take the de Groot bridge, near Neerpelt, and so obtain a foothold on the other side of the waterway. To the east, 11th Armoured Division was paying for the failure to push out from Antwerp and gain crossings over the Albert Canal: on 6 September, the division captured a small bridgehead, but the Germans counter-attacked and the success could not be exploited. Two days later, 11th Armoured was switched from one side of the British front to the other in order to protect Guards Armoured Division's right flank, leaving behind 50th (Northumbrian) Division striving to capture another bridgehead over the Albert Canal at Gheel. The shortage of fighting troops up forward was becoming apparent.

For XXX Corps, the problem, of course, was supplies, and the transport required to fetch forward all the ammunition, fuel, food and everything else needed to keep the corps fighting and moving. Despite the delay that had occurred in making the break-out from the Normandy bridgehead, the Allies had reached the Seine seventy-five days after the landings, fifteen days ahead of the date forecast by the SHAEF administrative planners. By early autumn they were a full two months ahead of schedule, but they had failed to capture a major port, and their bombers had smashed the French railway system with such success that the material could not be transported by rail. Nearly everything was being brought forward by truck from the beaches, which now lay 300 or more miles to the rear. To compound the problem, both humanity and politics dictated that the newly liberated towns and cities of France should not be allowed to starve, the daily tonnage diverted to Paris alone being enough to have supplied three combat divisions with all their needs. To have opened Antwerp to shipping would have solved the problem. By the end of the war, 40,000 tons were being landed there daily, enough to maintain two million men, but it was to take three months to clear the sixty-mile long estuary that leads to the port, and the cost would be 30,000 British and Canadian serviceman killed, wounded and captured.

This shortage of supplies dominated Allied strategy. Either whatever was available could be spread equally between the different army groups and armies, thus reducing all advances to a common norm, or priority could be given to a single sector, allowing a major effort to be made there while movement was slowed or halted elsewhere. That, to put the subject in the simplest terms, was the root of the celebrated 'broad' and 'narrow' front arguments between Eisenhower and Montgomery, in which the former pressed for advances to be made along the full length of the Allied front, and the latter sought to concentrate his resources for a decisive blow at a vital point. This was not just a difference of opinion between the two commanders, but something which had bedevilled Allied planning in Tunisia, in Sicily, in Italy and during the Normandy fighting, its roots planted deep in the disparate strategical and tactical theories of the two countries – years after the end of the war, the 'broad-front' philosophy was still being expounded at American staff colleges, to the astonishment of visiting Commonwealth officers. After the victory in Normandy, Montgomery believed that the Germans might be beaten quickly provided that pressure upon them was maintained, and that this could be effected only by developing a single major thrust: as he saw it, there were two alternatives, either

21

to capture the Ruhr by means of an encircling movement, or to cross the Rhine higher up between Karlsruhe and Frankfurt, and drive from there into the heart of Germany. Not only did Montgomery favour this 'narrow-front' strategy, but he wanted it to be directed towards the Ruhr. This industrial complex, with Holland and Belgium, was producing 65 per cent of Germany's crude steel and 56 per cent of her coal, and its loss, it had been calculated, would bring the war to an end in three months. The defence of so vital an industrial complex, Montgomery considered, would force Hitler to concentrate whatever reserves he could scrape together, and there they would be defeated on ground of the Allies' own choosing, thus allowing the Americans to the south of Twenty-First Army Group to sweep forward into the centre of the Reich.

There were considerations other than those of pure strategy. With extreme reluctance, Montgomery had handed over control of ground operations to his Supreme Commander on 1 September, the day he was promoted field-marshal, a sop both to the British public and to his own self-esteem. Now he commanded only the largely British and Canadian troops of Twenty-First Army Group, whereas Bradley's newly formed Twelfth Army Group controlled the US First, Third and Ninth Armies, while, moving up from the south, was General Jacob L. Devers's US Sixth Army Group, which had landed on the Côte d'Azur on 6 August, and which contained US Seventh Army and French First Army. The trouble was that, in order to make this northern thrust to the Ruhr, Montgomery would not only need to be given priority in supplies, but he would also have to have US First Army under his command to give support on his right flank. It would also mean that Eisenhower would have to halt the advance of Lieutenant-General George S. Patton, commanding US Third Army, whose brilliant handling of the Normandy break-out and the subsequent pursuit across France had made him as much of a public idol in the United States as Montgomery had become in the United Kingdom. There could be no question of American opinion, either civilian or military, being persuaded that Patton should be stopped, with victory apparently just within his grasp, in order to allow Montgomery to win the war.

Montgomery's ambitions, both personal and for his country's arms, matched the lucidity of his strategic thinking. He was, however, incapable of comprehending the sound political reasons behind the decision not to give him virtual control of the ground battle in Western Europe. Nor was the situation made any easier by the fact that his personal relations with many of his peers and most of the senior members of Eisenhower's staff at SHAEF were so unhappy (during the coming months they were to deteriorate still further). His legendary arrogance and condescension did not endear him to his allies, and what some saw as an over-cautious method of fighting the Normandy battle had not enhanced his military reputation among the many senior officers only too ready to see that reputation destroyed, even though his victory, based on the British holding the left flank and drawing the enemy armour upon themselves while the Americans broke out of the bridgehead, had clearly gone as intended. He was not an easy subordinate, and he knew it, but his distrust of the senior staff at SHAEF, British and American alike, equalled their dislike of him. There was much truth in the words he wrote to his close friend and confidant, the then Major-General Frank Simpson, Director of Military Operations at the War Office, in September:

> I am not so happy about the senior British generals at SHAEF. Not only are they inefficient and of no use; I fear they are also disloyal to us and instil poison whenever possible. I have not had a visit from any of them since the party began ... the American staff from SHAEF visit me but not the British staff.

On 4 September, after he had captured Brussels and Louvain, Montgomery reiterated his ideas to Eisenhower, pleading for a single thrust towards Berlin, backed by all available transport and supplies, in order to end the war. His reasons carried weight. The lines of communication of the American armies were longer than his. Dieppe was about to be brought into use, and Antwerp would be available as soon as the Scheldt was opened; with German resistance apparently at a low ebb, at the time there seemed to be little reason why Antwerp should not be opened to shipping reasonably quickly. Eight armoured divisions and two armoured brigades were well placed to lead an offensive into Germany which could be supported by tactical aircraft flying from the United Kingdom.

Eisenhower's reply to this reasoning, however, was considered by Montgomery to be unrealistic. The Supreme Commander's signal repeated his intention to advance on a broad front, and he insisted that success should be exploited by breaching the Siegfried Line, crossing the Rhine on a broad front, and seizing both the Saar and the Ruhr. At the same time the ports of Le Havre and Antwerp should be opened. On the other hand, Eisenhower did concede that Montgomery's flank of the Allied front should have priority for supplies, although he failed to spell out the details. The manner in which Eisenhower's reply arrived emphasised to Montgomery the inadequacies of his Supreme Commander's arrangements for fighting the land battle. Since 1 September, Eisenhower had been operating from an advanced headquarters on the west side of the Cherbourg peninsula, 400 miles distant from the fighting. Neither telephone nor radio-telephone linked him with his three army groups, and his signal, despatched on 5 September, arrived in two parts, the second section before the first, at 0900 hours on 7 September and at 1015 hours on 9 September.

At the time, Eisenhower was almost immobilised as the result of a knee injury, but on 10 September he managed to fly to Brussels to see his importunate subordinate. The meeting, held in the Supreme Commander's aircraft, started badly. Brashly, the Field-Marshal plugged his ideas for ending the war, doing little to disguise his reservations about the quality of his senior's generalship. Seething with rage though the American was, a pat on the knee and the words 'Steady Monty. You can't speak to me like that. I'm your boss', elicited an apology and set the meeting on better lines. Montgomery then proceeded to outline his latest ideas.

On 4 September, Eisenhower had placed his sole strategic reserve, Brereton's First Allied Airborne Army, in support of Montgomery's army group, a decisions which had been made easier by Bradley's lack of enthusiasm for airborne operations and by his desire to use the transport aircraft to supply Patton instead. An operation by British 1st Airborne Division and the Polish Parachute Brigade Group had then been planned to combine with the forward movement of XXX Corps from Brussels and Antwerp, the aim being to speed this advance by seizing the great bridges over the Maas at Grave, the Waal at Nijmegen and the Neder Rijn at Arnhem. Code-named 'Comet', this operation had been discussed at brigade level as early as 4 September, and had been due to start on the 8th. That day, postponements had been received, first for twenty-four hours, and then for a further forty-eight.

The proposal which Montgomery now made to Eisenhower was that the full available power of Brereton's Airborne Army should be used to capture Arnhem – in effect a more powerful 'Comet'. More than four divisions would be parachuted or landed in German-occupied Holland. These forces would seize the crossings over the three major rivers and a number of lesser waterways which intersected XXX Corps' line of advance. The latter would now thrust forward to Arnhem and beyond towards the Ijsselmeer (which, before it was closed to the ocean before the war began, had been known as the Zuyder Zee), so cutting off the German forces in western Holland. However, as the Vice-Chief of the Imperial General Staff, Lieutenant-General Sir Archibald Nye, was to signal to his chief, Field-Marshal Sir Alan Brooke, who was in Quebec with Churchill at the time, the primary object of the operation was to advance to the neighbourhood of Munster, with victory in that area been exploited towards Berlin. On 13 September, the day this signal was despatched, Montgomery was to signal the War Office: 'hope we shall now win the war reasonably quickly'. For all that hope, he was only too aware that before he could press on towards Berlin, the Ruhr had to be captured and the 100,000 to 150,000 Germans in western Holland had to be eliminated.

Three factors seem to have influenced Montgomery's choice of the Arnhem route into Germany, as opposed to a north-easterly, more direct, thrust to cross the Rhine at Wesel (a course of action favoured by Dempsey and for which Montgomery's staff had been preparing plans), although no firm evidence on the subject exists as this was to be the only one of the Field-Marshal's battles that, afterwards, he could never be persuaded to discuss. First, an advance in this direction would outflank the more northerly defences of the Siegfried Line. Second, there was the danger that the strength of German fighter and flak defences in the Ruhr was such that any airborne landing in the Wesel area would be far too expensive in casualties; it is significant that such an operation was one of the few possible uses for airborne troops never studied by Brereton's staff. The third consideration, and the one that probably influenced Montgomery most strongly, was the signal he received from the War

Office informing him that the first of Hitler's new rockets – the deadly V2s – had hit London on 8 September, and had been launched from bases in western Holland. Clearly, a force breaking through at Arnhem, rather than at Wesel, would be closer to these bases, and therefore able to deal with them more quickly.

The arguments in favour of the Wesel alternative were that a crossing there offered a shorter route into Germany, with one less major river to negotiate (the Waal joins the Rhine south-east of Arnhem, but north-west of Wesel). Furthermore, an offensive aimed in this direction would avoid opening a gap between the British forces and, on their right, US First Army, which was due to attack along the axis Liège-Cologne. Among the several informed critics of Montgomery's choice of route subsequently was the late Major-General R.F.K. (David) Belchem, the Brigadier, General Staff (Operations) at Twenty-First Army Group HQ, who at the time was standing in for Major-General Sir Francis (Freddie) de Guingand, Montgomery's Chief of Staff, who was away sick. After the war Belchem insisted that Montgomery had committed a major error in not entering Germany by way of Wesel, claiming in a television interview that German generals with whom he had discussed the battle had stated that opposition in the area was virtually non-existent, and that the British could have 'bicycled along the road to Wesel' almost unopposed.

Eisenhower's welcome for Montgomery's proposal was more than enthusiastic. It seemed that an imaginative use had at last been found for First Allied Airborne Army, precisely the type of operation that both Arnold and Marshall had been seeking. As the Supreme Commander was to write to Montgomery after their meeting at Brussels: 'I must say that it is not only designed to carry out most effectively my basic conception with respect to this campaign but it is in exact concordance with all the understandings that we now have', thoughts that the recipient of the letter, if put to it, would have expressed in fewer words. For his part, the Field-Marshal was satisfied. To him it now appeared that British forces, led by himself, had been given the opportunity of striking the final blow against Germany: if the drive to Arnhem succeeded and Montgomery's forces broke through towards the Ruhr and the North German Plain, it would be hard indeed for Eisenhower to deny him the resources needed to finish off the war in the West.

But the problem of supplying Twenty-First Army Group had not been properly resolved at the 10 September meeting. In what appears to have been an attempt to extract a precise commitment, Montgomery signalled Eisenhower on the following day to say that the operation could not start before 23 September at the earliest, or even three days later, because of the shortage of supplies; and, at the same time, he warned his superior that delay would enable the Germans to stiffen their resistance, signs of which had already developed in the fighting along the canals. Montgomery recorded that on 12 September, as a consequence of this signal, Eisenhower's Chief of Staff, the American Lieutenant-General Walter Bedell Smith, visited him at his tactical headquarters and told him that he was to get the bulk of what he needed. Patton would be halted, and the larger part of Bradley's logistic resources would be switched to US First Army, operating on Montgomery's right. At the same time, three newly arrived American divisions would be grounded and their transport used to carry supplies to the British army group. With the promise of this support, Montgomery now agreed that the operation could start on 17 September, just five days later.

On 13 September, however, Montgomery received a confirmatory signal from SHAEF which did not quite match the notes he had made after his meeting with Bedell Smith. In it he was told that the US Communications Zone would transport 500 tons of supplies daily to the Brussels area by truck, and that, in addition to this, he would receive a daily airlift of a further 500 tons – this last, however, would be suspended during the airborne operation. The signal also stated that US First Army was to receive supplies adequate for its task. As the basic supply needs of an immobilised division were some 200 tons daily, as against 450 tons for one engaged on an operation, the extra priority given Montgomery would, after 16 September, allow him just enough to keep two more divisions in the field.

Such a last-minute decision on so vital a question as supply and re-supply was the result of the haste in which the operation had been planned, born of the need to strike again before the Germans could scrape together sufficient reserves to withstand the Allied thrust. This lack of time to plan effectively was to have serious and far-reaching consequences on the outcome of the battle. Weeks had been available to plan the airborne operations in Sicily, but still the time allowed had been insufficient; months had been spent on the preliminaries to the airborne landings in Normandy. Now, for this, the largest and most complicated airborne operation to date, just seven days were provided.

CHAPTER TWO

'TO GRAB THE BRIDGES WITH THUNDERCLAP SURPRISE'

At Montgomery's tactical headquarters on 10 September, while Eisenhower and the Field-Marshal were arguing about the future conduct of the war at Brussels airport, General 'Boy' Browning awaited the outcome of their meeting. Soon after it had ended, the airborne commander learned from Montgomery the details of the tasks allotted to First Allied Airborne Army in the coming offensive. In Operation 'Comet', a single reinforced division was to have been used to seize the river and canal crossings which barred the road between the Meuse-Escaut Canal and Arnhem. Now the full available strength of the Airborne Army was to be committed to the same task. 'Market-Garden' was to be the code-word – 'Market' for the airborne part of the operation, and 'Garden' for the northwards advance of British Second Army to link up with the airborne forces.

At 1430 hours on the same day Browning landed in England, bringing with him a tentative plan, the main outlines of which, including the divisional tasks, Montgomery had himself sketched in. When he arrived at First Allied Airborne Army HQ at Sunning-hall Park, Ascot, he was informed by his army commander, General Brereton, that he and his corps headquarters would be responsible for the army side of 'Market'. By 1800 hours he was outlining the plan to thirty-four commanders and staff officers assembled in

Brereton's office. Reading from south to north, US 101st Airborne Division was to seize the crossings along the stretch of the corridor which was to be opened between Eindhoven and Veghel. Next, US 82nd Airborne Division had to capture the two great bridges over the Maas river at Grave and the Waal at Nijmegen. Lastly, in Browning's terse phrase, the role of British 1st Airborne Division was 'Arnhem bridge – and hold it'. Meanwhile, Second Army would fight its way northwards to link up with each airborne division in turn, the distance between the Meuse-Escaut Canal, Second Army's start-line, and Arnhem being sixty-four miles. The bridges, Brereton insisted at the meeting, must be grabbed 'with thunderclap surprise'. He placed 1 Polish Independent Parachute Brigade Group under command of the 1st Division, while 52nd (Lowland) Division would be in reserve, standing by to be flown in to landing-strips north of Arnhem as the situation permitted. As Montgomery graphically described the planned operations to the War Office in London, 101st Division was to lay a 'carpet' of airborne troops to assist the advance of the ground forces, and 82nd and 1st Divisions would put down 'two large dining-room carpets'.

Well practised though Browning's listeners were at planning airborne operations, the one he now outlined was not only of unprecedented complexity and boldness, but there were only seven days available in which to plan and launch it. Indeed, D-day had not in fact been finally settled when this first meeting was called, and it was therefore possible that everything might have to be tied up even more quickly. Although the British and the Poles had done a certain amount of groundwork when making their preparations for 'Comet', decisions would now have to be taken, in a very short time, on such involved questions as the allotment of tasks to divisions, the allocation of transport aircraft, the choice of dropping-zones for the paratroops and landing-zones for the gliders (called, in the jargon, 'DZs' and 'LZs'), the choice of flight-paths, and the planning of air re-supply. At the same time, arrangements had to be made with the various air forces, based both in Britain and on the Continent, for the preliminary bombing of targets, for photographic reconnaissance, for fighter protection for the long and vulnerable columns of troop-carrying aircraft and glider-tugs, for flak suppression, and for fighter-bombers to give close support to the airborne troops once

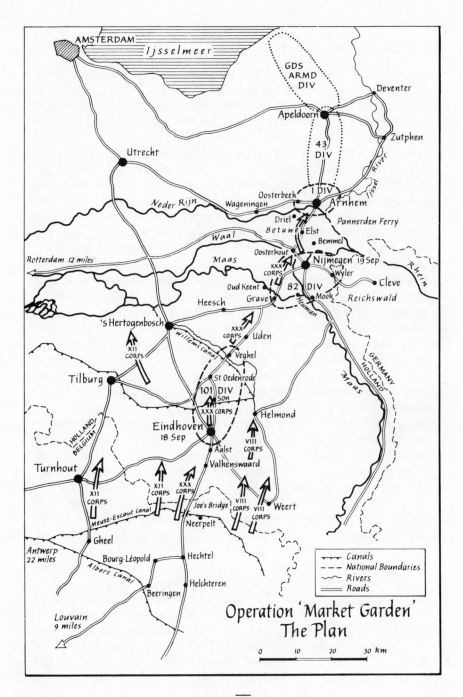

AMSTERDAM

Ijsselmeer

GDS ARMD DIV

Deventer

Apeldoorn

Zutphen

Utrecht

43 DIV

Neder Rijn

Oosterbeek

Wageningen

Oosterbeek

I DIV

Arnhem

Driel

Pannerden Ferry

Betuwe

Elst

Waal

Bemmel

Ijssel River

Rotterdam 12 miles

Maas

Oosterhout

XXX CORPS

Nijmegen 19 Sep

Wyler

Cleve

Rhein

Oud Keent

82 DIV

Mook

Reichswald

Heesch

Grave

'S Hertogenbosch

Willems Canal

XXX CORPS

Uden

Veghel

Maas

XII CORPS

St Oedenrode

GERMANY

HOLLAND

Tilburg

101 DIV

Son

XXX CORPS

Helmond

Eindhoven
18 Sep

VIII CORPS

HOLLAND
BELGIUM

Aalst

Turnhout

Valkenswaard

XII CORPS

XXX CORPS

VIII CORPS

VIII CORPS

Weert

Joe's Bridge

XII CORPS

Meuse-Escaut Canal

Neerpelt

Antwerp
22 miles

Albert Canal

Gheel

Bourg-Léopold

Hechtel

Beeringen

Helchteren

Louvain
9 miles

| Canals |
| National Boundaries |
| Rivers |
| Roads |

Operation 'Market Garden'
The Plan

0   10   20   30 km

they were on the ground. Formation and unit commanders, from divisional generals to the lowliest squad or section corporals, had in turn to plan their part in the coming battle, a sequence that would culminate in every individual soldier knowing just what he had to do from the moment he touched down on mother earth.

Some details, such as equipment loads and battle-drills, were standardised, the former the subject of detailed loading-tables, but for all that the interlocking work at a multiplicity of levels was vast in scope and complicated in detail. Nor did it make matters any simpler that three allies and two fighting services were involved, and that the staff of First Allied Airborne Army had worked together for little more than a month. With some 35,000 troops to be briefed and then moved to the twenty-four take-off airfields scattered between Lincolnshire and Dorset, Brereton was justified in making it clear to his senior commanders at the initial conference on 10 September that any decisions arrived at must stand.

There was little doubt in the mind of Major-General Roy Urquhart, commanding 1st Airborne Division, that he had been presented with the most difficult task of the three. Browning thought much the same. When briefed by Montgomery, he had asked how long he was expected to hold the Arnhem bridge. 'Two days', snapped the reply. 'We can hold it for four, but I think we might be going a bridge too far', was Browning's now-famous response. It was the first time that American airborne troops had fought under British command. This was not too popular a decision, especially with General Ridgway, who had hoped to be placed in charge of the operation, and there could be no question of Browning risking Americans on what could prove to be 'a bridge too far'. In any case, the two American divisions had both taken heavy casualties during the Normandy invasion and the subsequent fighting, while the British 1st Division had not been in action since 1943 and was very much seeking a challenge. After a summer of continual training, interspersed by the planning of one abortive operation after another, morale was flagging. On 17 August, Browning had felt the need to take the unusual step of sending a circular around the division in which he had said that he fully realised 'the irritation and disappointment which all ranks feel' at the postponement of an operation planned to cut off the retreating Germans in the Paris-Orleans gap. Expressing his understanding of the fact that criticism of the direction of affairs is likely to follow disappointment, he promised all ranks of the division that they were being kept for the decisive blow. Now, with 'Market Garden', it seemed that the 'decisive blow' was about to be struck. Few doubted that this time the operation would go ahead, and the officers and men of 1st Division were as determined to get into the war in North-West Europe as their commanders were to see them used in that theatre.

Brereton's first task, commanding as he did both the troops and the air transport, was to decide whether the operation should be carried out by day or by night. All previous Allied airborne operations had taken place in moonlight, and nearly all had been marked by navigational errors and resultant scattered landings. Eisenhower, when he had appointed Brereton to his new command, had emphasised his anxiety about the navigational qualifications of the transport crews, and he had ordered Brereton to keep him in touch with the progress of their training. As it happened, there was no moon during the week starting 17 September, thus putting any large-scale night landing out of court; it was fortunate, therefore, that the Allied day-fighters had by this time won almost complete air superiority over the European battlefield, and that, with fighters in plenty to escort the transport columns and to suppress the flak by strafing the gun-sites, a daylight operation was feasible. On the other hand, the German night-fighters were still a serious threat, and the radar-controlled flak guns could be almost as dangerous by night as by day.

Having settled upon a daylight operation, Brereton's next concern was to allocate the available transport aircraft to the three divisions. Large though his fleet was, it could carry only some 16,500 troops in a single lift, less than half Browning's total airborne force. To land the greater part of the corps on the first day of the battle would, therefore, need two sorties, the first of which would have to take off from its bases in England in the dark. The advice Brereton was to receive from his air commanders was conflicting. Air Vice-Marshal Leslie Hollinghurst, commanding 38 Group, RAF, and a pioneer of airborne warfare, had the task of co-ordinating the plans of the two RAF groups (38 and 46) which, with 130 USAAF Dakotas, were scheduled to lift 1st Airborne Division in to Arnhem. While Hollinghurst was ready to allow his crews to fly to Arnhem twice in the day, taking off in the dark on the first sortie, Major-General Paul L. Williams, the commander of IX Troop Carrier Command, USAAF, and the co-ordinator of the air transport plan as a whole, had different views. In the preceding months his aircraft had been doubled in number, without a corresponding increase in ground staff. As a result, he advised Brereton that there would not be enough time for maintenance and for the repair of battle damage if two sorties were flown on the first day; he added that the extra flying necessary to make two sorties would produce crew fatigue. The advice was strangely out of character. Williams was known among both British and Americans for his general helpfulness and for his drive, and it was largely because of the respect in which the soldiers held him that they accepted what he had to say with little argument. Brereton proceeded to act in accordance with Williams's views – only one sortie would be flown on the first day.

The consequence of this decision was that the arrival of Urquhart's 1st Airborne Division at Arnhem would now need to be spread over three days, the implications of which Brereton may have failed to grasp, lacking as he did any intimate knowledge of the problems of the ground battle. Montgomery, however, spotted the snag in the plan as soon as the details reached him in Belgium, and he sent Brigadier Belchem to Ascot by air in order to urge Brereton to change his mind and allow a double lift for the troops who were to tackle Arnhem. But Brereton stood firm, probably rightly so in the circumstances, since by the time Belchem arrived it was too late to change the plan so radically. As Brereton had insisted at the first planning conference, this was the type of fundamental decision which, once made, must stand if confusion were to be avoided.

The details of airlifts and routes for the transport aircraft were settled at the second planning conference, held at HQ IX Troop Carrier Command at 0900 hours on 11 September. Almost immediately Urquhart, as was the habit of airborne commanders, began to prod Browning for a larger share of the first lift, concerned that 1st Airborne might well have obtained more but for the fact that the greater part of the transport fleet was American. Browning responded by pointing out that the priority in airlift had to be from 'bottom to top', as he expressed it, so ensuring that there would be no hitch in seizing the more southern bridges. The momentum of the advance of Horrocks's XXX Corps had to be maintained.

In consequence, US 101st Division was apportioned the largest share of the airlift on the first day, and 1st Division the smallest. For all that, Urquhart was not too badly served. Different records provide slightly different figures, but it seems that he received a first lift of 480 aircraft, 110 fewer than 101st Division, but only 40 less than 82nd Division. Urquhart, however, decided to take fewer infantry and a greater proportion of supporting arms, with their transport, than either of the two American divisional commanders, both of whom dropped their nine parachute battalions on the first day. In contrast, Urquhart lifted slightly less than six battalions on this first day. Had he chosen to delay the arrival of his field artillery until the second day, and if Browning had not decided to use thirty-six of the available aircraft to lift his own headquarters into the battle on the first day, most of 1st Airborne Division's infantry could have been brought in on the first lift.

After the second conference on 11 September, and before the divisional commanders flew back to their formations to prepare their detailed plans for the operation, another and possibly even more controversial question had to be settled. The DZs and LZs had to be chosen, decisions which, once made, were just as difficult to change. Here again, a strong clash of interests developed.

Airborne troops are, of necessity, lightly armed, and are thus more suitable, in the absence of heavy supporting fire, for defence than attack. The essence of the use of such forces is that they should not have to fight a hard battle to gain their objective, but should drop on it – or as near to it as possible – so increasing their chances of seizing it by surprise. There was, then, no doubt at all in Urquhart's mind that his troops should land on either side of the Neder Rijn, straddling the main Arnhem highway bridge, and as close to it as possible. But the final decision on everything concerning the fly-in rested with the air forces. Hollinghurst, knowledgeable though he was of the problems of airborne troops and keen though he always was to do all he could to help the soldiers, was unable to agree with Urquhart's ideas. Flak around Arnhem had been reported as being formidable: 112 light and 44 heavy AA guns were said to ring the area, and air reconnaissance had further reported a number of mobile units and flak barges in the neighbourhood, information that had been confirmed by bomber crews flying to the Ruhr. Especially heavy was the flak said to be defending Deelen airfield, seven miles to the north of Arnhem; the transport aircraft would run straight into this fire after they had released their gliders or dropped their paratroops. Only a week earlier, the available information about the German air defences had been far less disturbing. In the 38 Group operation order for 'Comet', air crews had been warned only that:

> The route to the target area has been chosen with due regard to the main enemy flak emplacements and the main roads along which mobile flak is likely to be encountered. Heavy A.A. guns protect Nijmegen, and Arnhem is within range of heavy flak covering Deelen airfield. It should be borne in mind that, with a fluid ground situation, fire from mobile flak of any calibre may be met almost anywhere within range.

The source of the information about this rapid build-up of German flak in Holland has yet to be traced, but it may have come from the Dutch Resistance. Long after the war, a copy of what purports to be a flak map, dated 11 September, was given to Major-General John Frost in Arnhem: on it are marked the positions of 100 or so heavy and light guns in the southern part of the city and suburbs, and just south of the river.

Because of this threat from flak, Urquhart was obliged to accept a number of large open expanses of heathland and farmland as DZs and LZs, all of them lying between four and nine miles west of the three Arnhem bridges,* a formidable distance to cover quickly on foot without forfeiting surprise. There were, however, compensations. The areas chosen were perfectly suited for the job, level and unimpeded, and only initially light opposition was expected from the enemy. For once, therefore, a tidy drop might be expected, one that should result in Urquhart's units assembling and moving off towards their objectives as cohesive fighting units.

The feasibility of landing small glider-borne *coup-de-main* parties near the highway bridge was discussed and rejected, despite the strong support given to the proposal by Colonel G.J.S. Chatterton, Browning's senior glider pilot. On the night of 5 June 1944, before D-Day in Europe, the seaborne landings in Normandy, British 6th

---

* Besides the main road bridge over the Neder Rijn, the chief target, there was also a pontoon bridge some half a mile to the west, and a railway bridge west of the town, but east of Oosterbeek.

Airborne Division had seized the bridges over the Orne and the Caen Canal in just such a manner. Similar operations for 'Comet' had been planned against the three major bridges at Grave, Nijmegen and Arnhem, the landings to take place before first light, a task the Royal Air Force was only too capable of accomplishing. Whether the proposal to land troops at or near Arnhem bridge was turned down because of the increased flak reported around the bridges, or whether it was thought inadvisable further to complicate the already involved flight-plan, does not appear to have been recorded.

It has often been stated that another reason for not putting a part of 1st Airborne Division down nearer to the Arnhem bridges was the unsuitability of the polder south of the river for landing gliders or paratroops. In the event, it turned out that the Allied air photographic interpreters had exaggerated the dangers of this boggy ground with its numerous dykes, and members of the Dutch Resistance who were interrogated by the intelligence staff of First Allied Airborne Army made the same error. Afterwards, it was to become clear that gliders could have landed without too severe losses, and paratroops without any difficulty at all. In discussing this, it has often been forgotten that the Poles were, in any case, scheduled to drop on to this polder on the third day of the battle.

New to the airborne arm, Urquhart had commanded a brigade group in the Sicilian and Italian campaigns with great success, and before that had fought in the Western Desert. Given command of 1st Airborne Division early in 1944, it was afterwards said that his relative inexperience of airborne matters inhibited him from arguing his case forcefully with his air force colleagues, a criticism which anyone who knew him can refute without difficulty. In any case, Browning, as his corps commander, was far better placed to argue such matters as the need for *coup-de-main* parties, or for the major landings to be made nearer to the main objective.

In some ways Browning's background and experience was the reverse of Urquhart's. Appointed in October 1941 to raise and command 1st Airborne Division, he had spent three years training troops and studying the problems of airborne warfare, but he had never been given the opportunity of leading these troops into action. During the First World War, he had proved himself as a very gallant junior officer, but his experience of handling anything larger than a

37

battalion, even on training, was meagre. A professional Grenadier, he possessed all the virtues as well as some of the defects of his background. He was devoted to the interests of his men, and they in their turn both liked and admired him, despite a barrier of reserve which few succeeded in penetrating. His staff appreciated his ability to decentralise – to give his orders and then leave people to get on with it. Like others who were to attain high rank during the war, he had never attended the Staff College.

Although Browning possessed many of the characteristics which American officers often admired in their British colleagues, he never managed to establish sound relationships with his allies. He could at times seem overbearing and, always immaculately turned-out, some saw him as rather too dapper. And the austerity of his outlook could give an impression of arrogance. Ridgway, when he first met Browning in North Africa, supposed that it was only natural that 'he should seem to be a bit patronising in his manner towards those who had considerably less experience than him'. Perhaps worse, the Americans did not trust him. One reason was that he clearly knew all the 'right' people and was known to use them as the need arose. As the then Brigadier-General 'Jim' Gavin, the commanding general or US 82nd Airborne Division during 'Market Garden' and the most reasonable of men, was afterwards to write about the events preceding the Normandy invasion:

> General Ridgway ... cautioned me against the machinations and scheming of General F.M. Browning, who was the senior British airborne officer, and well he should have. For although the Americans had provided most of the troops and the airlift, the British seemed determined to take command of the total Allied airborne effort.

Brereton and Browning had little in common. The American airman was a tough and stony-faced character, not ready to change his mind, and is said to have been embittered by his unfortunate experiences in the Far East, when the Japanese destroyed the larger part of his command drawn up in neat lines on the ground at Clark and Iba Fields. At times the new job seemed to leave him a little bewildered. This recently formed First Allied Airborne Army, a joint inter-Allied comand of both soldiers and airmen, was a fresh concept in warfare, and even for someone of Brereton's wide combat and staff experience in two world wars, it was taxing. Realising that he knew little about ground operations, perhaps rightly he seems to have left the details to the soldiers.

It was not long before the two generals clashed. Among the plethora of possible operations which had poured off the desks of the airborne planners at the end of August had been 'Linnet', a scheme to seize key points ahead of the advancing Second Army. Cancelled because the ground troops had moved too quickly, it was immediately replaced by 'Linnet 2', a similar operation planned for 4 September and aimed at capturing crossings over the Meuse south of Douai. Because this operation was laid on with such speed that there were no maps available for the junior commanders, Browning objected strongly, unwilling as he was to see his troops thrown carelessly into battle. He became so incensed when Brereton overruled his objection that he threatened to resign. To the Americans, this smacked of a refusal to obey an order, and it shook them to the core that a man of Browning's calibre and reputation should have thought it necessary to make such a threat. On the day after this row, however, 'Linnet 2' went the way of its abortive predecessors, and Browning withdrew his threat.

Although Browning did attempt to persuade his air force colleagues to reconsider their plans for 'Market-Garden', it was difficult for him to make a stand. No one can offer to resign twice in ten days. In any case, it was difficult either for him or for Urquhart to insist on an air plan of a more hazardous nature; air losses of up to 40 per cent had been forecast for the existing plan. It had been much the same before Normandy, when Air Chief-Marshal Sir Trafford Leigh-Mallory, C-in-C of the Allied Expeditionary Air Force, had vehemently and unceasingly opposed Montgomery's plan to drop three airborne divisions on the flanks of the seaborne invasion force, forecasting losses of 75 to 80 per cent among the transport aircraft. It was fortunate that Eisenhower had overruled his objections, for of the 805 transports which had brought in the airborne troops, just 20 were lost. But such caution was, in some ways, understandable. It was difficult for the air commanders to forget the frightful losses that both the RAF and the USAAF had suffered over Europe from German flak and fighters. And the slow-moving Dakotas, flying low in their rigid formations, lacked not only defensive armour and armament, but even self-sealing petrol tanks.

CHAPTER THREE

'BUT THE GERMANS, GENERAL, THE GERMANS'

Over the years, much has been written of the accuracy of the intelligence put out to the 'Market' commanders and troops about the German forces they were likely to encounter. For the earlier Operation 'Comet', in which a single division was to have carried out the task given to a complete corps in 'Market', the information was explicit indeed. 1 Airborne Division Planning Intelligence Summary No.2, dated 7 September, read:

> ... it is reported that one of the broken Panzer divisions has been sent back to the area North of ARNHEM to rest and refit; this might produce some 50 tanks. We may therefore reckon that the forces from ROTTERDAM to the German frontier might comprise a regt from 719 Div, a regt from 347 Div, remnants of 70 Div, a few mobile bns, some scraped up static troops and one Panzer division much the worse for wear. To-day's photographs, together with ground reports from Dutch sources, indicate that the main direction of German movement is NW to SE; not only has 347 Div come down, but many of the SS Training units which were near AMSTERDAM are now quartered in the excellent barracks at NIJMEGEN. There seems little doubt that our operational area will contain a fair quota of Germans, and the

previous estimate of one division may prove to be not far from the mark; moreover it would not be surprising to find the high ground South of NIJMEGEN, Pt 83 (7456) is the highest point in Holland – protected as it is by the MAAS-WAAL Canal to the West, the MAAS to the South, and the WAAL to the North [*sic*], and guarding a vulnerable outpost of the Fatherland's frontier, has been made into a hedgehog defensive position ...

The prediction, therefore, was that the single British airborne division and the Polish brigade would be opposed by a force of much the same size, but one that included the battered remnants of a Panzer division equipped with some fifty tanks.

'Comet' was an operation which had aroused small enthusiasm among its prospective participants. Despite their anxiety to get into the war while it still lasted, even some of Urquhart's more junior commanders had reservations about its chances of success. At one battalion briefing, a company commander, on hearing the task allotted to a colleague, had leaned over to him and whispered 'That should provide you with either a Victoria Cross or a wooden one'. On another level, Major-General Stanislaw Sosabowski, the commander of 1 Polish Independent Parachute Brigade Group, having listened to Urquhart propounding the 'Comet' plan, could not stop himself blurting out 'But the Germans, General, the Germans'. Old enough to be the father of most of those present, this outspoken and often tactless general had first seen action in 1914 as a corporal in the Austrian army fighting the Russians. After a lifetime of war, the apparently nonchalant attitude of some of his young British colleagues often upset him.

Sosabowski's criticism was justified. Precise and disquieting though the intelligence was about the Germans in Holland, especially those around Arnhem and Nijmegen, the endless good news current since the German collapse and retreat in mid-August had persuaded nearly everyone, from general to private soldier, that the war in Europe had reached its final stages.

At the time, intelligence was coming from a number of sources, the most important of which was undoubtedly Ultra, the code-name for the top-secret system whereby, using Enigma machines, German codes were deciphered and the decrypts passed on to commanders. Details of Ultra were only officially released to the public in 1978.

The historians Ralph Bennett and the late Ronald Lewin, the former for four years a member of the team at Bletchley Park where the information was intercepted, deciphered and analysed, have both discussed the Ultra material which threw light on the dispositions and movements of the German forces before 'Market Garden'. The information was both alarming and detailed. A series of intercepts had traced the course of the withdrawal of II SS Panzer Corps after the failure of its counter-attack at Falaise, where, it had been revealed, the corps had lost 120 tanks. It had moved in an easterly direction, through Evreux and Soissons, but on 5 September its staff was ordered north to Eindhoven to direct the refit of three panzer divisions, one of which was the 9th SS. On the previous day this division, together with 10th SS Panzer, had been ordered to rest and refit in the Venlo-Arnhem-s'Hertogenbosch area, except for those elements still operational. On 9 September it had been discovered that the German Army Group B had asked for air reconnaissance in order to find out whether the main Allied thrust was aimed at Aachen or Arnhem, and this message was complemented by two others, dated 14 and 15 September, which indicated that the Germans judged that the Allies were intending to move on both sides of Eindhoven towards Arnhem. A further message dated 14 September reported HQ Army Group B at Oosterbeek, a village some four miles west of Arnhem. Other intercepts revealed the exact progress of the German retreat up the Channel coast towards the Scheldt estuary, and showed the numbers of men ferried across the estuary to the Dutch mainland, to escape eastwards through the Beveland isthmus and thus threaten the left flank of British Second Army as it advanced northwards.

Information radioed by Dutch Resistance groups matched this signal intelligence, but the exact details of what was received have proved hard to trace. It seems, however, that by 10 September the Allies knew from these Dutch sources that battered panzer divisions had been sent to Holland to refit, and that Eindhoven and Nijmegen had been named as reception areas for them. By 15 September, further and more detailed intelligence had located 9th SS Panzer Division firmly in the triangle formed by Arnhem, Zutphen and Apeldoorn.

This information was evaluated as it was received by the widely separated major headquarters involved in 'Market Garden', and was then passed lower down the line in the shape of intelligence summaries and reports. The limitations on the use of Ultra were, however, severe. Because of the paramount need to protect the source, no signals were passed below the equivalent of army headquarters, and anything reaching corps or divisional headquarters arrived in the shape of a disguised operational order or instruction. Nor could a commander order, on the strength of Ultra decrypts, that something be done which might reveal to the enemy that his signal traffic was being read: for example, a concentration of tanks could not be bombed until Ultra had been confirmed by, say, air reconnaissance.

In charge of intelligence at Twenty-First Army Group was Brigadier E.T. (Bill) Williams, who, like other senior members of the Field-Marshal's staff, had served Montgomery ever since the desert battles and possessed his complete confidence. Privy, of course, to the Ultra intelligence, and so aware of the strength of the opposition the airborne divisions were likely to encounter, Williams briefed his master on the dangers of the operation on the evening of 10 September, after the latter's meeting with Eisenhower, but failed to persuade him to change his mind. A few days later, Williams tried again, as did Belchem, both of them pointing out what they saw as flaws in the plan, but to no effect. It was, Williams remembers, unfortunate that de Guingand, the Chief of Staff, was away ill – only he might have succeeded in dissuading Montgomery.

These were not the only warnings Montgomery received. On 15 September, just two days before the operation was due to start, Bedell Smith, informed that there might be two panzer divisions in the area and that they were probably to be equipped with tanks from a depot a few miles from Nijmegen, obtained permission from Eisenhower to visit Montgomery. His object was to warn the latter either to put down a second division in the Arnhem area, or to move one of the American divisions, scheduled to drop further south, up to Arnhem. The visit was abortive. Smith recalled that Montgomery ridiculed the suggestion and waved his objections aside. This behaviour was, however, understandable. It is hard indeed to comprehend how either Smith or Eisenhower thought that a plan of the complexity of 'Market Garden' could be changed so radically without imposing a major delay.

In the matter of intelligence First Allied Airborne Army was not always well served. For some reason, possibly because the headquarters was of such recent creation, it received only a limited amount of Ultra material; in fact, Browning's corps headquarters received most of its intelligence direct from Twenty-First Army Group, rather than from First Allied Airborne Army HQ. Lewin has described how Wing-Commander Asher Lee, recently posted to the Airborne Army headquarters as air intelligence officer, found evidence of enemy armour at Arnhem. He then proceeded to brief himself on Ultra files located elsewhere, to which he still possessed access. Alarmed by what he found, Asher Lee took the information to Brereton, who told him to fly over to see Twenty-First Army Group. Asher Lee did so, but he seems to have been unable to make contact with anyone of adequate seniority, and there the matter seems to have rested.

Although he did not have access to Ultra, Browning's senior intelligence officer at Airborne Corps HQ, Major Brian Urquhart (he was no relation to the general), had been concerned by the Dutch underground reports which he had seen. As a result, on 12 September he requested oblique air photographs of the Arnhem area. Three days later they arrived, and upon them he identified tanks close to the DZs and LZs of 1st Airborne Division. But Browning, when Major Urquhart showed him the photographs, played down the evidence and arranged for the intelligence officer to be sent on sick leave on the grounds of nervous exhaustion.

Urquhart was twenty-five years old, young for the job even in 1944, and in the manner of the young he may have pressed his case with rather too much enthusiasm. He was overworked and perhaps suffering from the strain of being involved in the planning of one airborne operation after another. Moreover, he had done little to disguise his alarm at the assumption of most of his colleagues that the Germans were no longer capable of effective resistance, and at what he saw as a universal determination to get into the action at almost any price. It seems likely that the 'Market Garden' affair brought things to a head. In no way an emotional individual, in the post-war years he established a high reputation in a very senior post in the United Nations.

The information about the enemy which Browning issued to his division on 13 September, before Major Urquhart tackled him with the news about the tanks, read as follows:

The enemy is fighting determinedly along the line of the ALBERT and ESCAUT canals from inclusive ANTWERP to inclusive MAASTRICHT. His line is held by the remnants of some good divisions, including Parachute Divisions, and by new arrivals from HOLLAND. They are fighting well but have few reserves. The total armoured strength is probably not more than 50-100 tanks, mostly Mark IV. There is every sign of the enemy strengthening the river and canal lines through NIJMEGEN and ARNHEM, especially with flak, but the troops manning them are not numerous and many are of low category. The flak is sited for dual purpose – both AA and ground.*

This seems to have been as much as Browning's divisional commanders were ever told, and General Urquhart, who complained after the war that his intelligence staff had been scratching around for 'morsels of information', was informed by Browning that his division was not likely to encounter more than a German brigade group supported by a few tanks.

Browning's after-battle report admits that he believed that the enemy were 'in no fit state to resist another determined advance', and that, 'once the crust of resistance in the front line had been broken, the German Army would be unable to concentrate any other troops in sufficient strength to stop the break-through.' This seems to have been the nub. The report of the British 1st Airborne Division uses a different form of words for the same theme, although Urquhart himself afterwards wrote that he had 'no illusions about the Germans folding up at the first blow'. Others felt much the same. Sosabowski considered that the way in which his British allies discounted the possible German resistance was 'arrogant optimism completely unjustified'. The thirty-three year old Brigadier J.W. (Shan) Hackett, the commander of Urquhart's 4 Parachute Brigade, whose battle experience all but equalled that of Sosabowski (of whom he was a close friend), understood only too well how the Germans reacted to a dangerous threat. What Hackett and Sosabowski particularly deprecated was the tendency of airborne planners to set up an operation as a sort of 'airborne picnic', to

---

* It is worth noting that the formidable German 88-mm anti-tank gun had been designed originally as an anti-aircraft weapon – it proved excellent in either role.

which the enemy were added as an afterthought. Hackett called it 'cooking up the airborne battle and then adding the enemy in as pepper and salt to taste'. In general, however, the euphoria was still widespread, the feeling prevailing that the Germans were on the run and the airborne troops were about to deliver the coup-de-grâce.

One puzzling aspect of these intelligence summaries issued by Airborne Corps is the contrast between that provided for 'Comet' and that for 'Market'. The earlier one contains the explicit reference to the panzer division refitting north of Arnhem (information probably originating from the Dutch), to the SS training units which had moved to Nijmegen, and to the infantry in the operational area probably adding up to a division. All these details are absent from Browning's intelligence summary for 'Market', despite the extra information that had become available to the higher headquarters since 7 September. It is hard to find an explanation for this discrepancy. In planning such an operation in such a limited space of time, a corps intelligence staff can do little more, of course, than collate the information being received from above and pass it on. As with so much else, the handling of intelligence for 'Market' was plagued by the wide separation between the headquarters and the short time available for consultation. In Belgium and in France, the HQs of Second Army, Twenty-First Army Group and SHAEF were all involved; in England there were First Allied Airborne Army and I Airborne Corps. In addition there were the various air force headquarters. Some information came to one place, some to another. Nor did the low standing accorded to field intelligence by the British during the Second World War help; at an American corps headquarters such intelligence would have been handled by an officer either one or two grades senior to the major usually employed on the task at British HQs.

Browning was in no way the man to endanger his troops by suppressing information that he believed to be true. It has been reported that he was uneasy about the task set him in 'Market', and his possibly off-the-cuff 'bridge too far' comment to Montgomery bears this out. Like any other professional soldier, he was itching to lead into action the troops he had been training for so many years, and to see the worth of airborne troops incontrovertibly established. But despite these pressures, there can be no grounds for any suggestion that he deliberately hid information, either from General

Urquhart or from anyone else. His conduct at the time of 'Linnet 2' is sufficient mark of his integrity. Nor would he have been justified in proposing that the 'Market' operation should be cancelled on the information he had received – and that from an officer in whose judgement he had lost confidence. To have made such a stand would, in any case, have been a pointless gesture from his point of view. This time his resignation would have been accepted, and there were plenty of experienced airborne commanders waiting in the wings to replace him, Ridgway among them.

If he had been privy to the Ultra information, Browning might have acted differently, but there was no question of his being given full access to it. The risk of compromising Ultra was the primary consideration; as Wavell is said to have remarked in 1941, 'Better lose Crete than lose Ultra'. Williams remembers how intelligence staff at Twenty-First Army Group, not knowing intimately all those with whom they were dealing in the tangle of headquarters concerned with 'Market Garden', did not dare to risk even a paraphrase of Ultra which might imperil so vital a secret. It is possible that if Brereton had allowed himself to become rather more deeply involved in the planning for the battle, he would have ensured that the gist of what became known through Ultra was passed to Browning in some guarded fashion, but it was not to be.

The one person who could have cancelled 'Market Garden', even at a late stage, was Montgomery himself. The boldness of the plan was uncharacteristic of the man, and it was not in his nature to hazard the lives of his troops without good cause. This was especially so in the autumn of 1944 when, after five years of war, the British manpower tap was running dry, and formations were being disbanded and their men reassigned to other units because of the lack of replacements. Why then did Montgomery disregard the accumulation of evidence about the increasing German presence in the area where the airborne divisions were to land, not to mention the advice of senior members of his staff in whose judgement he had the greatest confidence?

Firm in his conviction that a single thrust to, and perhaps beyond, the Ruhr, would smash Hitler's remaining armies, the Field-Marshal had staked his reputation on such a 'narrow front' thrust in all his long arguments with Eisenhower. It was the chance he had been seeking to end the war in the West quickly, to end it before

Christmas, and so avoid another winter of conflict. The German armies had collapsed in disorder before they had even fled over the Seine, and there was good reason to believe that the same collapse could happen once more if they were again hit hard. And it would be British troops, led by Montgomery himself, who would have won the final victory. The role of a commander is to judge the risks and take the decision: Ultra could be misinterpreted, Dutch information inaccurate, reconnaissance photographs misleading. After the chaos of the German retreat across France, a report of two panzer divisions refitting in Holland meant little in terms of men and tanks. Montgomery could have cancelled the operation, but he certainly knew that more battles are lost through indecision than by bold action. His reasons for not wavering were sound indeed.

CHAPTER FOUR

'... IT WAS EVIDENT THAT THE INITIAL FLIGHT ... WOULD BE HAZARDOUS'

The war-weary people of eastern and southern England had long grown accustomed to seeing vast numbers of bomber aircraft gathering in the late evening light, forming up before starting out over the coast towards their targets in Europe. But what summoned everyone out of their houses and into streets and gardens on the lovely morning of Sunday, 17 September 1944, was something altogether different, something on a scale that neither they nor anyone else had seen before. First there was a faint drone in the distance, and rapidly this swelled to a throbbing roar as the planes came into view – Dakotas, Stirlings, Albermarles and Halifaxes, many of them towing gliders behind them. Five miles across, the long columns filled the sky. In places the spectacle lasted for over an hour. The aircraft flew on over the North Sea, over Europe, where the Belgians and Dutch who saw them, as well as the people in England, felt sure that such an armada must herald the final and victorious battle of the war. Even those members of the three airborne divisions who watched it from their sealed camps, waiting themselves to fly to Holland on the next day or the day after that, were astounded by the scale of it all. It brought both excitement and relief. At long last their waiting seemed to be over, provided the weather held.

49

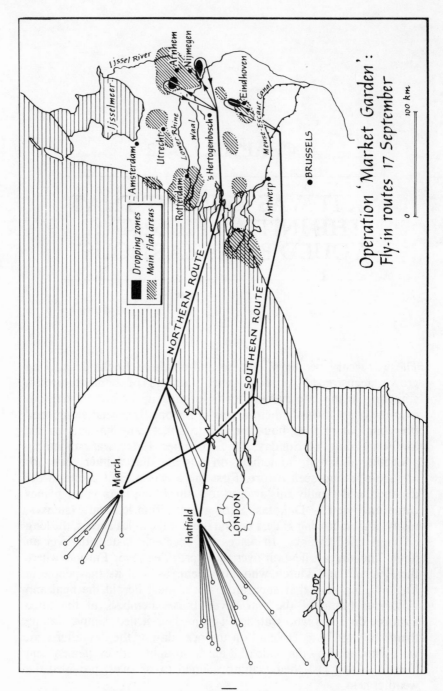

Operation 'Market Garden':
Fly-in routes 17 September

0   100 km

NORTHERN ROUTE

SOUTHERN ROUTE

March

Hatfield

LONDON

Dropping zones
Main flak areas

Ijssel River

Ijsselmeer

Arnhem
Nijmegen
Eindhoven

Amsterdam

Utrecht
Lower Rhine
Waal
Meuse-Escaut Canal

Rotterdam
s'Hertogenbosch

Antwerp

BRUSSELS

It was the largest force of transport aircraft ever assembled. From twenty-two airfields, most of them around Grantham or in the Swindon-Reading area, 1,534 troop carriers and 491 gliders took off to converge at fixed points around the coast, before splitting into two columns to cross the ocean. By the northern route, which passed over the Dutch island of Schouwen, travelled the British 1st and the US 82nd Airborne Divisions; by the southern, which ran just south of Antwerp before turning north-east towards Eindhoven, flew the US 101st. Beacons marked the rendezvous and the points of departure on the coast, and marker-boats helped to keep direction across the sea. It was ideal flying weather. Receiving a favourable forecast for the following day, Brereton had made the final decision at 1900 hours on 16 September: the operation would go ahead as planned, with H-hour timed for 1300 hours, Continental time, on the 17th. The weather forecast proved accurate. By 0900 hours on D-day ground fog had cleared from the airfields, and all the way over the sky was clear, with only a slight haze and some cloud over the target area.

During the night of 16-17 September and on the following morning, 1,395 bomber and 1,240 fighter sorties were flown by the Allied air forces in support of the operation. In darkness, 282 Lancasters and Mosquitoes of Bomber Command hit a single important flak position and four German airfields from which enemy fighter squadrons threatened the airborne landings; one of the latter targets was a base for the new, fast and dangerous Messerschmitt 262 jets. American B-17 Flying Fortresses attacked a fifth airfield. The results were excellent: so cratered were the runways that on the following morning no fighters could take off, while the attacks had been so designed that they avoided indicating to the Germans that anything unusual was about to occur. Early on the next morning, the day of the landings, 821 Flying Fortresses of the US Eighth Air Force, escorted by 153 P-51 Mustang fighters, dropped 3,139 tons of bombs upon 117 separate flak positions. The results were reported as '43 good, 24 fair and 50 poor'. At the same time more Lancasters and Mosquitoes hit three coastal batteries around Walcheren Island in the Scheldt estuary, and the British Second Tactical Air force (TAF), flying from its bases in Europe, attacked barracks at Nijmegen, Cleve, Arnhem and Ede; 212 fighters of the US Ninth Air Force then hit the flak positions once again. The vulnerable transport columns were guarded by P-51 Mustangs, P-38 Lightnings and P-47 Thunderbolts of the US Eighth Air Force, and by Spitfires, Tempests and Mosquitoes of the Air Defence of Great Britain, 60 per cent of the aircraft flying escort and the rest carrying out anti-flak patrols. In all, nearly 1,000 Allied fighters or fighter-bombers were in the sky at the same time. The only enemy aircraft encountered were some fifteen Focke-Wulf 190s which challenged American fighters near Wesel: seven were shot down, the Americans losing only a single fighter. During the entire day, the Allies lost just twenty-three fighters and bombers from all causes.

At the transport take-off airfields, the sheer power of the scene, the massed rows of gliders and aircraft parked in their threes and stretching right across the grass and tarmac, impressed even the most cynical of the soldiers – and cynical not a few of them were after a long summer of cancelled operations. Few men lacked their private fears, but the very size of the undertaking, allied to the meticulous preparations in which they had taken part, produced in most a happy confidence, for though there had been little time in which to argue out the larger issues, the briefing of the troops had in no way been skimped. A little later, as the airborne soldiers sat in the dark, tunnel-like fuselages, those who could see out of a Dakota's door (which was left open in flight), or who could crane their necks to peer through a small window, caught glimpses of the vastness of the aerial armada, proof of the complete superiority over the enemy attained by the Allied air forces.

But as England disappeared from view and the sun glistened on the sea below them, thoughts of flak intruded upon those soldiers who had remained awake, some of them reading the Sunday newspapers, some munching their sandwiches or opening the large thermos flasks of tea provided for the flight. The air-sea rescue launches, dotted at intervals across the sea, were pleasantly comforting, but no one was under any illusions about the damage the German anti-aircraft guns might inflict upon these slow-moving columns. It was perhaps fortunate that few of the troops realised that their Dakotas lacked self-sealing petrol tanks. In the event, however, there proved to have been small cause for worry. As the British 1st and the US 82nd Divisions crossed the narrow band of beach that marked the Dutch coastline, hardly anyone was to have this peaceful journey interrupted. Light flak from a barge was quickly silenced by a fighter which dived to deal with it, and some heavy flak guns on the shore caused little damage. Over the targets themselves, only seven aircraft were to be damaged by anti-aircraft fire.

The daylight drop, the small amount of flak, and the excellence of the complicated air plans were between them to produce the first accurate large-scale landing ever carried out by Allied airborne troops. Twelve British Stirlings and six American Dakotas of the Pathfinder Force, flown by specially selected crews, had travelled ahead of the main columns and, twenty minutes or so before the main landing, troops of the army pathfinder units had jumped from these aircraft over the DZs and LZs. Once landed, they set up the Eureka homing beacons, laid out the white indicator panels, and made ready the smoke signals, all of which would be used to guide in the main force. As they finished their task, the sky started to fill with aircraft. Hundreds of gliders, released from their tugs, swept earthwards. Fast-falling specks suddenly coalesced into clouds of different-coloured parachutes, an oddly gay and peaceful scene.

So thorough had been the briefing that the roads, rivers and buildings unfolding beneath them seemed almost familiar to the men peering through the open doors of the Dakotas, their attention from time to time distracted by the Allied fighters weaving in and out of the transport columns, as they waited for the green light to flicker on and the scream of 'GO' to shrill in their ears. When it sounded, the bulky figures, burdened with 'chutes (a reserve also, in the case of the Americans) moved awkwardly towards the door to follow their leader out into space. The parachute soldiers made a bizarre sight. Tied to their legs were bags crammed with weapons, radios, ammunition, mines and every sort of bulky equipment. Strapped beneath their jumping jackets, their haversacks produced a quaint effect of advanced pregnancy. Once in the air, however they became altogether different beings, their now-open parachutes billowing in the sky and their weapon-bags, released from their thighs, swinging from long cords beneath them. Although they were helpless and vulnerable for the minute or two they were in the air, exhilaration tended to overcome fear, their main worry for the moment being the risk of injury when they landed. As it was, the few Germans troops encountered around the DZs and the LZs either made good their escape or fired a few shots before looking for someone to whom to

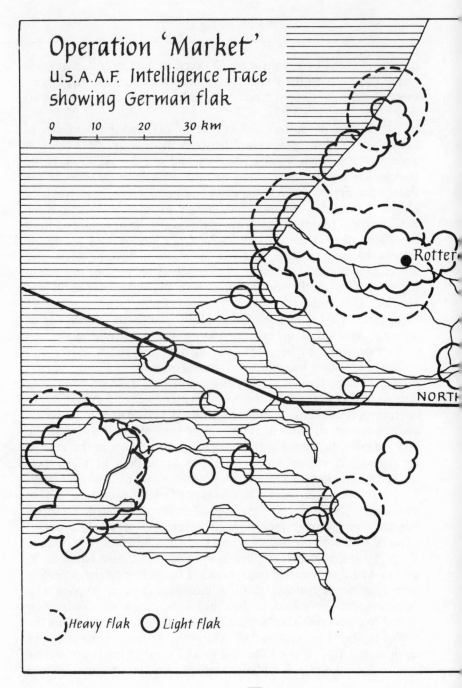

Operation 'Market'
U.S.A.A.F. Intelligence Trace
showing German flak

0   10   20   30 km

Rotter

NORT

⌒Heavy flak ◯Light flak

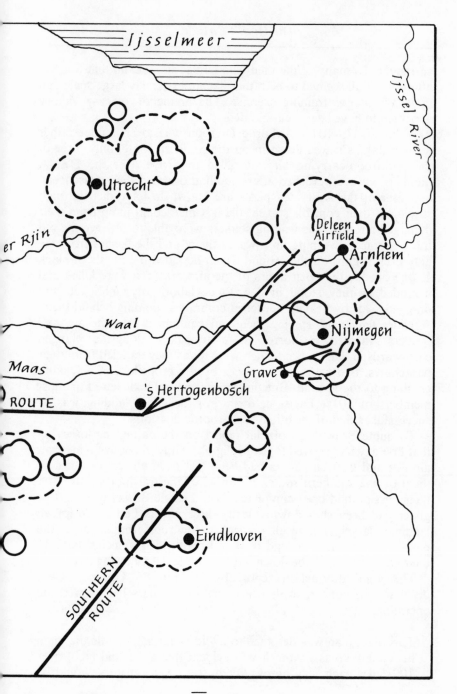

IJsselmeer

IJssel River

Utrecht

Deleen
Airfield

Arnhem

er Rjin

Waal

Nijmegen

Maas

Grave

's Hertogenbosch

ROUTE

Eindhoven

SOUTHERN
ROUTE

surrender. To many of the men who landed in Holland that Sunday afternoon it all seemed to be rather like an extremely large-scale and unusually lifelike training exercise. The prediction of easy victory appeared to have been well-founded.

Although US 101st Airborne Division was to encounter rather heavier flak as it was flown in on the southern route, only three of the paratroop-carrying aircraft failed to arrive over the DZ. A number, however, crashed after they had dropped their passengers, and four of the American pilots are known to have died through staying at their controls so that the last men could jump from their damaged aircraft. The waiting soldiers were able to observe the red trails of tracer sweeping up towards them, and the flashes from the anti-aircraft guns on the ground which heralded the bursts of black smoke outside the open doors of the aircraft. Men were killed and wounded as they stood in line, to be laboriously unhooked and dragged aside by heavily burdened comrades standing behind them. A glider fell apart, spilling men and equipment into the air, and soldiers watched in horror as a transport alongside plunged earthwards in flames. Some men were hit as they dangled from their parachutes: two were cut to pieces by the propellors of a Dakota crashing to the ground. But these were the unlucky few. For most members of 101st Division, their drop or glider landing was as successful as that of the other two airborne divisions.

To quote Browning's official report on the battle, the losses on that first day had proved to be 'negligible'. Only thirty-five American aircraft and thirteen gliders had been lost from all causes, most of them on the southern route, and most of the transports only after their mission had been completed. Not a single British transport or glider had been shot down; twenty-three gliders had made forced landings, largely the result of broken tow-ropes, but most of the passengers managed to find their way, with their vehicles, back to their base airfields, to be flown into the battle the following day.

The joint after-action report by 38 and 46 Groups, RAF, discusses the concern with which the air planners had viewed the operation:

This flight plan was designed to avoid as far as possible the main heavy flak areas ... but it was evident that the initial flight over 100 miles each way across enemy occupied territory would be hazardous. Flak in the target area was being rapidly built up in the week before the operation, and although anti-flak sorties were ordered, appreciable losses were expected.

A later paragraph in the same report reads:

The great discrepancy between the expected and the actual losses calls for comment. On the basis of the flak map and reports showing a very rapid build-up of flak just before the date of the operation, losses up to 40% were predicted ... it is hardly credible that flak positions of the density predicted by intelligence can have been occupied, but it is noticeable that on the occasions when fighter cover was lacking, losses to flak were higher than the average, suggesting a reluctance to open fire when fighters were in the area.

The flak around Deelen airfield is said to have been dismantled completely before 'Market Garden' started, and air photographs of the country south of the Neder Rijn taken on 19 September (D-plus-2) reveal no signs of anti-aircraft guns. It would seem that the air forces had greatly overestimated the strength of the flak, and had failed to appreciate the ability of their aircraft to smother it. Dutch civilians reported seeing Germans abandon their guns; hardly surprising, perhaps, in view of the crushing power of the Allied bombers and fighters.

In fact, the air support provided for the operation could well have been greater still. The complicated programme was the outcome of meetings held on 12 and 15 September at the rear headquarters of the Allied Expeditionary Air Force in the United Kingdom. These meetings should have been attended by representatives from all the many air forces involved in the operation, but the officer from Second Tactical Air Force missed the second conference, albeit through no fault of his own. The consequence was that his formation headquarters did not know until 16 September that the fighters under its command were to attack yet more flak positions, and thus, with insufficient time to rearrange the programme, some targets were never engaged. The days to come would demonstrate an equally inadequate liaison on air support for the troops once they had landed.

The planning for 'Market' had been very much marked by a repetition of the unfounded pessimism which had presaged the D-Day airborne operations in Normandy. Brereton and his air force commanders had not been well advised. As a result *coup-de-main* glider parties were not used to make surprise attacks on the major bridges, and 1st Airborne Division was landed up to eight miles distant from its main objective. If a request had been made for paratroops of US 82nd Airborne Division to drop on either side of the Nijmegen bridges, undoubtedly the answer would have been the same – too difficult, too dangerous.

CHAPTER FIVE

'SIGNAL FAILURES WERE NO NEW PHENOMENON'

The town of Arnhem has been likened to Cheltenham, and its surrounding countryside to that around Aldershot. The city itself possessed much of the dignity of the Gloucestershire spa. With its wide roads, solid prosperous houses and pleasant surburbs, it provided a comfortable retreat for equally dignified retired colonial officials and planters, and was a prosperous commercial centre as well. To the north of the Neder Rijn lay the Surrey-like woods, sandy and interspersed with open stretches of heathland and scattered with villages, patches of farmland and neat housing estates. There was little of the conventional tourist-poster Holland, no dykes, tulip-fields, windmills or canals. This was the Dutch hill-country of the cyclist and walker, rising in places to as much as 300 feet above sea level, like the Groesbeek Heights, rather similar country, lying to the east of Nijmegen along the border with Germany. Only in the Betuwe district between Arnhem and Nijmegen was the traditional countryside of Holland to be found, the polderland sprinkled with villages and orchards.

It was on the open heath and farmland west of Arnhem that Urquhart's British 1st Airborne Division was obliged to make its landing. Five stretches of country had been chosen for the purpose, three of them north of the Arnhem-Utrecht railway (of which the furthest lay eight miles as the crow flies from the road bridge), and

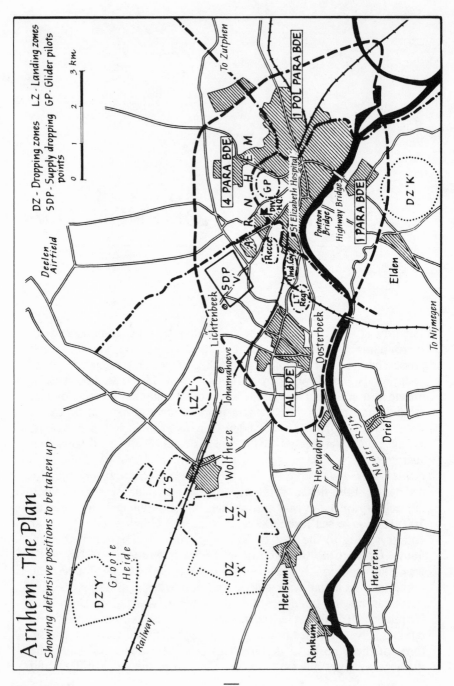

Arnhem: The Plan

Showing defensive positions to be taken up

DZ - Dropping zones   LZ - Landing zones
SDP - Supply dropping   GP - Glider pilots
points

3 km
0 1 2

To Zutphen

1 POL PARA BDE

4 PARA BDE

A R N H E M

GP

Div HQ

St Elizabeth Hospital

Recce

2nd Coy

LT
Regt

Pontoon
Bridge

Highway Bridge

1 PARA BDE

DZ 'K'

Elden

To Nijmegen

Deelen
Airfield

SDP

Lichterbeek

Johannahoeve

LZ 'L'

Oosterbeek

1 AL BDE

Wolfheze

Heveadorp

Neder Rijn

Driel

LZ 'S'

LZ
'Z'

DZ
'X'

Heelsum

Heteren

DZ 'Y'

Groote
Heide

Railway

Renkum

the other two lying between the railway and Heelsum village near the river. Closer to the city, just to the east of the area called Lichtenbeek, another, smaller field had been earmarked for subsequent supply dropping. 1 Polish Independent Parachute Brigade was to drop on the polderland south of the river and close to the main bridge, but this was not planned to happen until the third day (19 September), when Arnhem would have been captured and any flak eliminated.

Urquhart had decided to carry, in the first lift on Sunday, his 1 Parachute Brigade, the bulk of 1 Airlanding Brigade, his own headquarters, and a high proportion of the divisional troops,* including two of his three batteries of 75-mm field artillery. The rest of his division, other than the Poles, largely 4 Parachute Brigade and its supporting arms, was to follow on the second day. As has already been said Urquhart's arrangements contrasted with those made by the two American airborne divisional commanders. Taylor and Gavin both decided to drop three regiments of parachute infantry (each US regiment being equivalent in numbers to a British parachute brigade) on the first day. Influenced by the possibility of a quick German reaction to the landing, Urquhart had given guns and other supporting arms priority over infantry, so providing 1 Parachute Brigade with some fire support, little though it was, to help the troops force their way through the city towards the bridges.

Because Urquhart had not been allowed to land any gliders close to the bridges he had decided on the next best thing, a *coup-de-main* to be carried out by 1st Airborne Reconnaissance Squadron, a task that aroused misgivings in the mind of Major Freddie Gough, the unit's commanding officer. Designed to probe forward for information, rather than perform a frontal assault such as Urquhart's plan envisaged, Gough's unarmoured jeeps were singularly ill-suited for such a venture, despite the devastating fire-power of the twin Vickers 'K' machine-guns mounted on each vehicle.

Behind the Recce Squadron, whose task was to rush the bridges as soon as the jeeps had been reunited with those of the squadron's men who had dropped by parachute, 1 Parachute Brigade would

* The military expression used to designate that part of a division other than infantry or armour.

61

follow on foot, leaving the Airlanding Brigade to hold the DZs and LZs for the second lift on D-plus-1, a necessary precaution once the Germans had been alerted to the possibility of the initial landing being reinforced. The plan was that, on the second day, the Airlanding Brigade would be joined by 4 Parachute Brigade, and both would then move to link up with 1 Parachute Brigade in defending a box-like perimeter around Arnhem against any German counter-attack, a perimeter which the Polish Brigade would thicken when it arrived on the third day. From the Westerbouwing bluff, east of the suburb of Oosterbeek, on the left flank to the bridge over the Ijssel on the right, a twelve-mile front had to be held, a huge task for a single lightly armed division in wooded and built-up country such as this.

At 1300 hours on 17 September, exactly on time and twenty minutes after 21st Independent Parachute Company, the division's pathfinders, had landed, the first of the gliders began to sweep down on to the heather and the plough. It was fifty minutes before the last had landed. As the flimsy craft were guided by their pilots in to the soon-crowded LZs, some flipped over on to their noses, often crushing the occupants under the jeeps or guns as they did so, others smashed in to trees, while still others collided. It was hardly surprising that most parachute soldiers viewed the method of conveyance of their glider-borne colleagues with a strong distaste.

Then, at 1400 hours, those same paratroops began to land, on a DZ adjacent to the area where their division's gliders had already arrived. Ninety minutes later, men and vehicles had married up, and each unit was ready to do battle. While 1 Airlanding Brigade remained to guard the DZs and LZs for the next landings, 1 Parachute Brigade was moving off towards Arnhem.

Commanded by Brigadier Gerald Lathbury, the officers and men of this experienced brigade knew very well that they were the élite of a crack division. Formed in 1941, their German enemies had bestowed upon them the epithet 'Red Devils', the colour of their headgear matching the manner in which they had fought during the Tunisian campaign, in which the brigade had suffered 1,700 casualties in four months of bitter battles during the winter of 1942-3. Despite the unfortunate inaccuracy of the drop in Sicily the following summer, the tenacity with which the small number of 1 Parachute Brigade's men who succeeded in reaching the Primosole

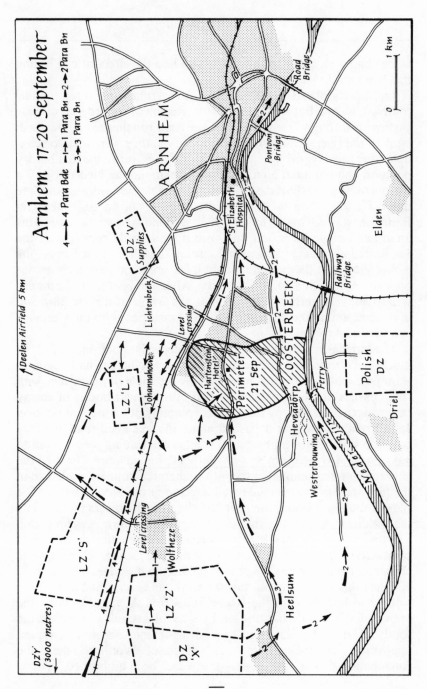

Arnhem 17-20 September

4 ➤ 4 Para Bde   1 ➤ 1 Para Bn   2 ➤ 2 Para Bn
           3 ➤ 3 Para Bn

↑ Deelen Airfield 5 km

DZ 'Y'
(3000 metres)

LZ 'S'

DZ 'V'
Supplies

LZ 'L'

Lichtenbeek

Level crossing

Johannahoeve

Level crossing

Wolfheze

LZ 'Z'

DZ 'X'

ARNHEM

St Elizabeth
Hospital ■

Hartenstein
Hotel

Perimeter
21 Sep

OOSTERBEEK

Heveadorp

Westerbouwing

Nedei Rijn

Ferry

Railway
Bridge

Pontoon
Bridge

Road
Bridge

Elden

Polish
DZ

Driel

Heelsum

0   1 km

bridge had then clung to their objective had the effect of confirming this reputation.

Lathbury's plan was to advance into Arnhem on three parallel routes. His 2nd Battalion, Parachute Regiment he ordered to pass eastwards through Heelsum, using the road running along the north bank of the river. Advancing upon the town, they were then to seize, first, the railway bridge, and afterwards, in turn, the temporary pontoon and the main highway bridge spanning the Neder Rijn. To the north, the 3rd Battalion was to approach the bridges along the main Utrecht-Arnhem road while, further north still, the 1st Battalion was to make for the high ground above the city. This approach on such a wide front, with only a single company of the 1st Battalion retained as brigade reserve, had been based upon the assumption that the brigade would meet only comparatively minor opposition, and that of poor quality. After the operation, Lathbury was to admit his error in not keeping the whole of the 1st Battalion in reserve, and in the misreading of the threat posed by the Germans in and near Arnhem.

The familiar routine of units sorting themselves out on the DZ, so much like a training exercise until the first few bullets had begun to skim past, had been interrupted by only a couple of skirmishes with small parties of Germans. One or two other similar bodies of enemy troops were dealt with by the leading company of Lieutenant-Colonel John Frost's 2 Para as it pushed along the tree-lined road, country only too suitable for ambushes. Then, as the leading men started to pass through Heveadorp and Oosterbeek, the advance assumed the character of a triumphal entry into a liberated country, rather than the first stages of what could well develop into a bloody battle. The jugs of milk and water, the fruit and the orange flowers pressed into the soldiers' hands by the delirious Dutch were welcome and heart-warming, but they began to become a distraction as well. And soon German resistance started to harden. Some SS men were captured. An armoured car proved difficult to dislodge.

While this was going on, further north, as Gough had feared, the worst had happened to the Recce Squadron. Advancing along the railway line towards the bridges by way of a track running to the south of it, the jeeps had run straight into resolute German opposition. To the east of the village of Wolfheze, near the Johannahoeve farm, the leading troop had been ambushed, and no way of skirting the enemy position had been found. Frost was on his own, although he had no means of knowing it: there seemed to be something wrong with the radios, and little or no information about the rest of the battle was reaching him.

Frost had planned that his C Company would capture the railway bridge, cross it, and then approach the main highway bridge from the south bank of the river. Stiff resistance had been expected from the flak gunners who had been reported in the area, but when C Company swept forward across the open ground to seize the railway bridge no more than a few harmless shots were fired from the southern bank. As the leading troops started to cross, however, there came a huge explosion and the southernmost span curled into the air on top of them. A small German demolition party had successfully destroyed the bridge. Two other crossing places still remained, however, the pontoon bridge to the east and, beyond that, the main highway bridge.

Meanwhile, the rest of the brigade was not making very quick progress. Tough German resistance had twice held up the leading troops of 3 Para, the second time just east of the Hartenstein Hotel in Oosterbeek, and the high, close-meshed wire fencing around the trim suburban gardens was hampering efforts to outflank the enemy. The German mortar fire was devastatingly accurate, and casualties soon started to mount. The story was much the same further north. Here 1 Para had encountered some German armour on the Ede-Arnhem road, and the battalion had, as a consequence, taken to the woods which lay between the road and Wolfheze, and which stretched down to the north side of Johannahoeve. By nightfall one of the companies of this battalion had already lost half its strength.

As the sounds of battle on the roads leading into Arnhem echoed faintly back across the woods and houses to the LZs and DZs, most of Brigadier P.H.W. (Pip) Hicks's 1 Airlanding Brigade was enjoying quite a peaceful evening. Made up of 1st Border Regiment, 7th King's Own Scottish Borderers (KOSB) and 2nd South Staffordshire Regiment (of which two companies were to arrive by the second lift), the brigade had suffered like everyone else in Sicily from a scattered landing. Arnhem, the brigade's second airborne operation, had been quite different. The operation had started in a tidy manner, with the brigade landed accurately and all but complete, and now, with a few prisoners in their possession (including a surly female Nazi who at first had refused to accept even a cup of tea for fear of poison), the two and a half battalions settled down to guard the LZs and DZs for the arrival of the second lift planned for the next day. Only one or two slight skirmishes were to disturb what proved to be a quiet night.

Meanwhile Urquhart himself had been watching 1 Parachute Brigade's advance into Arnhem as best he could. Soon after 1st Airborne's general touched down in his glider, he had discovered to his dismay that the Divisional HQ signallers were having difficulty in raising anyone at all on their radios, either his own brigades and units, or the other headquarters of the Airborne Corps down south. It was clear that the range of the sets was not adequate for the task in such closely wooded and built-up country. There was little surprising in this. As Urquhart afterwards wrote, 'signal failures were no new phenomenon', but the consequences were most serious. Lacking any news of what was happening either to 1 Parachute Brigade or to the Recce Squadron, Urquhart set off towards Arnhem to find out for himself, with his signaller in the back of the jeep vainly trying to make contact on his command net with the other units.

Urquhart first drove down the narrow and winding road to the river, where he overtook the rearmost troops of 2 Para. In his view the troops were advancing far too slowly, and this he made clear to them. Frost he failed to contact, for the battalion commander was up ahead, urging his troops forward as Urquhart was doing behind him. From the river route, the general then returned to the axis of 3 Para's advance, the centre road into Arnhem, where he contacted Lathbury. Not long before he had observed graphic evidence of the battle, a smashed German staff car around which were sprawled four bodies, one of them that of Generalmajor Kussin, the Feldkommandant of Arnhem, ambushed by 3 Para as he drove past on his way towards the city.

The slow progress being made in this area also worried Urquhart. The reality of battle still escaped some of his troops: a number, he learned, were even knocking on the doors of the houses of these hospitable and welcoming Dutch folk, politely asking them for permission to search the buildings for Germans. Urquhart well understood the problem. Many of his men were in action for the first time, while others had not seen any fighting for a year or so: in such circumstances men could take far too much notice of a few odd bullets. All three airborne divisions involved in 'Market Garden' were initially to behave in much the same way, even though the Americans had only recently been withdrawn from the Normandy fighting. On their first day in action units had to find their second wind, a recurrent problem with airborne troops. To men suddenly immersed in battle, the contrast with the tranquillity of the home base could be severe – it took them just a little time to settle down. Much the same applied to the machinery of command: in the early stages of an operation, headquarters tended to creak a little.

In conversation with the 1 Parachute Brigade commander, Urquhart discovered that Lathbury was also suffering from communication problems similar to his own. Not only was Lathbury unable to raise Divisional Headquarters but he was in only sporadic touch with his three battalions. Then, as the two officers were discussing the problems of the battle, Urquhart's jeep was hit by a mortar bomb and his signaller was wounded. At the same time he learned that the Germans were between himself and his Divisional Headquarters. Out of touch with nearly everyone, he decided that the best thing he could do was to stay with Lathbury, where he could at least bring some influence to bear upon what was the vital section of the battle. Soon it was dark, and Lathbury decided to halt 3 Para, by that time rather scattered and disorganised, with its forward company some 800 yards short of the Hartenstein Hotel in Oosterbeek. The advance, the brigadier decided, would be renewed at dawn.

Frost, on the other hand, who had seen more fighting than most people, valued the cover of darkness. In 1941, as a company commander in 2 Para, he had led the famous night raid against the German short-range radar station at Bruneval on the French coast, the first successful British airborne operation of the war, and for which he had been awarded the Military Cross. Later, first as second-in-command and afterwards as commanding officer of the same battalion, he had fought throughout the Tunisian winter campaign of 1942-43 (during which he had won the Distinguished Service Order), and in the invasions of Sicily and Italy. His experience had led him to believe that the Germans were reluctant to fight at night, a gap in the military skills of these accomplished soldiers of which he made sound use, for it certainly proved to be the case at Arnhem. It was, however, something of a paradox that many

German soldiers tended to believe much the same about their enemies, especially the Americans.

Acting on their colonel's principles, 2 Para kept moving. After the railway bridge had been blown, A Company, in the lead, had for a time been held up along the line of the railway by patrolling German armoured cars, and by machine-guns and snipers firing from the high ground just to the north, a wooded area called Den Brink. Helped by B Company, which managed to work around the back of this feature, A Company infiltrated through the back gardens of some of the houses along the road, and pushed on into the dusk. Ignoring bursts of German fire that swept across the road and overrunning a small body of troops that tried to bar the way, Frost's men swept on past the pontoon bridge, the centre section of which they found dismantled. Six hundred yards more and they had reached the north end of the main road bridge, which was intact and unguarded. The company quickly occupied some high and solid buildings overlooking the main road ramp leading up to the bridge itself, and here, as the evening progressed, more troops arrived. First came Frost with his headquarters, followed by the larger part of 1 Parachute Brigade Headquarters (from which Lathbury had by now become separated), a number of Royal Engineers, a platoon of Royal Army Service Corps and Gough with a small part of his Recce Squadron.

Gough had arrived more by accident than anything else. Just before his leading jeep had been ambushed south of the railway, an unfounded rumour had reached Divisional Headquarters that most of the gliders carrying the Recce Squadron's vehicles had failed to arrive. As a result Gough had received an order to report to Urquhart. Still searching for his divisional commander, he had found his way to the bridge by the lower road which, as it proved, was by then the only practical way to enter Arnhem and reach the road bridge, although during the night a part of 3 Para's C Company did manage to slip down the line of the railway to reinforce Frost further. Gough's chapter of accidents was typical of the confusion of a battlefield, particularly one in which the communications fail to function. Three battalions and a reconnaisance squadron had been despatched to seize and hold the bridge over the Neder Rijn. By nightfall on the first day one end of the bridge was indeed in British hands, but it was held by only part of one battalion and a handful

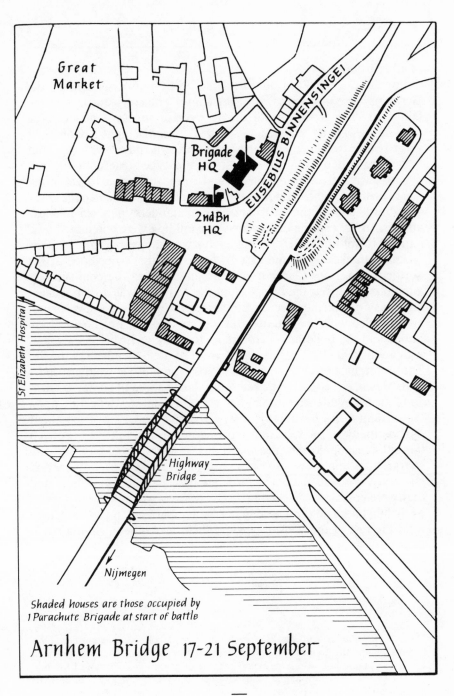

Great Market

Brigade HQ

2nd Bn. HQ

EUSEBIUS BINNENSINGEI

St Elizabeth Hospital

Highway Bridge

Nijmegen

Shaded houses are those occupied by
1 Parachute Brigade at start of battle

Arnhem Bridge 17-21 September

of other troops.

For although 2 Para now held the north end of the bridge, the Germans were in possession of the south. The consequences of the failure to drop troops south of the river or to use a glider-borne *coup-de-main* party had become clear. During the night A Company was to make two attempts to rush the southern end of the bridge, but both were halted from fire from a pill-box-type structure built into the roadway of the bridge itself, and from an armoured car firing from further back. Among the wounded was Lieutenant Jack Grayburn, one of the two platoon commanders involved in these attacks. In the end the defenders of the pill-box were eliminated by a flame-thrower and a PIAT*, but as this was happening the Germans counter-attacked from the eastern flank of Frost's positions at the northern end. Four German lorries then added to the confusion by attempting to cross the bridge from the south. It was a complicated and noisy engagement, lit by the flames of the now-burning lorries, and it ended with the counter-attacks repulsed, the north end of the bridge and the buildings surrounding it firmly in British hands, and with about 100 Germans captured, most of them members of the SS. The Germans, however, were still in possession of the southern end.

By dawn, Frost had gathered round him a force of some 500 men and four 6-pounder anti-tank guns with their crews. Reflecting upon the certainty of a hard battle during the day, he was worried about the possibility of the Germans blowing the bridge, but the heat from the still-burning lorries prevented his sappers from tackling any charges that might already be in position. Nevertheless, both he and his men were well pleased with what they had accomplished, and they were confident of speedy relief. XXX Corps' tanks were expected by lunchtime on the Tuesday, 19 September and, in any case, help from the rest of the division, behind them in Arnhem, should reach them very soon.

---

* Projector Infantry Anti-Tank, a small rather crude-looking weapon fired by a two-man team, the gunner lying prone with the weapon pulled into his shoulder. Firing a 3-pound hollow-charge bomb capable of penetrating 75 mm of armour, the PIAT was a formidable and invaluable infantry weapon, despite its seeming crudity.

CHAPTER SIX

'THE DROP WAS BETTER THAN HAD EVER BEEN EXPERIENCED'

Except for 1 Parachute Brigade, the British and Polish troops who were to land in Operation 'Market' had seen far less action than either of the two American divisions. Many members of Brigadier-General Jim Gavin's 'All American' 82nd Airborne Division had already jumped three times into battle, in Sicily, at Salerno, and in Normandy – Gavin himself was among them. More than one British observer has described the division as having been composed of the best fighting troops he had ever been. The 101st Airborne Division, the 'Screaming Eagles', commanded by Major-General Maxwell D. Taylor, had fought in only the one campaign, but that had been Normandy. There, together with the 82nd, the division had held the right flank of the Allied bridgehead; the 101st had stayed in the line for three weeks, the 82nd for five. Of the 11,730 officers and men of the 82nd who landed in Normandy, 5,429 were to be reported as killed, wounded or missing; the casualties of its sister division numbered 4,670.

It was perhaps understandable, therefore, that the attitude of mind of these combat-hardened Americans differed from that of most of the members of the British division. The large number of newly arrived American reinforcements were just as keen to see action as any other airborne troops, but among the officers and enlisted men there was no lack of battle-experienced veterans, many still recovering from their wounds, only too ready to disabuse a rookie of the so-called 'glamour' of war. The two divisions were, in effect, powerful and professional fighting machines, well run-in and lubricated by a mixture of know-how, pride and and youthful enthusiasm. Moreover, their members were fortunate in being commanded by two outstanding generals. Taylor, like Ridgway, his corps commander, was later to head his country's armed forces; before taking command of the 101st Division, he had led the divisional artillery of the 82nd in Sicily and Italy. Gavin – 'Slim Jim' to his men – was a lean, tought ex-ranker, a quiet and courteous man with a penetrating mind. At thirty-seven, he was the youngest divisional commander in the United States Army (he was to be promoted major-general while in Holland), and he had previously led 505 Parachute Infantry Regiment* in Sicily and in Italy. He had then acted as Eisenhower's airborne adviser during the planning for the invasion, and had served as assistant divisional commander of the 82nd during the Normandy battle. After the war he was to reach four-star rank and become the United States Ambassador in Paris.

The initial response of both these men to 'Market Garden' was a little muted. Both were concerned that their divisions would not be arriving in a single lift, and by the extent of their tasks. Gavin's chief of staff protested that two divisions, not one, were needed for the job facing the 82nd. Taylor, whose division was to come under command of XXX Corps as soon as it had landed, had initially been ordered to spread his division over seven separate areas along a thirty-mile stretch of the main axis of advance. 'Stepping stones' would, perhaps, have been a more appropriate simile than 'carpet'. When Taylor complained, Brereton despatched him to Belgium to discuss the matter with Montgomery himself. It was a measure of the detail of Montgomery's orders to Browning that the army group commander's permission was now required before changes could be made to the divisional commander's plan. In his turn, Montgomery sent Taylor to see General Dempsey, the commander of British Second Army (Taylor was, after all, to come under command of XXX Corps), and a change of plan was agreed.

The result of Taylor's visit was to reduce the task of his division to seizing and holding a fifteen-mile stretch of road, something

---

* A US regiment is equivalent in numbers to a British brigade.

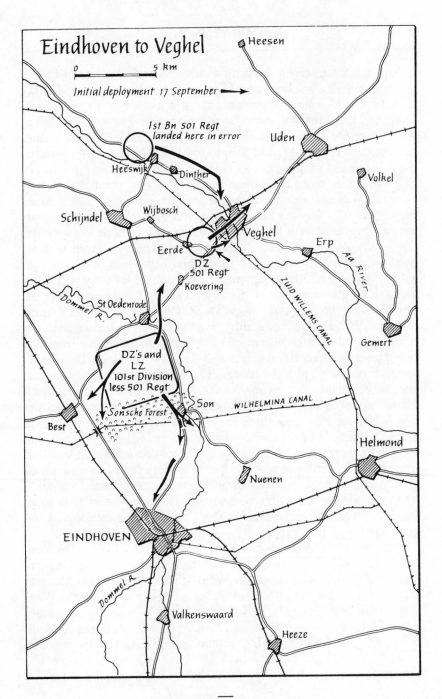

Eindhoven to Veghel

0   5 km

Initial deployment 17 September ➤

Heesen

1st Bn 501 Regt
landed here in error

Uden

Heeswijk   Dinther

Volkel

Schijndel   Wijbosch

Veghel

Eerde

Erp

DZ
501 Regt

Koevering

Aa River

St Oedenrode

Dommel R.

ZUID WILLEMS CANAL

DZ's and
LZ
101st Division
less 501 Regt

Gemert

Son   WILHELMINA CANAL

Sonsche Forest

Best

Helmond

Nuenen

EINDHOVEN

Dommel R.

Valkenswaard

Heeze

rather more manageable, but still a daunting task. Determined upon a tidy drop, Taylor chose two DZs and an LZ in the centre of his area, from which his troops could fan out towards their objectives. Dropping just north of the village of Son, 506 Parachute Infantry was ordered to capture the road bridge over the Wilhelmina Canal, just south of the village, and then to move still further south towards Eindhoven and its bridges. As with Arnhem and Nijmegen, heavy flak had been reported around Eindhoven, the result being that General Williams, as co-ordinator of the air plan, had refused permission for troops to be dropped south of the Wilhelmina Canal: the consequences were that 506 Regiment was not able to tackle the Son bridge from both ends simultaneously, and was faced with an eight-mile march from its DZ to its final objectives in Eindhoven.

To the north of 506 Regiment, 502 Parachute Infantry was given the task of guarding the LZ for later lifts, and of seizing the road bridge over the Dommel river at St Oedenrode. Taylor's third regiment, 501 Parachute Infantry, was to land a little further to the north, just outside the village of Veghel, its objectives the road and railway bridges over the Aa river and the Willems Canal. Despite his background as an artillery officer, Taylor decided to leave his guns and his glider infantry regiment behind for a later lift (larger than a British airborne division, the American counterpart possessed the four infantry regiments – three parachute and one glider-borne – and twice the numer of field artillery pieces, thirty-six in all). One reason for Taylor's arranging to bring his artillery in on a later lift was that his division would be so dispersed after landing that he would not be able to site his guns in a position where their concentrated fire could be switched from one area to another. Another was that support from the XXX Corps artillery would be available as soon as the guns arrived within range.

The task of 82nd Division, landing to the north of 101st Division, was even more complicated. As well as capturing and holding the great bridges which spanned the Waal at Nijmegen and the Maas at Grave, Gavin had also to seize the crossings over the Maas-Waal Canal which connected the two rivers and provided yet another obstacle to the advance of XXX Corps. But that was not all. South-east of Nijmegen, the ground rose through the wooded suburbs of the city to the Groesbeek Heights, a plateau some 300 feet above the rivers. In the north, around the holiday centre of

Berg-en-Dal, this plateau fell steeply to the polder bounding the Waal; to the east it extended from Groesbeek in a flat and rolling plain which stretched towards the Reichswald Forest and Germany. Enemy armour had been reported as sheltering in his forest.

Browning's Operation Instruction No.1, signed on 13 September, had ordered 82nd Division to 'seize and hold the bridges at Nijmegen and Grave ... The capture and retention of the high ground between Nijmegen and Groesbeek is imperative in order to accomplish the Division's task'. At a conference on 14 September, Gavin recorded that Browning was even more explicit, instructing him that he should not attempt the Nijmegen bridges* until all other missions had been successfully accomplished, and the Groesbeek-Berg-en-Dal high ground firmly in American hands. Afterwards, Browning stood by this decision; he was, Gavin remembers, vehement about the matter.

Gavin agreed with Browning that this hilly country was the key to the battle, and that, without it, the bridges at Grave and Nijmegen would be untenable and the right flank of Second Army would be left unprotected as its troops advanced over the Maas and the Waal. He decided, therefore, to use two of the three regiments of parachute infantry that would be dropped on the first day to seize the Groesbeek Heights; with them would come his headquarters and an artillery battalion equipped with 75-mm guns.† In this area would also land Browning's advanced Corps Headquarters. The third parachute regiment would be put down north of Grave, its objectives the canal bridges and the northern end of the bridge over the Maas at Grave; a single company was also to be put down at the southern end of this 1,800-foot span so that both ends would be attacked simultaneously.

Because of this decision to give priority to capturing the Groesbeek Heights, Gavin was faced with holding a perimeter twenty-five miles in circumference with three lightly armed regiments, a task that left him with no alternative but to scatter his troops in small detachments covering the more important road and track junctions. It can be argued that this dispersion could have been avoided. The highway bridge at Nijmegen cannot be observed

* A railway bridge and, east of it, a massive road bridge.
† Each of these pieces was broken down into seven parachute loads in order that they could be dropped with the infantry.

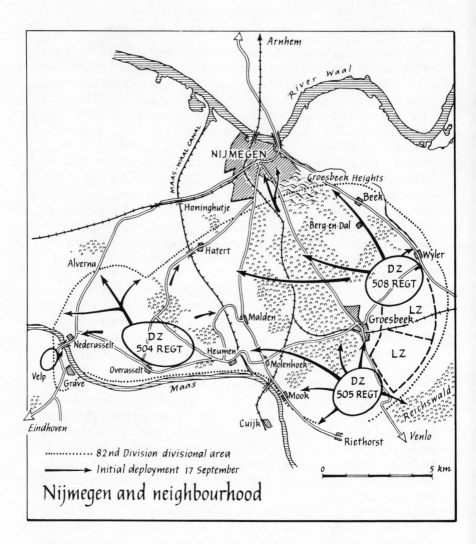

Arnhem

River Waal

MAAS-WAAL CANAL

NIJMEGEN

Groesbeek Heights

Beek

Honinghutje

Berg-en-Dal

Hatert

Alverna

Wyler

DZ
508 REGT

LZ

Malden

Groesbeek

LZ

Nederasselt

DZ
504 REGT

Heumen

Molenhoek

LZ

Velp

Overasselt

Maas

DZ
505 REGT

Gråve

Mook

Reichswald

Eindhoven

Cuijk

Venlo

Riethorst

·············· 82nd Division divisional area

⟶ Initial deployment 17 September

0   5 km

Nijmegen and neighbourhood

from high ground two miles to its east, for this ridge bends away to the south. A much smaller perimeter, extending only some three miles from the centre of the city, would have still denied the Germans observation over the two Nijmegen bridges. It was, of course, a temptation to secure for the second and subsequent lifts the excellent DZs and LZs on the Groesbeek Heights. But other areas were available, both south of the city and on the north bank of the Waal, not ideal but similar to the ground south of the Arnhem bridges upon which it was planned to land the Poles. The air forces would, of course, have refused to drop troops on the first day so close to the flak reported around Nijmegen, but if the capture of the city and the bridge had been given first priority and then achieved, the flak would have been eliminated by the time the second lift flew in.

Gavin has described how his staff officers criticized the British 1st Airborne Division plan, with its DZs and LZs so far from the bridges, and how relieved they were at not having to take part in such an operation. It was, therefore, something of a paradox that he was to be faced with exactly the same problem, a drop eight miles away from the Nijmegen bridge, involving a final approach march through thickly wooded and built-up country.

A short time before take-off (sources vary as to exactly when), Gavin decided that the plan was shaping up so well that he could risk sending a single battalion against the Nijmegen road bridge. As a result, he instructed Colonel Roy E. Lindquist of 508 Parachute Infantry, the more northerly of the two regiments dropped on the high ground, to commit one of his battalions against the Nijmegen bridge as soon as possible after landing, but authorised him to stop this attack if the degree of enemy resistance from other directions was such that he might not be able to hold the rest of the sector. The exact wording of these orders has gone unrecorded, but, as their originator was later to admit, they were 'a bit ambiguous'.

US 82nd Division was put down as accurately as the British had been outside Arnhem. 'The drop', Gavin recorded, 'was better than had ever been experienced'. Of the German base troops and flak crews in the area, only a few found the courage to fire more than a shot or two before trying to escape or surrender. They can hardly be blamed. Few sights can be more terrifying than that of several thousand paratroops descending in a cloud on top of you. 'It was surprising', Gavin also wrote, 'to find out how well flak batteries could be handled by small parachute units jumping directly upon them'. That evening, members of the Dutch Resistance, who had appeared and offered their services to the Americans, were guarding 400 German soldiers, some of them drunk, or so the tale had it. But then they had after all been captured on a Sunday afternoon, their day off.

Guided in by pathfinders, Colonel Reuben H. Tucker's 504 Parachute Infantry began to land just north-east of Grave at 1313 hours. Assisted by the company which had dropped south of the Maas, the bridge at Grave was quickly in American hands, the speed and determination of the attack having prevented the Germans from destroying it. By nightfall, the Americans had occupied Grave itself, abandoned by its 400 defenders. Another of Tucker's companies had captured the easternmost of the four road bridges which spanned the Maas-Waal Canal, that at Heumen, near Mook. It was well that it did. Two of the other bridges were blown before the Americans could reach them, and for some reason the fourth was not tackled until the following morning.

That night, parties of 505 Parachute Infantry, which had dropped on the southern stretch of the Groesbeek Heights, had linked up with Tucker's men; to everyone's relief, Dutch civilians had reported that the rumours of German tanks in the Reichswald were untrue, information that was later to be confirmed by patrols. From previous experience, Gavin was totally confident that his division could handle the German infantry, but he was only too aware of his lack of adequate anti-tank weapons. So far, all had gone well. Casualties had been few, and only the one task had still to be completed – the capture of Nijmegen and its bridge.

The tasks with which Lindquist's 508 Regiment were to cope, after they had dropped just to the north of 505 Regiment, were numerous and involved. As well as holding the high ground from Nijmegen through Berg-en-Dal to the village of Wyler, and then south to Groesbeek, Lindquist had to deploy a battalion to block enemy movement south from Nijmegen, and had also to help 504 Regiment in seizing the two northernmost bridges over the Maas-Waal Canal. In addition, he had to secure the LZs south of Wyler and earmark a battalion for the assault on the Nijmegen highway bridge. His orders were that this unit was not to be diverted until the situation on the high ground had clarified, but it soon became obvious that there was

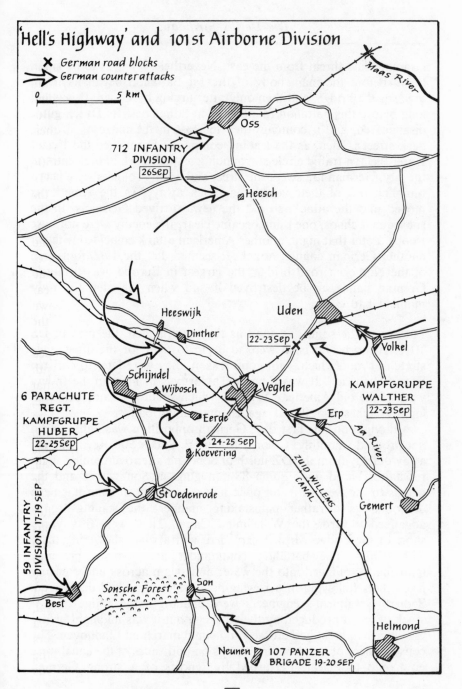

'Hell's Highway' and 101st Airborne Division

✕ German road blocks
→ German counterattacks

0   5 km

Maas River

Oss

712 INFANTRY DIVISION 26 Sep

Heesch

Heeswijk

Dinther

Uden

22-23 Sep ✕

Volkel

Schijndel

Wijbosch

Veghel

KAMPFGRUPPE WALTHER 22-23 Sep

6 PARACHUTE REGT. KAMPFGRUPPE HUBER 22-25 Sep

Eerde

Erp

✕ 24-25 Sep

Koevering

Aa River

59 INFANTRY DIVISION 17-19 SEP

St Oedenrode

ZUID WILLEMS CANAL

Gemert

Sonsche Forest

Son

Best

Helmond

Neunen

107 PANZER BRIGADE 19-20 SEP

no immediate threat from the east. Nevertheless, it was to be seven hours before the main body of the 1st Battalion began its move towards the bridge, and then only after urging by Gavin. It was not long before this battalion found itself in difficulties. Its Dutch guide disappeared, and a company became lost in the maze of strange, dark streets. Then, as the leading company approached the Keizer Karel Plein, a traffic circle surrounding a small park in the centre of the city, German fire swept the street and enemy soldiers were heard tumbling out of their vehicles a block away. As the Americans moved into the attack, so did the newly arrived Germans. In the subsequent chaos, one thing became clear; the enemy were not base troops. Later that night, another American attack coincided with yet another German counter-attack. It seemed that the 1960-foot span of the Nijmegen road bridge, the largest in Europe, was firmly in German hands, to be destroyed if and when they felt the right moment had come.

Further to the south, as soon as they had landed, the men of US 101st Airborne Division were to begin to fight for the fifteen-mile stretch of road which, with good reason, they were later to christen 'Hell's Highway'. It was a battle Taylor was to liken to the Indian wars of the old American West, in which small garrisons defended long stretches of railroad against marauding bands.

Although, on this first day, German opposition was light, all did not proceed smoothly. Colonel Robert F. Sink's 506 Regiment got away quickly from the DZ north of Son, and after overcoming slight resistance based upon some 88-mm guns in Son village and the woods to the west of it (an operation carried out in what has been described as a rather painstaking manner) the leading troops advanced towards the Wilhelmina Canal. They were fifty yards short of the bridge when it exploded with a roar, showering them with debris. The battalion commander and two of his men immediately plunged into the water and swam across under enemy fire, others following in a rowing-boat which they had discovered. Soon the regiment's engineers were building a footbridge from a stock of wood produced by the villagers, but it was midnight before the whole regiment had crossed and could march on Eindhoven. The consequences of not dropping troops on both sides of the canal were now only too clear. Perturbed by reports of a strong German garrison in Eindhoven, and lacking any news of the progress of XXX Corps because his radio link was in a missing glider, Sink was reluctant to enter a city of 100,000 inhabitants in the dark; with his leading troops no more than a mile beyond the Wilhelmina Canal, he obtained his divisional commander's permission to halt for the night. In the words of the official historian of the US Army, this was, perhaps, a 'rather conservative approach'. It had been planned that the regiment would reach Eindhoven two hours after it had dropped.

Just over three miles to the west of Son, another bridge crossed the Wilhelmina Canal. To guard against the risk of the Son bridge being blown, a company of 502 Regiment was ordered to capture this crossing, which lay near the village of Best. After getting lost in the dark and wooded country, only a single platoon actually arrived there, and this small body of men was then beaten off its objective. Learning that a column of a dozen German vehicles had brought up reinforcements, Colonel John H. Michaelis, the regimental commander, decided to send the rest of the battalion to help. A mile short of Best, mortar and artillery fire hit the Americans, who then dug in for the night. Further north, however, another battalion of the same regiment had captured the crossings over the Dommel river at St Oedenrode, and 501 Regiment had secured Veghel and the bridges over the Willems Canal, both forces with little trouble.

All in all, there had been little to choose between the speed of progress of the two American divisions and that of the British in Arnhem. Battle-experienced though most of the troops were, there was a certain tendency towards stickiness during the first few hours after arrival, not only among the forward units but in the machinery of command as well – just at the time when the greatest effort was demanded.

CHAPTER SEVEN

'A TALE YOU WILL TELL YOUR GRANDCHILDREN'

On that same morning of 17 September, Lieutenant-General Brian Horrocks was at his command post. Its position was a little unusual, the flat roof of a large factory overlooking the Meuse-Escaut Canal. Spanned by the De Groot bridge, renamed 'Joe's Bridge' by Horrocks in tribute to Lieutenant-Colonel J.O.E. (Joe) Vandeleur's Irish Guards, who had seized it on 10 September and subsequently held it against determined German counter-attacks, a small bridgehead on the far side of the waterway provided a jumping-off point for the start of XXX Corps' sixty-four-mile advance towards Arnhem. Around the corps commander, hidden and camouflaged among the woods and farms, were 350 guns ready to support the initial attack. Zero hour was dependent upon the airborne landings taking place as planned, but, just before 1300 hours, Horrocks heard on his radio that the operation was on. Soon the armada came into view, flying low overhead, and he gave the order for the artillery programme to start. Thirty minutes later, the first tank of the Irish Guards, still the leading unit of Guards Armoured Division, began to edge forward along the road.

On 12 September, two days after he had briefed Browning, Montgomery had summoned Horrocks to meet him at a forward airfield. There he had outlined his plans for 'Market Garden' and the part XXX Corps was to play in the operation. They knew one another well. 'Jorrocks', as he was known throughout the British Army, was Montgomery's man. At Dunkirk, he had led first a battalion and then a brigade in the division commanded by Major-General Montgomery. Then, in 1942, Montgomery had summoned him out to the Western Desert to take command of XII Corps before the battle of El Alamein; later Horrocks had turned the Mareth Line with X Corps, and then, in command of IX Corps, had directed the breakthrough which led to the capture of Tunis and the end of the war in North Africa. Hit in the chest and stomach during an air raid just before the Salerno landings, he was fortunate to survive, but it seemed certain that a very distinguished career had ended. In July 1944, however, Montgomery judged him fit enough to join him in France to take over command of XXX Corps, valuing Horrocks's presence so highly that he was ready to overlook the periodic bouts of high temperature and sickness, the legacy of his wounds, that were to plague the corps commander.

In August, when Montgomery had been hoping to persuade Eisenhower to back an advance on the left flank of the Allied front with everything available, he had visualised a forty-division thrust into Germany. Now the main assault was to be carried out by just XXX Corps, advancing on a single-division front, and with that division all but confined to a single road. To reach the Ijsselmeer, Horrocks had only Guards Armoured Division, 43rd and 50th Infantry Divisions, 4 Armoured Brigade and the Princess Irene Brigade of Free Dutch. Deployed along the line of the Meuse-Escaut Canal on his left and right were XII and VIII Corps. Given initial objectives to seize bridgeheads across the canal, XII Corps was then to protect the flank of XXX Corps by extending its positions to the Maas river. VIII Corps was to act in the same way on the right, advancing to Helmond, due east of Eindhoven, but the supply situation was such that at the start of the battle the corps could only maintain forward a single infantry division.

At 1100 hours on 16 September, Horrocks had assembled his senior officers, most of them of the rank of lieutenant-colonel or above, in an ugly, nondescript cinema in the small Belgian mining-town of Bourg Léopold. The late Major-General Hubert Essame, then a brigade commander in 43rd Division and the author of the division's vivid history, recorded the occasion – the squalid surroundings, the gaiety and optimism laced with tension, the old friends shouting greetings to one another, the appearance of those present.

> The variety of headgear was striking [he wrote] ... No one deigned to wear a steel helmet. The Royal Armoured Corps affected brightly coloured slacks or corduroys. The Gunners still clung for the most part to riding breeches or even jodhpurs. Few had retained their ties, but wore in their place scarves of various colours, dotted with white spots. Snipers' smocks, parachutists' jackets, jeep coats, all contributed to the amazing variety of costume.

Like Wellington, Montgomery was more interested in how his officers fought than what they wore.

Down the aisle of the cinema strode the tall, angular 'Jorrocks', looking, one or two of those present thought, not too well. His bubbling sense of fun and his tremendous charm were qualities that stood him in good stead. And, added to this, his long record of success in battle provided the ingredients needed to inspire confidence in those who worked for him. Standing erect in front of an enormous sketch map of eastern Holland, he opened with the words, 'This is a tale you will tell your grandchildren'; the aside, 'and mighty bored they'll be', had the intended effect. In after years, Horrock's eloquent hands and mesmeric eyes made him a master of the television screen; anyone who watched his performances can judge the clarity and self-confidence with which he set out to explain XXX Corps' forthcoming and complex operations.

Loops of violet tape encircled the objectives of the three airborne divisions, and through them ran the line of arrows marking the single road along which Guards Armoured Division was to thrust to the Ijsselmeer. Speed was essential, Horrocks emphasised, something that Montgomery had emphasised to him. If the major bridges at Grave, Nijmegen and Arnhem were found to be destroyed, the Guards were to fan out to the flanks to allow 43rd Division, travelling behind them, to build new bridges. 9,000 sappers, together with stockpiles of bridging material, were ready near Bourg Léopold in case the worst happened. Once the Neder Rijn had been crossed, 43rd Division was then to seize crossings over the Ijssel at Deventer

Lt-Gen Lewis H.
Brereton, commanding
First Allied Airborne
Army, 'an odd choice to
lead an inter-Allied
command'.

Maj-Gen Matthew B.
Ridgway, commanding
US XVIII Corps,
'undoubtedly the most
experienced senior
airborne commander at
the time' – he had hoped
to be given command of
the airborne operation.

Lt-Gen F. A. M.
Browning, commanding
the British Airborne
Corps (left), and the
Deputy Supreme
Commander, Tedder,
discussing plans with an
American brigadier-
general before the start
of 'Market'. Browning
could at times be
overbearing and . . . the
austerity of his outlook
could give an impression
of arrogance'. A
threatened resignation
by him had earlier
shaken the Americans.

Maj-Gen R. E. Urquhart, commanding British 1st Airborne Division (right), with an unidentified RAF officer, Col Warrack, the division's ADMS (background), and two of the journalists who went on the operation, Fairford Airfield, Gloucestershire, before take-off on 1 September. The aircraft is a Horsa glider. 'There was little doubt in [Urquhart's] mind . . . that he had been presented with the most difficult task'.

Maj-Gen Maxwell D. Taylor, commanding US 101st Airborne Division, who fought his 'Screaming Eagles' with skill, courage, and panache.

Brig-Gen Jim Gavin, commanding the 'All American' US 82nd Airborne Division, getting ready for the flight – 'a lean, tough ex-ranker . . . with a penetrating mind'.

Lt-Gen Brian Horrocks, commanding XXX Corps, with his personal tank, shortly before the start of the operation. 'It is possible,' wrote Urquhart, 'that for once Horrocks's enthusiasm was not transmitted adequately to those who served under him'.

British airborne soldiers inside a C-47 Dakota, before jumping, 17 September. 'Beneath their jumping jackets, their haversacks produced a quaint effect of advanced pregnancy'.

Members of the divisional staff of US 82nd Airborne Division before jumping from their C-47. US paratroops had a reserve parachute, unlike the British, seen here strapped to each man's front.

A Horsa glider lifts off, towed by an Armstrong-Whitworth Albemarle bomber.

'The Belgians and Dutch . . . felt sure that such an armada must herald the final and victorious battle of the war.' Gheel, Belgium, 17 September, as 101st Airborne Division sweeps over on the southern route.

'Garden' – British Second Army convoys moving up towards Holland. 'Traffic control and staff work of a very high standard indeed would be needed to avoid chaos'.

Horsas on one of 1st Airborne's LZs, 17 September. A ring charge in the glider's fuselage could be detonated after landing, blowing the rear half of the aircraft free to ease unloading.

1st Airborne's paratroops arrive, one hour after the gliders, some of which can be seen on the ground. The transport aircraft are C-47s.

Brig Gerald Lathbury, who commanded 1 Parachute Brigade at Arnhem. He was wounded early in the battle, but eventually escaped over the Neder Rijn after 1st Airborne's withdrawal.

Brig Pip Hicks, commanding 1 Airlanding Brigade, who took over command of the division on 1 September when Urquhart and Lathbury were separated from their HQs. At forty-nine he was old for an airborne brigadier, and feeling ran high when he and Hackett met on the 18th.

The LZ near Wolfheze on the 17th. The first two gliders to land, bringing the HQ of 1st Airborne's Royal Artillery party, having collided slightly, are unloaded. Second from left, carrying haversacks, is Lt-Col Sheriff Thompson, 1 Airlanding Brigade's Artillery Commander.

The first German prisoners, captured by the British near their DZ on 17 September, are searched while Dutch civilians look on.

The presence of journalists and official photographers with 1st Airborne Division meant that many of the surviving pictures, although of excellent quality, are rather 'posed'. The crossroads at Wolfheze on 17th September – the weapon in the centre foreground is a PIAT, while a Bren gun is manned across the road.

and Zutphen, and behind it 50th Division would be moving forward in reserve.

The problems which Horrocks faced were clear to all present. They were fourfold. First there was the danger that the Germans might destroy one or more of the main bridges: to replace them would take time. Then there was the enemy. Horrocks's battle-wise audience was only too aware how German resistance had hardened north of Brussels. The fighting to capture the canal crossings and the key road centres had been grim, the Corps' opponents often fresh young paratroops, newly arrived at the front, well led and apparently well organised, a contrast indeed to the Dutch SS battalion and the old men of 719th Coastal Division, veterans of 1918, previously reported in the area. Casualties had been high: the Guards had lost 598 killed, wounded and missing in ten days as compared with the 1,400 men lost in the entire Normandy campaign. A mark of the quality of the German resistance had been the 150 enemy dead counted around the cross-roads at Hechtel, and the 220 wounded among the 720 prisoners captured. The third problem was the sixty-four-mile length of road to Arnhem, in its early stretches running through farmland, heath and woods, passable in many places to tanks but easy to defend. But further north, it crossed soft polder on a high dyke, making the deployment of vehicles all but impossible. Most of the way forward, artillery and aircraft would be needed to blast a passage for the armour. The fourth and last problem concerned the 20,000 vehicles which would have to travel along this road; in places they would need to drive two abreast with southbound traffic prohibited, but traffic control and staff work of a very high standard indeed would be needed to avoid chaos.

Throughout his explanation of the plans for the coming battle, Horrocks radiated his usual sparkling confidence, and he has recorded that failure never entered his head, although he knew that it would be a very tough battle. For all that, doubts seem to have existed, and understandably so. On 19 September, the third day of 'Market Garden', Lieutenant-General Neil Ritchie, the commander of XII Corps, was to write to congratulate the commander of his 15th (Scottish) Division on the manner in which his troops had fought so gallantly on the left flank, so removing some of the pressure from XXX Corps. The letter included these words:

I know that you would like to know that General Horrocks, commanding the 30th Corps, told me yesterday [18 September] that he had grave doubts as to the possibility of his being able reasonably quickly to break out of his bridgehead in Operation 'Market Garden'.

If such misgivings did exist, they might have been greater still if Horrocks had been granted access to the Ultra intelligence which had been accumulating during the previous ten days.

A lonely figure, burdened with the responsibility for thousands of lives, watched the advance start the following day. For some ten minutes all went well. 100 yards ahead of the leading tank of 2nd Irish Guards rolled the barrage of shells and, further ahead still, rocket-firing Typhoons hammered the German positions. Riding on the outside of the second squadron of tanks were infantrymen, fellow 'Micks' of the 3rd Irish Guards – altogether a family affair. Even the commanding officers of the two units were cousins, Joe and Giles Vandeleur, travelling in their scout cars behind the leading squadrons. But, as the barrage lifted, anti-tank guns and Panzerfausts (the German equivalent of the PIAT), hidden on either side of the road, came to life. In two minutes nine of the leading tanks were blazing. Then began a stubborn fight, seemingly confused, but in reality orderly. Typhoons, directed on to their targets by radio contact cars, swept in at tree level to attack the German positions, and the artillery switched to these now revealed targets. As every other weapon within range poured in yet more fire, the infantry leaped off the tanks to complete the destruction of the Germans. As Horrocks wrote, 'It was a classic example of perfect co-ordination between the RAF and the Army'. By nightfall, the Irish Guards had reached their first objective, the small red-brick village of Valkenswaard, its streets filled with Dutch cheering their liberators.

The leading troops of Guards Armoured Division had travelled seven miles but were still six miles short of Eindhoven, their objective that first evening, and where they should have met 101st Airborne Division. At Valkenswaard, Joe Vandeleur, in overall command of the Irish Guards Group, was told by the chief of staff of the Guards Armoured Division to wait until the next morning before moving forward, his reason being that news had come through that the bridge at Son had been blown, and that bridging material would have to be brought forward. This was something of a *non sequitur*, because the blowing of the bridge had created an urgent need to reach it as quickly as possible so that preparations for the repairs could be started. Horrocks, however, has defended the decision on the grounds that the men had been fighting hard and the tanks needed to be serviced. This was undoubtedly so. The Irish Guards *had* been fighting hard, very hard indeed, but other troops were available both from Guards Armoured Division and from 50th Division. Certainly some of the officers of the Irish Guards themselves found it hard to understand why the advance should have been halted. It is difficult indeed to explain why an infantry battalion was not produced to probe forward in the darkness to discover the locations of the next enemy positions and to endeavour to ease the Germans out of them. Horrocks wrote later that 'there was a desperate urgency about this battle which I had rarely experienced before or since'. At times an awareness of this urgency was undoubtedly there. At others it was possibly missing.

General Horrocks has also suggested that the Guards were a little stereotyped in their methods, working always in regimental groups – Grenadier tanks with Grenadier infantry, Welsh tanks with Welsh infantry, a system he described as not calculated to get the full value from the mobility of an armoured division. Major-General Verney, the division's historian, has said much the same, commenting that this grouping sacrificed some of the flexibility inherent in an armoured division.

The programme for the advance seems to have been as follows:

Eindhoven	1715 hours	17 September
Veghel	2400 hours	17 September
Grave	1200 hours	18 September
Nijmegen	1800 hours	18 September
Arnhem	1500 hours	19 September

This matches British 1st Airborne Division's expectation of relief within forty-eight hours and Horrocks's specification in his orders that Arnhem was to be reached 'if possible in forty-eight hours'.*

* Something of a mystery hangs over the source for this timetable, which is printed in Albert A. Nofi (ed.), *The War Against Hitler: Military Strategy in the West* (New York, 1982). The present writer and others have failed to trace this programme in either the instructions for or the reports on the operation.

Given the distances to be covered, the difficulties of the ground, and the manner in which the Germans had fought during the previous ten days, it is hard to see how such a programme could have been thought feasible, especially as the destruction of even one of the major bridges would have wrecked it completely. If, however, XXX Corps had pressed on that first evening, the first stage, at least, might well have been completed on schedule. As it was, at the end of Sunday 17 September the battle closed down for twelve hours, with Guards Armoured Division six miles south of Eindhoven and the Americans four miles north of the city.

CHAPTER EIGHT

'OH, HOW I WISH I HAD EVER HAD SUCH POWERFUL MEANS AT MY DISPOSAL'

Just as Generalfeldmarschall Walter Model, the commander of German Army Group B, was about to sit down to lunch at his headquarters in the Tafelberg Hotel at Oosterbeek, the news reached him that Allied gliders had begun to land two miles away to the west. Members of his staff have described the panic that ensued. Convinced that the object of the landing was to eliminate him, Model rushed for his staff-car, spilling as he did so the contents of the case into which he had crammed a few belongings. Within minutes, his staff had removed operation maps and orders, and the headquarters transport was loaded and being driven away from the direction of the landing, down the road into Arnhem. As the Germans afterwards officially admitted, the attack had come as a complete surprise. The Ultra information regarding the location of the headquarters had been quite correct.

Hitler had chosen Model as the man to salvage the wreckage cast back towards Germany after the débâcle in Normandy. From 17 August he had been commanding both his own army group and filling the post of Commander-in-Chief West, but on 5 September Generalfeldmarschall Gerd von Rundstedt had been recalled from retirement to take over the more senior appointment. This released Model to concentrate his ruthless energies on halting the advance of Twenty-First Army Group, a seemingly impossible task with Brussels and Antwerp lost, and a sixty-mile undefended gap open between the latter and Maastricht. Only fifty-four years of age – young, that is, for a senior German general – Model was a man of humble origins who had acquired all the outward marks of the traditional officer class. One of his greater strengths was his ability to stand up to the Fuehrer, an almost unique quality among the members of the German higher command, and, loyal though he was, he would disregard pointless orders when the need arose. He was also one of the few whose faith remained unshaken in his leader's promises that the new and revolutionary weapons under production would, even now, bring victory to the Reich.

The demoralisation that had occurred when the German armed forces fell back from the Seine was something new in their history. Trucks loaded with officers, their terrified mistresses and accumulated loot reached the Rhineland before being stopped and their occupants arrested. Naval troops discarded their weapons and sold their spare uniforms. In Holland, 5 September was to be remembered as 'Mad Tuesday': on that day the flood of panic reached its heights, with German servicemen and civilians, and their Dutch collaborators, pouring eastwards in every type of vehicle, official and commandeered, their terror fed by a succession of false rumours.

With the greater part of the German Fifteenth Army for the time being cut off in the Channel Ports and around the Scheldt estuary, the only troops at first available to Model to stem the Allied advance were those of 719th Coastal Division, reinforced with Luftwaffe ground staff and an unreliable Dutch SS battalion. But, as the Generalfeldmarschall began to move this slight force to the line of the Albert Canal on 4 September, unexpected help arrived. Retreating towards the Rhineland with the shattered remains of three divisions, including his own 84th, Generalleutnant Kurt Chill perceived the danger. Acting on his own initiative, and without orders, he set up rallying points along the canal on 4 September to catch the conglomeration of fleeing troops, most of them from base units, and knit them into his own depleted formations. Three days later Kampfgruppe Chill was in being, and fighting to delay Guards

Armoured Division as the latter sought to expand its bridgehead over the canal at Beeringen.

Two days earlier, the Allies had learned, again through Ultra, that patrols similar to those deployed by Chill had been established on the bridges across the Rhine, information that had the effect of reinforcing still further the sanguine expectations of those Allied commanders and staff officers privy to the intelligence.

For the Germans, yet more reinforcements were on the way. On 4 September, Hitler's headquarters had ordered Generaloberst Kurt Student to form the First Parachute Army, and to place himself under Model's orders to block the Antwerp-Maastricht gap. The innovator of airborne warfare and the victor of the successful airborne attacks against the Low Countries in 1940 and Crete in 1941, Student had not held an operational command for three years, the losses suffered in the capture of Crete having destroyed Hitler's faith in the efficacy of airborne troops. Student's new army hardly merited the title, consisting as it did of the scratch units already in position along or near the Albert Canal, with some 20,000 paratroops and 10,000 Luftwaffe men now scraped together in Germany. It was, he later wrote, 'improvisation on the grandest scale'. During the next two weeks, Student was to throw these units into the battle as and when they arrived from their bases scattered throughout Germany. First to appear was the 2nd Parachute Battalion, to be followed by 6 Parachute Regiment, freshly equipped and reinforced after the hard fighting it had been through, in a ground role, in France. Then came barely trained troops, organised into five regiments, three of them formed into 7th Parachute Division and all of them without artillery or other heavy weapons. 5,000 convalescent paratroops, shaped into yet more *ad hoc* units, completed Student's force.

Further reinforcements were arriving from another direction. As Ultra was accurately reporting, German forces were being ferried back across the Scheldt estuary and through the Beveland isthmus. Among these troops was 245th Infantry Division, a force of small fighting value which came under Student's command on 16 September; 59th Division followed it the next day, again a division in name only, but it did contain 1,000 good infantrymen and some engineers, together with a replacement battalion and thirty guns. On 23 September, at the height of the Arnhem battle, an intercepted summary provided the Allies with the complete picture: a total of 82,000 German soldiers, 530 guns, 46,000 vehicles and 4,000 horses had, by that date, crossed into western Holland from the vicinity of the Scheldt estuary. The consequences of the Allied failure to clear that vicinity were all too clear.

Initially, Student's area of responsibility extended back to a line running roughly along the Maas and Waal rivers; north of this line, Model left the operational command in the hands of the Commander Armed Forces Netherlands, General der Flieger Friedrich Christiansen, who controlled only a hotch-potch of small training and administrative units. As with Christiansen's troops, in Germany itself, east of the Reichswald, the Corps Feldt had been organised, named after the cavalry general placed in command of it. As well as training, service and Luftwaffe units, it contained a last few reserves of the 'ear' and 'stomach' battalions, made up of men suffering from complaints particular to those parts of the body.

On 7 September there had arrived in Christiansen's area the headquarters of Obergruppenfuehrer Willi Bittrich's II SS Panzer Corps, the HQ whose movements back from Normandy had been so accurately monitored by Ultra, as had been the progress of its 9th and 10th SS Panzer Divisions, the 'Hohenstaufen' and the 'Frundsberg' respectively. Originally, Model had ordered these two divisions to the Arnhem area so that they could be reinforced and replenished with armour and weapons. But on 9 September he instructed the Hohenstaufen to continue on its way back into Germany.

For long after the war it was widely believed that the remnants of these two panzer divisions had been placed outside Arnhem deliberately in anticipation of a possible airborne landing there, the Allied plans having been betrayed by a Dutch double-agent. The story had a basis of truth. The traitor was a man named Christian Lindemans, known from his appearance and behaviour as 'King Kong'. Succumbing to threats that his imprisoned brother and his former mistress would be executed by the Germans if he did not work for them, Lindemans had been controlled by the Abwehr (German military intelligence) since 1943, infiltrating the Belgian Resistance and betraying the Dutch end of an air-crew escape route into Spain. On 15 September, a German patrol had picked him up after he had made his way through the Allied lines with a message from a Canadian intelligence officer instructing the Dutch Resistance to hold Allied escapers for the time being, rather than pass them along the current escape route. Incredibly, Lindemans had been told that the reason for this order was the opening of an Allied offensive on 17 September, which was to be accompanied by an airborne operation in the vicinity of Eindhoven. Lindemans had, in fact, left the Allied lines on 10 September, the day Montgomery briefed Browning for the operation, so it is highly unlikely that the Canadian intelligence officer could have known anything about 'Market Garden'. It was fortunate, to say the least of it, that the Abwehr officer who cross-examined Lindemans decided that the information was not reliable, and, as a result, did nothing about it for two days, by when it was too late. The mischance which resulted in Lindemans's fortuitous revelation of the date for the start of 'Market Garden' is still a mystery.

The imminence of a large-scale operation was apparent to the Germans, and they had every reason to anticipate that it would involve the airborne forces known to be ready and waiting in England. Intercepted RAF tuning trafic indicated that something was about to happen, as did German knowledge of Allied air reconnaissance sorties over Nijmegen and Arnhem. Each day Model's senior intelligence officer warned him of the obvious indications of a coming offensive, and, as good intelligence officers should do, he and his colleagues examined all the possibilities. This the Allies knew from the Ultra intercepts, which in turn revealed the way in which their possible intentions were being discussed by German intelligence. In one clearly reasoned signal, Model's staff forecast an American armoured thrust into the Ruhr by way of Roermond, covered by a British attack towards Nijmegen with the First Allied Airborne Army landing fifty miles east of the Rhine once that river had been reached, just the sort of operation which would have appealed to the powers in Washington. A seaborne landing in northern Holland, supported by an airborne assault, was also feared. What never seems to have been envisaged was this thrust of Montgomery's towards Arnhem: the siting of Model's headquarters just outside the city, and the surprise that greeted the landing of British 1st Airborne Division, provide ample confirmation of this.

When Model fled from Oosterbeek, he made for the headquarters of II Panzer Corps at Doetinchem, some twenty-five miles east of Arnhem, pausing as he passed through the city to order the

Feldkommandant, the ill-fated Generalmajor Kussin, to radio the Fuehrer's headquarters with the news of the Allied attack. When the signal arrived, it upset Hitler. 'If such a mess were to happen here', he complained, his entire supreme headquarters, Goering, Himmler and Ribbentrop included, would provide what he described as a 'worthwhile catch', well worth the possible loss of a couple of airborne divisions. Model also was, for the moment, shaken by the unexpected attack: before getting down to business with Bittrich, he wasted the latter's time by relating to him the details of his personal escape from the British assault.

An experienced and a highly competent officer, Bittrich had, as was to be expected, anticipated the orders Model was about to give him. News of the British landing had reached him five minutes after it had started, through the Luftwaffe communication network, and it was not long before he learned that Nijmegen and Arnhem appeared to be the principal objectives. Using the Dutch civilian telephone network, his main channel of communication within his corps, he ordered 9th SS Panzer Division to reconnoitre towards these two cities, and, at the same time, to occupy the Arnhem area, destroy the forces that had landed near Oosterbeek, and hold the Arnhem bridges. To 10th SS Panzer Division he gave the tasks of moving to Nijmegen, occupying the main bridges in strength, and holding bridgeheads south of the Waal. Bittrich had immediately grasped the essentials of the problem. If the Allied advance could be stopped at Nijmegen, the eventual destruction of the British at Oosterbeek would be guaranteed. Model saw no reason to amend this bold plan, one that is said to have been influenced by Bittrich's opinion of the capabilities of the British soldier – amazing in defence, but lacking in initiative and boldness in the attack, a view not uncommon among German officers. Model had every confidence in his corps commander, an unusual Obergruppenfuehrer. Shortly after the start of his career as a regular officer, Bittrich had transferred to the Waffen SS in order to speed his promotion. After Normandy, his unrestrained criticism of Hitler's conduct of the war became known to his Fuehrer, and only Model's determination not to lose such an outstanding officer prevented him from being recalled to answer for his conduct.

Various and conflicting estimates have been made of the strength of these two panzer divisions, no official records having survived the war. It seems certain, however, that each was the equivalent of a reinforced infantry regiment with a few tanks, the 9th Division a little stronger, not least in armour, possessing as it did a company of some twenty Mark V Panthers. When this division had arrived in the Arnhem area, it still numbered some 6,000 men, but a battalion was then detached to strengthen Student's First Parachute Army further south. When Obersturmbannfuehrer Walter Harzer, 9th SS Panzer's chief of staff and temporarily in command, received the orders from Model to move the division back to Germany, he was also instructed to hand his vehicles and weapons over to 10th Panzer, which was to stay in Holland and reform there. By 17 September, some of Harzer's men had already left, and some of his equipment had been transferred; as a shrewd professional officer, however, he was reluctant to have another lay hands on that equipment, especially with an Allied attack clearly imminent. Harzer therefore arranged for many of his heavy weapons and vehicles to be immobilised, and then reported them as unserviceable. The consequences were that, when the landings occurred and before he could carry out Model's orders and move his units into action, some of his equipment had to be unloaded from railway flats, and some of it made serviceable again. Furthermore, the units were scattered in a triangle around Arnhem, Zutphen and Apeldoorn, and many of his men were out of camp, enjoying the September sunshine or quenching their thirsts. For all that, within a short time – the exact hour is unrecorded – part of the armoured reconnaissance unit from 9th SS Panzer had crossed the Arnhem highway bridge, heading for Nijmegen. By 1700 hours, four hours after the British drop, a battle group with armoured cars and light tanks was advancing through Arnhem towards Oosterbeek. This says much for the efficiency of the division, some of whose men had had less than twelve weeks' service and were commanded by officers of whom many were recovering from their wounds.

Meanwhile, to the west of Arnhem, other German troops were entering the battle. General der Flieger Christiansen had already organised his miscellany of administrative and training units into a defensive force under a senior member of his staff, Generalleutnant Hans von Tettau. Among the more useful units in what has been described, inaccurately, as the 'Division von Tettau', were Sturmbannfuehrer Eberwein's SS Depot Battalion, Standartenfuehrer

Lippert's NCOs' School, and Sturmbannfuehrer Hans Kraft's SS Panzer Grenadier Training and Depot Battalion, the last-named split between Oosterbeek and Arnhem, and consisting of thirteen officers, seventy-three NCOs and 349 half-trained soldiers, most of them between seventeen and nineteen years of age, and a high proportion of them unfit. They were, however, well led and equipped and with light dual-purpose flak and anti-tank guns, and with mortars, machine-guns and flamethrowers.

The Allied air attack carried out on the morning of 17 September had caused Kraft to alert his men for action. Forty-five minutes after the British gliders had begun to land, he had ordered one of his companies to attack the LZ and the rest of the battalion to position itself along the line of the Oosterbeek-Wolfheze road, appreciating correctly that the British objectives were the Arnhem bridges. It was his men who were to be responsible for the skirmishing on the LZ, for the ambush of the Reconnaissance Squadron alongside the railway line, and for the initial delay to the battalions of 1 Parachute Brigade as they advanced towards Arnhem, thus winning time for the 9th SS Panzer Division battle group to reach the city and halt the advance of the 1st and 3rd Parachute Battalions. Student afterwards wrote that 'the foremost British parachute brigade ... lost too much time whilst overcoming the resistance by weak German garrison and units of the Luftwaffe'. Kraft was of the same opinion. Afterwards, he managed to bypass all intermediate headquarters and send his report on the battle direct to Himmler, thereby winning from the Reichsfuehrer SS well deserved praise and promotion. Possibly he exaggerated his exploits (he was not alone in this), but his part in delaying the advance of 1st Airborne Division had been appreciable. The report, while in general complimentary to the British, criticised their resolution when attacking. In reading such criticisms, however, it is well to remember that it takes only a few steadfast men with machine-guns and mortars to halt virtually unsupported attacks, however resolute, by lightly armed infantry moving along wide and straight boulevards.

The other two improvised SS units of von Tettau's force were too far away to reach the fighting on that first afternoon, but some men from a Dutch SS battalion carried out rather half-hearted attacks against a company of the KOSB which was guarding the Groote

Heide,* the furthest west of the DZs, for the arrival of the second lift the following day. Raised to guard a concentration camp at Amersfoot and recruited from jailbirds and youngsters earmarked for slave-labour in Germany, the last thing they had anticipated was being ordered to attack British paratroops. It says much for the training of the German officers and NCOs in charge of them that they could hold such men together, especially as they were commanded overall by a nervous and unmilitary Sturmbannfuehrer, a comic-opera figure from the Tyrol.

The Germans encountered initially by US 82nd Airborne Division after landing and during the first unsuccessful probe towards the Nijmegen bridges were a similar mixture of base and training units, among them the troops who had surrendered so quickly near Groesbeek. But those whose arrival at the Keiser Karel Plein had coincided exactly with that of the foremost American company were the leading troops of the reconnaissance unit from 9th SS Panzer, so expeditiously despatched by Bittrich southwards across the Arnhem bridge before Frost's men had reached it.

In much the same way, 101st Airborne Division had met only rear area troops that first day, an exception being at the bridge over the Wilhelmina Canal near Best, where troops of the German 59th Division had repulsed the company of 502 Parachute Infantry which had been despatched to seize it. On 17 September, as soon as this division had arrived in his area from eastern Holland, Student had ordered it out of its trains to be flung straight away into the battle. At the same time, he had instructed two battalions of convalescent paratroops to recapture the bridges taken by the Americans at St Oedenrode and Veghel.

That first day, the toughest resistance had been encountered by Guards Armoured Division, which had been forcing its way through what was then Student's best formation, 6 Parachute Regiment, known from about this time as Kampfgruppe Walther after its commander, Oberst Walther. Supporting this Kampfgruppe was a fresh unit of twenty-five armoured vehicles – Panther tanks and assault guns.

The Allies had reason to be grateful that so many of the bridges

---

* Also known as 'Ginkelsche Heide' or 'Ginkels Heath'.

had fallen into their hands undamaged on the first day of the battle, especially as most of them had been prepared for demolition and were under guard, with an officer appointed to detonate the charge if need be. One reason for this good fortune was, of course, the mixed quality of the troops defending the bridges: it is pertinent that the first forty-seven Germans captured by 1st Airborne Division belonged to twenty-seven separate units. But, as Student was to comment, the failure to destroy the bridges was proof also of the paralysing effect of surprise by airborne troops, although the German airborne general was a prejudiced witness. Another German officer described the descending masses as appearing to suffocate every living thing on the ground, a near-accurate metaphor for the drop on the Groesbeek Heights, when the German flak-gunners broke and ran as Gavin's men descended on top of their guns. For all that, the German machinery of command had withstood the assault. Nowhere was there any delay in preparing or launching counter-attacks against the Allies. The British and Americans were out of luck in being faced with officers of the calibre of Model, Bittrich, Chill, Walther, Harzer and Student.

As Student watched the immense stream of tugs and gliders flying low over his headquarters, he turned to his chief of staff and lamented, 'Oh, how I wish I had ever had such powerful means at my disposal'. But, as with Bittrich and every other senior German officer, Student's reaction to the danger was sharp. He was later to claim that his task was made the easier because he gained possession of the detailed plans for the Allied airborne landings, including objectives and times and places of subsequent lifts, within hours of the operation being launched. According to the German general, the papers were recovered from the body of an American officer whose glider was shot down on the first day. The story has still to be verified.

CHAPTER NINE

'THEY PROVED TO BE AMONG THE BRAVEST AND AND MOST PATRIOTIC PEOPLE WE HAD LIBERATED'

Those few British officers and officials who were privy to such matters were deeply mistrustful of the Dutch Resistance, and with good reason. Not that there was any question of German repression having broken the spirit of the people of the Netherlands, nor was there any lack of volunteers ready to risk everything to fight the occupying power. Instead, the misgivings sprang from a bitter series of events. Links between London and the Resistance in German-occupied Holland had been established as early as 1941, but some of the first agents of the Special Operations Executive* to be dropped by parachute had been captured, and had then succumbed to threats and torture. The outcome was the notorious 'Nordpol', the German code-name for the subsequent operation in which captured British radios and codes were used to ask for yet more Allied agents to be dropped into Holland. These in their turn were captured, to suffer the same wretched fate as their

---

* The British clandestine organisation whose role was primarily the support of resistance movements in occupied countries. Its American equivalent was the Office for Strategic Services (OSS).

predecessors. Only at the end of 1943 did SOE discover that its circuit supposedly functioning in Holland was almost completely under enemy control. During twenty months, fifty agents had been caught. When the German officers responsible for the coup realised that the game was up at last, they were so smugly pleased with themselves that they sent a final message to London in clear, bragging of their success.

Not until after the landings in Normandy did the Allies attempt to drop more agents into Holland, and then only in small numbers. However, as British Second Army approached the Dutch frontier and it seemed probable that Holland would fall as easily as Belgium had done, further men were parachuted in, as were sizeable quantities of weapons. At once information began to flow back to London, some of it accurate, such as the reports of enemy armour around Nijmegen and Eindhoven, some of it less so, as was to be expected from underground groups. On 31 August 1944, an order from SHAEF had marked the setting-up of the Dutch Forces of the Interior, which was from now on to include the paramilitary wings of the Resistance, under the command of Prince Bernhard of the Netherlands. On 17 September, the day of the Allied invasion of Holland, the London-based Dutch Government-in-Exile called for a general strike on Holland's railways, one of a number of measures, including sabotage, asked of the Forces of the Interior; the raising of the Resistance was, however, limited to the areas over which 'Market Garden' was to be fought.

Dropped with the Airborne Corps on the first day were four of SOE's four-man 'Jedburgh' teams, each of which contained Dutch and other Allied officers; one of the teams accompanied 1 Parachute Brigade at Arnhem. Their charter was comprehensive: as well as helping to requisition transport, the Jedburgh teams were ordered to contact the Resistance in order to produce information, to arrest any Dutch Nazi sympathisers, and to prevent civilians moving into the battle area. In addition, a party of Dutch commandos landed with 1st Airborne Division, their tasks, so far as can be gathered, duplicating those of the Jedburgh teams. And, two days earlier, a four-man Belgian Special Air Services party had been dropped to a waiting Dutch reception north-west of Arnhem, its purpose more far-reaching – to gather information about enemy troop movements, especially on the roads leading east out of Utrecht, and to look for

V2 launching-sites and rocket-carrying transport.

17 September brought the Allies to Holland. Wearing their orange arm-bands,* the jubilant men and women of the Dutch Resistance poured out to meet their American and British liberators. For a long four years they had been living for this moment. But although there was enthusiasm in plenty, there was rather less sound organisation. There were a number of reasons for this. First there was the damage done by 'Nordpol', and the consequent lack of outside aid for the forces of the Resistance. Then there was the problem of too many competing bodies, although in western Holland the usual political split between left and right was missing, the Communist groups being confined largely to the industrialised eastern provinces. Co-ordination between the various groups was rare, largely because of the obvious dangers involved; and, in any case, the flat and densely populated country was ill suited to guerrilla action on a large scale, lacking as it does the *maquis* or mountains necessary for training and concealment.

The American airborne divisions made sound use of the local help so eagerly proffered. With US 82nd Division was Captain Arie Besterbreutje, a courageous and highly intelligent native of Nijmegen, who had already undertaken a number of hazarous missions into enemy-occupied Europe. General Gavin and he had landed together near Groesbeek village and straight away the two of them had become involved in a gun-fight, in the course of which Besterbreutje shot a German machine-gunner through the forehead. He then proceeded to contact the chief of the Groesbeek Resistance, who found him a telephone; with the assistance of a code, Besterbreutje was able to get in touch with Resistance groups both in Nijmegen and in Arnhem, and from these calls he was able to give Gavin the news that the British had landed and that all seemed to be going well. By the following morning the Dutchman had collected about 600 would-be fighting men, some of whom, armed with German weapons, had already been put to guarding the prisoners captured at Groesbeek. Arranging for others to be armed with the weapons of American casualties, Gavin suggested that these eager volunteers might be used to help prevent the demolition of the

* The Netherlands have been ruled for many years by the House of Orange – hence the national colour.

Nijmegen bridges by covering the approaches with snipers and cutting any wires leading to the structures; at the same time, he pointed out to these Dutchmen something that they already well knew – that to be captured fighting in civilian clothes would have but one outcome.

The greatest value of the Resistance, however, both to the 82nd and the 101st Divisions, was the intelligence these local men produced. Lacking, as the Americans did, ground reconnaissance units, and without any call on air reconnaissance either once they had landed, the Dutch became, in effect, the eyes and ears of the airborne soldiers. Both divisions were also to make good use of the Resistance for guiding their troops through strange streets and down country lanes. With the experience of eighteen months of war behind him, Gavin was later to record that 'they proved to be among the bravest and most patriotic people we had liberated'.

With the British, however, things were different. Although individuals attached themselves at one time or another to different headquarters and units of 1st Airborne Division, little was done to exploit the enthusiastic help the Dutch were so eager to supply. It may be that the general distrust for the Resistance among the British intelligence agencies had percolated through to the commanders and staff, and certainly Frost had been told not to trust the Dutch. Perhaps no one realised just what the Dutch could do to help, the British airborne staff being less experienced in campaigning in newly liberated countries than their American counterparts. Or perhaps a little of both reasons prevailed. Undoubtedly everyone had been warned that among the Dutch people were German sympathisers, knowledge that tended to make security-minded officers wary of offers of help. This attitude quickly became apparent to the Dutch, and as the battle progressed, and the likely outcome for Dutch helpers became uncertain, the British became even more chary of enlisting their help. Whatever the reasons, insufficient use was made of the Dutch during the battle, as Urquhart himself admitted.

Although they were short of effective radio communications, the German were to make good use of the civilian telephone system throughout the 'Market Garden' battles. This, however, had its drawbacks. Both Besterbreutje and his equally gallant and able opposite number with Urquhart, Lieutenant-Commander Arnoldus Wolters, were to learn much about German troop movements from the Dutch exchange operators, and they also used the system themselves to collect information from the Resistance groups. But it was a pity that when the British radio communications failed to operate effectively no one realised that the civilian telephone network might provide an alternative, even after a medical officer had made a successful call from a private house to the St Elizabeth Hospital in Arnhem. Possibly this is understandable. Security training in the British Army was extremely thorough, and the use of civilian circuits had certainly never been contemplated during training.

It was also unfortunate that, in Arnhem, the men of the Royal Corps of Signals failed to discover that yet another and perfectly secure communications system existed. Linking the electricity and waterway installations was a separate telephone system, unnoticed by the Germans as well until the middle of November. Through it, US 82nd Division in Nijmegen was to receive brief accounts of what was happening at the Arnhem bridge, but, in Arnhem especially, its use was never exploited as it might well have been.

The strike by Dutch railwaymen called on 17 September epitomised the latent quality of the Resistance. It demonstrated too the determination of so many ordinary men and women to do what lay in their power to rid themselves of the hated *'Moffen'* (their term of abuse for the Germans), regardless of what might happen to themselves and their families. This strike was to continue until the Netherlands were finally liberated at the very end of the war in Europe, despite the Germans' retaliatory embargo upon the movement of food during the winter of 1944-45 from the east of the country to the starving cities in the west. Equally resolute was the help provided to sustain and guide the many members of the airborne divisions who had landed or dropped wide of their targets into the middle of enemy-held areas, and so too was the succour that was later given to officers and men evading capture by the enemy. This was cold-blooded and unselfish gallantry of the highest order.

CHAPTER TEN

'A GROSSLY UNTIDY SITUATION'

Cn 18 September, in the tall buildings grouped around the northern ramp of the Arnhem highway bridge, Frost's men stood to arms just before dawn and waited for what the day might bring. Through swirling snatches of autumn mist, those whose positions overlooked the bridge itself could see the scattered bodies on the road, the still-smouldering remains of the German trucks that had tried to cross from the southern end during the night.

The riverside roads on the north bank ran through twin tunnels in this single soaring ramp, and around it jostled the narrow, congested streets of the old town, the roofs and upper storeys in places level with the raised roadway. In these houses the British had built their strongpoints, smashing out the glass from the windows and building barricades of furniture and books. Below, in the cellars, some of the Dutch owners still huddled with their families, barely comprehending the outcome of what, just a few hours earlier, had seemed to be a joyous liberation.

The defenders did not have long to wait. Into the open space opposite the house in which members of the headquarters of 2nd Parachute Battalion had barricaded themselves drove some truckloads of German soldiers. It was an error typical of what can happen in the confusion of street fighting. The British waited, holding their fire. Then a storm of bullets sliced into the crowded and

---

unprotected vehicles. Desperately drivers attempted to reverse, but few of the occupants survived the slaughter.

So began a savage battle which was to last for two hours. From nearby buildings Germans were shooting at anything that moved, while shells and mortar bombs smashed into the British-held buildings. Then, at 0930 hours, a column of German armoured vehicles drove across the bridge from the direction of Nijmegen, straight into the middle of Frost's encircling force. This was the 9th SS Panzer reconnaissance unit, hurrying back from Nijmegen over the bridge it had safely crossed less than twenty-four hours earlier. The first four vehicles managed to speed through unharmed, but the seven which followed all fell victim either to a 6-pounder anti-tank gun covering the bridge, or to PIATs fired from the houses overlooking the ramp. Some sappers on the eastern side under command of Captain Eric Mackay even managed to drop grenades from the upper window of their building into the open-topped armoured half-tracks. While this was going on, German infantry, supported by armoured cars and SP guns, pressed forward from the city side. In the end, however, the German efforts slackened, but for the rest of the day small parties continued to try to infiltrate the area. The shelling and the mortaring persisted, the latter relatively ineffective against the robust buildings, but the arrival of a 150-mm SP gun demonstrated how quickly the houses could be smashed into untenable heaps of rubble. Fortunately the gun was swiftly knocked out.

At nightfall, the British set fire to a small house near the river to provide light by which to shoot. They hardly needed to have bothered. Soon the building occupied by Frost's headquarters was ablaze, as was the one next door, although the fire in the former was soon quenched. An atmosphere of confidence, allied to self-congratulation, greeted Frost as he toured the positions held by his men that evening. Doubts, however, were starting to plague him. The larger part of his B Company had managed to reach him during the day, but C Company, which had been involved in the action at the railway bridge, was still missing. Ammunition was running short, and the only news about the progress of the rest of the brigade was a radio message giving the position of 1st Parachute Battalion as being just short of the railway on the outskirts of the city. Frost had also discovered that several of his SS prisoners belonged to 9th

Panzer Division, startling and worrying information to someone who had been told to expect light and low-quality opposition.

The report about 1 Para was only too true. After the battalion had encountered the German armoured cars and tanks on the Ede-Arnhem road the previous afternoon and had moved into the woods towards Johannahoeve, it had continued to clash with parties of the enemy – and to lose men – as it progressed southwards. At last it hit the Utrechtseweg, the route 3 Para was taking, and turned towards Arnhem. Then, at about dawn, a signal was intercepted from 2 Para at the bridge, asking urgently for reinforcements. Out of contact with his brigade headquarters, the battalion commander decided that he must strike for the bridge. Moving still further south, down to the river road, the battalion then hit the German positions along the railway embankment and around the high ground at Den Brink. It was unfortunate that 3 Para should also have side-stepped to the river road. As can so easily happen in the dark, when this battalion set off towards Arnhem at 0430 hours, after its night-long halt, the front of the column moved too quickly and the rear lost touch, so splitting the battalion. One of the consequences was that both General Urquhart and Brigadier Lathbury, who had together decided to stay with this battalion, became separated from their radio vehicles and thus lost the final remnants of any control either of them might have been able to exercise over the battle.

The accounts of what followed are confused. Somehow the leading troops of 3 Para succeeded in slipping past the Germans at Den Brink and reached the area just west of the St Elizabeth Hospital. By then there were only some 170 men of this front section of the battalion still on their feet. At the same time as the remnants of 1 Para were doggedly trying to force their way past Den Brink, German infantry, supported by a tank and some armoured cars, counter-attacked the survivors of 3 Para. In the muddled fighting around the small terraced houses, the units mistook one another for the enemy and opened fire. By nightfall neither battalion really existed as such, 1 Para having only some hundred man left and 3 Para little more, the former fighting just to the north-west of the hospital, the latter a short distance to its east. Intermingled among them were German infantry and armoured cars. Lathbury had been wounded about 100 yards away from the hospital entrance. Urquhart, his batman, and two other officers were holed-up in a house in a nearby street, unable to escape with a German SP gun and its crew just outside the door. During the fracas, the Divisional Commander had shot a German through a window with his revolver, an unusual experience for an officer of his rank.

Throughout the morning, all concerned with the conduct of the battle north of the Neder Rijn had been relying upon the arrival of the second lift to clear up an unsatisfactory but by no means hopeless situation. Not only would the lift bring 4 Parachute Brigade, with more guns and sappers, but it would also release 1 Airlanding Brigade from its negative but vital task of protecting the DZs and LZs for the second lift. The result of spreading the arrival of 1st Airborne Division over two days had become only too plain. If two sorties had been flown on the first day, the entire division, not just a single brigade, would have been available to secure the bridge on the first day. In fact, Urquhart might even have been better off without the second day's lift: with no requirement to hold the DZs and LZs, two complete brigades would have been available on that first afternoon to overcome the opposition in Arnhem and capture the bridge.

Because the larger part of 4 Parachute Brigade had seen much less of the war than had the members of 1 Parachute Brigade, its officers and men were possibly even more anxious to get into the fighting in Europe before it came to an end than were their more experienced rivals – rivals, it should be said, who they tended to regard with wary but unacknowledged envy. The brigade had been formed in Egypt in the winter of 1942-43 around a nucleus of 156 Parachute Battalion (itself raised in India in 1941, largely from long-service regular soldiers), which became one of the brigade's battalions, the other two being the 10th and 11th Parachute Battalions. Two of these units, 156 Para and 10 Para, had taken part in the invasion of Italy, landing by sea at Taranto, and had undergone some not-too-intense action against the German forces retreating up from the toe of Italy; 11 Para had dropped a company on the island of Cos in the Dodecanese in September 1943, the Italian garrison of which had welcomed the arrival of their liberators with some pleasure. In command of the brigade was Shan Hackett, who had made his mark as a fighting soldier in the Western Desert. He was also an outstanding linguist, historian and classicist, a rare combination in the pre-war British cavalry.

107

As Frost's force was in the process of destroying the German armour trying to cross the Arnhem bridge, Hackett and his men were contemplating with dismay the low cloud drifting over their departure airfields in England. After watching with considerable awe the first lift flying over their camps and billets on the previous day, and listening to the BBC news of the invasion that evening, the prospect of yet another cancelled operation was too much to be endured. But after several hours spent consuming large quantities of tea and thick sustaining sandwiches, the order to emplane arrived, four hours late.

The flight on the northern route was in no way so peaceful as that of the previous day. The now-alerted flak was active, and German fighters were about in strength. That morning, at 1100 hours, thirty Messerschmitts had bombed and strafed with machine-guns the LZ upon which the brigade's gliders were due to land, much to the surprise of its defenders, who, until then, had experienced convincing proof of Allied air superiority, having seen nothing at all of the Luftwaffe. This attack occurred at the exact time that 4 Parachute Brigade had been due to drop, which suggests that, if Student's account of the captured operation order is true, good use was made of the information. Ninety more German fighters attempted to attack the long column of transport aircraft as it neared its objective, but they failed to penetrate the overwhelming Allied escort. Standing in the open Dakota doors, waiting for the green light to jump, the paratroops could see below them, among the flooded fields, Dutch families waving from the roofs to which they clung. Then black puffs of smoke appeared among the aircraft, the white upturned faces of the flak gunners visible as Allied fighters dived to silence them. The damage inflicted upon the column was, however, surprisingly small, although one Dakota was seen to drop in flames and explode as it hit the ground, those who could see it wondering which of their friends were among the passengers.

The Groote Heide had been earmarked as the DZ for 4 Parachute Brigade. Since dawn, its defenders, the KOSB and a platoon of 21st Independent Parachute Company, the division's pathfinders, had been under increasing pressure from small parties of Germans, and as the first paratroops began to float down at 1500 hours on that glorious sunny afternoon they could see below them the smoke of battle and hear the crack of bullets. It was a considerable

108

relief to hit the ground, and even more so to discover that their arrival had persuaded the Germans either to leave or to surrender; the reception had been rather more spectacular than dangerous, but still it had cost the brigade a number of men killed and wounded. The battalions and other units collected themselves, ready to move, within the hour, but an unexpected hiatus then ensued: despite the fact that their arrival had been delayed by more than four hours, the move towards the brigade's objective north of Arnhem did not start until 1700 hours.

In the lead was 156 Para, taking the path along the north side of the railway, and soon all the units were joined by the transport and heavy weapons which had been landed in the gliders. Then, at about 2000 hours, an officer of the KOSB halted the leading troops to tell them that the Germans were holding a line running north and south along the Dreijenseweg, the road ahead of them leading into Oosterbeek. So it turned out. As the leading company approached the Dreijenseweg that night, a hail of bullets cut into the leading men. Faced with the near-impossible task of attacking an unseen and heavily defended position in the dark, the battalion's commanding officer decided to pull back his forward troops some 1,500 yards, there to organise a deliberate attack against what was, in fact, the forward defence line of 9th SS Panzer Division, although no one was yet to know.

With both Urquhart and Lathbury missing in Arnhem, Brigadier Pip Hicks, the commander of 1 Airlanding Brigade, had assumed command of the division early that morning. He was an excellent trainer of troops but, at the age of forty-nine, was old for an airborne brigadier, and early that summer Montgomery, who knew Hicks well, had sugested to Urquhart that he should be removed on these grounds to another command. He had stayed, however, and just before take-off for 'Market Garden' Urquhart had told his senior staff officer, Lieutenant-Colonel Charles Mackenzie, that Hicks would replace him if both he and Lathbury were to become casualties. Despite his age, Hicks was junior as a brigadier to Hackett, and Urquhart had omitted to inform the latter of his decision.

Learning about the parlous states of 2 Para at the bridge through the gunner radio net, the only one operating at the time, Hicks had decided to send the half-battalion of the South Staffordshires which had landed with the first lift into Arnhem to help 1 Parachute

Brigade, and to reinforce the brigade further with the rest of the battalion and with Hackett's 11 Para as soon as the second lift arrived. Soon after he touched down, Hackett met Mackenzie and learned what had been decided. He was not pleased. The news that one of his battalions was to be taken away from him disturbed him even more than the fact that Hicks was commanding the division. 4 Parachute Brigade, which he had raised and trained, was very dear to him. To remove a battalion, and to decide, without consultation, which battalion it was to be, was bad enough, but to feed units into the battle as night was approaching with no clear orders and no coherent plan, to fight in a strange built-up area where the enemy appeared to be gathering strength, was not, in Hackett's opinion, in any way sound. Furthermore, he was far from happy about the orders he now received from Hicks for the employment of the remainder of 4 Parachute Brigade. All in all, as he afterwards recollected, 'it was a grossly untidy situation'.

Feeling ran high when the two brigadiers met, although some accounts exaggerate the details of the incident. In the end, however, Hackett settled matters by outlining his own plan for the use of his own brigade, and to this Hicks gave his agreement. The following morning, it was arranged, 4 Parachute Brigade, less 11 Para but with the KOSB under command, would attack towards Arnhem, its first objective the high ground at Koepel just east of the Dreijenseweg, where the Airborne Cemetery now lies.

Urquhart's absence had resulted in a breakdown in command of the division at what, in retrospect, can be seen as the most critical stage of the battle. Hicks's errors were twofold. Not only did he despatch his newly arrived units into the untidy fighting at the edge of the city in such a haphazard manner, but he also failed to provide Hackett with clear instructions. It was a time when major decisions were needed. With the situation as it was on the second day, before the second lift arrived, one possible option would have been to change the plan for the use of 4 Parachute Brigade and drop it south of the Arnhem road bridge on the DZ planned for use by the Poles on the third day; this was something that could, admittedly with difficulty, have been arranged, since one of the few radio links still working was that to Browning's rear headquarters in England. An alternative would have been to abandon the attempt to force a way to the bridge, now surprise was so clearly lost, and instead establish a bridgehead around the high ground at Westerbouwing and the ferry-crossing it commanded at Heveadorp, there to await the arrival of XXX Corps and the heavy bridging. It is hard, however, to blame Hicks for failing to take far-reaching decisions such as these, even if it had occurred to him to do so. Urquhart was not known to be a casualty, and he could well reappear at any moment. The fault lay more in the fact that a British airborne division, unlike its American counterpart, did not possess a deputy commander. Given the circumstances, such an officer, had there been one, might well have thought himself fully justified in making a major and radical change to the original plan for the employment of the division. But Hicks could hardly have done so.

Urquhart has been censured (and sometimes by those who should know better) for becoming involved in the fighting in Arnhem and for failing to get back to his headquarters. It is a truism that a commander needs to be well forward so that he can see what is happening, and this is especially so when the situation is muddled and the communications faulty. Inevitably, airborne commanders were to find themselves in the thick of the fighting. It had happened to all three divisional commanders in Normandy, and in Italy in 1943 Major-General G.F. Hopkinson, Urquhart's predecessor as commander of 1st Airborne Division, had been killed by machine-gun fire while visiting 4 Parachute Brigade. During 'Market', both Gavin and Taylor were to become, at times, mixed up in the fighting, and Taylor was wounded. In the words of Gavin, who knew what he was talking about, 'the place for a general in battle is where he can see the battle and get the odor of it in his nostrils'. With his command net useless, Urquhart could only go forward to try to discover for himself what was happening.

Furthermore, everything might have been different if 1st Airborne Division's communications had functioned properly, both forward and to the rear. The heart of the problem lay in the fact that neither the sets nor their operators were up to the job. Urquhart's signals officers had expressed fears that the standard No.22 set used on the divisional net to communicate with brigades and divisional units was unlikely to work well with units widely separated and operating in thickly wooded and built-up country, and much the same applied to the brigade nets further forward, using the same equipment. The

No.22 set was also used to reach Browning's headquarters and that of XXX Corps. Ever since the division had returned from Italy at the end of 1943, attempts had been made to obtain a more powerful set. But these had been unsuccessful, the requests rejected on the grounds that the division was always likely to fight in an area no more than five miles across, and that, in any case, larger sets would require more gliders to lift them, and gliders were a scarce commodity.

For all that, it was possible to obtain good results from the No.22 set, although it was far from ideal for the job. This the divisional gunners demonstrated, as gunners had done before, displaying an expertise that seemed to be denied to other operators. When all else failed, it was the field artillery observation officer at the Arnhem bridge who passed to his gun position news of what was happening, this in turn being relayed to Divisional Headquarters. It was fortunate also that a detachment of the GHQ Liaison Regiment (known as 'Phantom') had landed with each division, their task being to pass information on the progress of the battle direct to the War Office in London. Their communications worked, as did those of the BBC correspondents landed with the 1st Division, whose sets operated with the help of a 100-foot aerial.

CHAPTER ELEVEN

'THE RETENTION OF THE HIGH GROUND SOUTH OF NIJMEGEN WAS OF GREATER IMPORTANCE'

At 0600 hours that same Monday morning, the second day of the battle, the Irish Guards at last began to edge up the road from Valkenswaard towards Eindhoven. Half-way there, near the village of Aalst, the first delay occured. The leading tanks were for the time being halted by a single SP gun, firing down the main road to which the British armour was confined. And, in this way, for the rest of the day a few German tanks and guns, covered by infantry hidden in houses, were able to hinder the advance. Attempts by other units of Guards Armoured Division to find a way around either flank failed, the frail bridges over the small waterways collapsing under the weight of the armour. Progress was made even more difficult because air support from the Typhoons was absent, the aircraft grounded by fog in Belgium, although the skies over western Holland were clear.

At about the same time as the Irish Guards moved off, Colonel Sink's 506 Parachute Infantry set off for Eindhoven from the small bridgehead the regiment had formed across the Wilhelmina Canal. Delayed by German patrols as they moved south, the Americans encountered little other resistance, but it was mid-day before they reached their destination, after eliminating a couple of 88-mm SPs on the outskirts of the city. Eindhoven was the first large city of the Netherlands to be liberated, and as the men of US 101st Airborne Division rounded up its German defenders, who amounted to no more than a company or so of rear-area troops, the place erupted into orange-hued carnival. Just after mid-day, two armoured cars of the Household Cavalry drove in from the north-west, having slipped around the surburbs, but it was a further five-and-a-half hours before the Americans heard the clanking of the Sherman tanks and were able to welcome the main column of Guards Armoured Division into the city. XXX Corps and the airborne troops had made contact, but twenty-four hours behind schedule.

Delayed only by the frenzied welcome of the people of Eindhoven, the Guards crossed the Dommel river, the Germans having failed to blow the bridges, and pushed on northwards towards the broken bridge across the Wilhelmina Canal at Son. Helped by the Americans, who had telephoned over the civilian network the details of the stores needed to repair this bridge, the sappers of the Guards Armoured Division were quickly at work. Meanwhile, further to the north, the other regiments of 101st Division had as yet experienced little trouble in safeguarding the main road from attack: during the Sunday night the Germans launched several minor assaults against 501 Parachute Infantry in the Veghel area (and were to do so again during Monday night), but these were repulsed with little difficulty.

Around Best, however, it was a different matter. With the Son bridge destroyed, that at Best had assumed much greater importance as an alternative route across the Wilhelmina Canal. As a result, both sides were pouring reinforcements into the battle. At first light on Monday Colonel Michaelis of 502 Parachute Infantry sent his 2nd Battalion to attack around the right towards the bridge, but the Americans found newly arrived troops of the German 59th Division to be already in position. Attacking across open fields without adequate supporting fire from heavy weapons, the paratroops were cut down by machine-guns, and the P-47 strike aircraft called in later that day to hammer the Germans made little difference to the outcome. This costly and unsuccessful attack provided proof again, if proof were needed, that without proper supporting fire even the best of troops could not overcome a determined enemy prepared to sit and fight it out. Unknown to

Michaelis, however, the attack had been a pointless exercise. Still fighting near the bridge were eighteen survivors of the platoon that had reached it during the Sunday night. At 1100 hours their foxholes were showered with chunks of steel and concrete as a tremendous explosion, unheard by the rest of their regiment, lifted the 100-foot span of the bridge into the air. Like the British, the Americans can sometimes draw inspiration from a costly failure. Even though 502 Regiment was later to play a major part in the fighting at Bastogne during the Battle of the Bulge, many of its men spoke with greater pride of the 2nd Battalion's unsuccessful attack at Best than of any other single event in the history of the regiment.

That afternoon, the second lift, although also delayed by the weather in England, brought welcome reinforcements to a now-over-stretched 101st Division. By glider there arrived two battalions of 327 Glider Infantry and the balance of the divisional troops, other than the artillery, 2,579 men in all. Only sporadic rifle fire from the edge of the LZ had interfered with the landing. The sorties were a success, no more than twenty-two gliders failing to arrive of the 440 that took off, but the supplies dropped by 121 bombers of US Eighth Air Force went sadly astray, only half being recovered by the troops on the ground. The arrival of 82nd Division's second lift was to be a quite different story, however.

To the north, in US 82nd Airborne Division's area, a company of Colonel Lindquist's 508 Parachute Infantry had made another attempt to reach the Nijmegen road bridge soon after daybreak on the 18th. Entering the city from the south-east, the Americans almost reached the traffic circle at the southern approach to the road bridge, which with the Hunner Park opposite is overlooked by the mediaeval tower and fortifications of the Valkhof. As they approached the circle, however, heavy enemy fire halted them. In some ways the fighting was rather similar to that taking place in Arnhem, although all on a smaller scale, as unco-ordinated attacks by small bodies of American troops without proper supporting fire met increased German resistance.

For the moment, however, Gavin was facing another and even more pressing problem. Having so vast an area to defend with his few troops, the LZs, especially those on the north side of the Groesbeek Heights, could only be protected by a handful of small patrols, all that he could spare. Early in the day, parties of Germans had started to filter into the area and to make a general nuisance of themselves. Information gathered from prisoners suggested, correctly as it turned out, that the German units consisted of no more than a collection of hastily assembled base troops, reinforcements and convalescents, but these had fought very stubbornly near Wyler. Only later did the Americans discover the reason for this. Wyler lay just inside Germany, and its defenders were striving to repel some of the first Allied troops to set foot inside the Fatherland. Gavin had also received other, and more alarming intelligence. Even though it had seemed clear enough on the evening before that the reports about German armour massing in the Reichswald were untrue, during the morning of the second day the chief of the Dutch underground told the American general that the Germans were in the forest in strength, in both armour and infantry.

It was perhaps fortunate that the 450 gliders of 82nd Airborne Division's second lift, like the reinforcements despatched to the other two divisions, were delayed by the weather. Worried by what reception the gliders might receive, Gavin ordered Lindquist to halt his attempts to reach the Nijmegen bridge and to return and secure the scantily guarded LZs instead. After a forced march from Nijmegen, the 1st Battalion of Lindquist's regiment arrived back on the Groesbeek Heights in the nick of time and, in the face of intense flak and small-arms fire, charged downhill to clear the LZ of the enemy. The Germans, of a calibre different from those fighting at Best and in Nijmegen, fled. In the words of the regimental report, it was 'a movie-thriller sight of landing gliders on the DZ as the deployed paratroops chased the last of the Germans from their 16 20-mm guns'. For the loss of only eleven men, the 1st Battalion killed fifty Germans and captured another 150. These American soldiers had spent an active twenty-four hours since they had arrived. The journey from the Groesbeek Heights and back was sixteen miles, they had dug a defensive position outside Nijmegen, and some of them had fought a nasty battle inside the city before returning to secure the LZs.

Although this second lift had arrived almost in the middle of the battle on the LZs, its losses had been small. All eight of the 57-mm anti-tank guns were landed safely, as were thirty of the thirty-six field artillery howitzers. And the subsequent supply drop was 80 per cent successful.

116

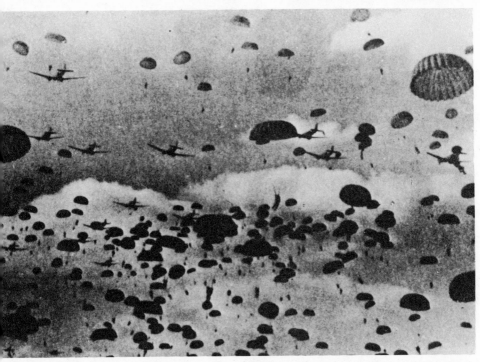

An unidentified US 82nd Airborne Division unit, possibly 505th Parachute Infantry, dropping near the Groesbeek Heights on 17 September.

A wrecked Waco CG-4A (Hadrian) glider which had collided with another on 506th Parachute Infantry's LZ near Son, early in the afternoon of D-day. 506th was part of US 101st Airborne Division.

Generalfeldmarschall Model, who narrowly escaped capture at his HQ at the Tafelberg Hotel on 17 September. Despite his surprise at the Allied landings, his response to the threat was swift and effective.

18 September – 4 Parachute Brigade's DZ burning. The DZ's defenders had been under increasing German pressure since dawn, but the arrival of the second lift persuaded the enemy to surrender or leave.

4 Parachute Brigade's drop, 18 September. 'As the paratroops began to float down, they could see below them the smoke of battle and hear the crack of bullets' – German soldiers firing on the British paratroops.

Brig Shan Hackett, commanding 4 Parachute Brigade – 'he was far from happy about the orders he now received from Hicks . . . All in all, as he afterwards recollected, "it was a grossly untidy situation".'

18 September. British troops, possibly 3 Para, moving down the Utrechtseweg. The photograph was taken by a Dutch woman author, Tony de Ritter, who lived in Oosterbeek at the time.

Members of Gough's Recce Squadron on the Utrechtseweg in Oosterbeek on D-plus-1.
Eventually some of them managed to reach Frost's position at the bridge.
506th Parachute Infantry with German prisoners in Eindhoven on 18 September, assisted by
Dutch police (in black uniforms). The German defenders 'amounted to no more than a
company or so of rear-area troops'.

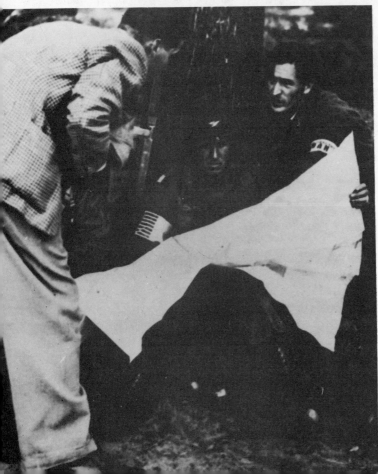

Col W. E. Ekman (centre), commanding 505th Parachute Infantry from US 82nd Airborne, giving out orders near Groesbeek. Browning stated that 'the retention of the high ground south of Nijmegen [i.e. the Groesbeek Heights] was of greater importance' than the capture of the Nijmegen bridges.

Col Howard R. Johnson, commanding 501st Parachute Infantry from US 101st Airborne, talking to two Dutch Underground members near 501st's DZ close to Veghel. 'The American airborne divisions made sound use of the local help', but with the British, 'little was done to exploit the enthusiastic help the Dutch were so eager to give.'

XXX Corps armour and transport in Eindhoven on 20 September – 'the place erupted into orange-hued carnival'.

Support for XXX Corps' advance up the road towards Arnhem. Infantry from 53rd (Welsh) Division (XII Corps) crossing the Meuse-Escaut Canal near Lommel by raft on 19 September.

A rare photograph, taken with an illicit camera, of the disastrous Polish glider landing near Johannahoeve on 19 September – 'the frantic Poles, landing in the middle of the confused battle, shot at anything that moved'. The glider is a Horsa, and supply canisters and parachutes can be seen on the ground.

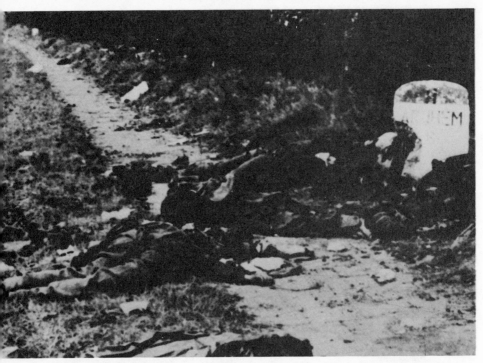

The Amsterdamseweg 6 kilometres (3¾ miles) from Arnhem, looking towards the city. A German photograph of British dead, their unit unidentified – possibly from the Recce Squadron, or from 1 or 10 Para.

Troops of US 101st Airborne Division near Son, after the link-up with XXX Corps. By then, the British ground troops were more than one full day behind schedule.

XXX Corps armour crossing the Bailey bridge at Son, built on the night of 18/19 September to replace the bridge destroyed by the Germans.

'Touch them and they react' – from left to right: Model, Bittrich, Knaust (a staff officer) and Harmel – the men who masterminded the defeat of 'Market Garden'.

Elsewhere, 82nd Division had strengthened its position during the second day's fighting. At about mid-day patrols from 504 and 508 Regiments captured the Honinghutje bridge over the Maas-Waal Canal, inexplicably neglected the previous day. Unfortunately the demolition charges were exploded by the Germans just as the Americans stormed it, which so weakened the structure that, later, the relieving columns had to be channelled across the Heumen Bridge, lying to the east, a much more circuitous route. Meanwhile, a battalion of 505 Parachute Infantry had cleared the German defenders out of Mook, a village strategically situated just to the south-east of Heumen on the main Venlo-Nijmegen highway, and a place already famous for the battle fought there during the German invasion of Holland in 1940.

One opportunity had been missed, however. Before dawn on Monday 18 September, Gavin, who had been snatching a short sleep at his command post near Groesbeek, was awakened by a train trundling towards Germany. No one had thought to block the railway line. A second train which approached an hour later was less fortunate: this time a round from a bazooka halted it, and the Americans rounded up its German passengers.

As soon as Gavin's second lift was safely down that Monday afternoon, Browning asked him to produce a plan for 82nd Division to seize the two Nijmegen bridges, one carrying the highway and one the railway. This was the division's primary task and had still not been accomplished, even though XXX Corps was scheduled to arrive in Nijmegen at 1800 hours. At the time, no news of XXX Corps' progress had been received – their tanks had still, of course, to reach Eindhoven. As for British 1st Airborne, all that was known about its progress was a telephone message passed by the Dutch Resistance over their public utility network, and received by 505 Parachute Infantry at 1040 hours on the Monday. It had read 'Dutch report Germans winning over the British in Arnhem'. Emanating as it did from the underground, this was little to go on, nor is it known whether the message reached Browning.

In response to Browning's request, Gavin produced a plan for a battalion of 504 Regiment to go straight for the two bridges, with 508 Regiment tackling them simultaneously from either flank. According to the journal of Gavin's Chief of Staff, however, details of which Gavin himself later confirmed, Browning had second

117

thoughts when he received the American plan to capture the bridges, affirming once again that 'the retention of the high ground South of Nijmegen was of greater importance'.

This decision was one of the very few Browning was called upon to make during the battle. His advanced headquarters, sited close to Gavin's command post, had been carried into Holland on the first day in its thirty-six gliders – gliders that might otherwise have been used to fly in a much-needed extra infantry battalion, either to Nijmegen or to Arnhem. There is little any senior commander can do to influence the course of events in the early stages of a battle, and this Browning was to discover. US 101st Division had come directly under command of XXX Corps as soon as it landed, and there was, in fact, little reason why Horrocks should not have assumed command of the other two airborne divisions as and when he reached them. Browning might, in fact, have been better placed in England at his rear headquarters, where he could have taken decisions on committing reserves, especially the air-transportable 52nd (Lowland) Division, as the situation developed, assuming, of course, that his communications worked as planned. But Browning, like many another, had long waited for the day when he would lead into battle the troops he had raised and trained. And this battle was likely to end the war in the West and bring renown to both his airborne troops and himself. In such circumstances, few men given the opportunity would have acted otherwise.

Soon after Browning's headquarters had arrived on the first day, his staff had captured a few German prisoners and radio communication was established with 82nd Division next door. Otherwise the corps was in touch with no one other than its rear headquarters in England, and there was to be little or no improvement on the second day: because of a shortage of cipher operators, even the link to England was of little value. 'Corps Signals in the field and at Airborne Base were totally inadequate in personnel and equipment and training', to quote Browning's report on the battle. The problem was that the headquarters was little more than an administrative and training organisation, ill-equipped both in men and equipment for the operational role recently and suddenly thrust upon it. These deficiencies were in no way the fault of its senior staff officers who had, throughout the summer, been working day and night on plans for a succession of complicated and abortive operations, and whose requests for extra men and material accomplished little. It was not only that Browning lacked a worthwhile job to perform in Holland – he was also short of the machinery with which to do such a job.

General Gavin is not alone in maintaining to this day that the decision to give priority to the high ground outside Nijmegen was correct. He was, however, a thrusting commander, and might perhaps have tackled the bridges in strength on the second day if Browning had not been there to forbid him to do so. He is remembered as having been somewhat in awe of his senior at the time: Browning was a much older man who had earned a brilliant reputation as a junior front-line officer in the First World War. It is certain, however, that if a decision had been taken at the outset to hold a tighter perimeter around Nijmegen, then spare battalions would have been available to attempt to seize and hold the bridges until Guards Armoured Division arrived.

CHAPTER TWELVE

'IT IS AGAINST TEXT-BOOK TEACHING TO BREAK OFF AN ENGAGEMENT AND WITHDRAW FROM THE BATTLEFIELD IN BROAD DAYLIGHT ...'

The Dutch Resistance had sound reasons for the report they had passed over the telephone to 82nd Division outside Nijmegen: 'Germans winning over the British at Arnhem'. By nightfall on the second day three separate battles were being fought there, one at the north end of the highway bridge itself, one by the four battalions struggling to reach 2nd Parachute Battalion defending the bridge, and one around Oosterbeek. All three were self-contained, and all were going badly. To the unfortunate Dutch civilians, cowering in their cellars as the din and smoke of the battles eddied down the streets, it was clear that all was not well. To those who ventured to leave their shelters, the sight of shattered bodies lying in the roads outside, or of fresh German units driving into the city, provided a grim contrast with the joy that had greeted the airborne troops such a short time before.

Despite everything, many of Frost's soldiers faced their second dawn at the bridge with confidence. Although they had seen heavy fighting the previous day and had inflicted considerable losses upon the German SS troops, their own casualties, except among Mackay's sappers on the eastern side of the ramp, had not been too serious. Most of the British troops were manning well constructed barricades in solid houses; 6-pounder anti-tank guns covered the wider of the roads leading into the complex of buildings they were defending; two 3-inch mortars were well dug-in on an open space outside the headquarters; and the battery commander of the 1st Light Regiment, Royal Artillery, was in radio contact with his 75-mm howitzers, sited near the church at Oosterbeek, and was using them to help break up the German attacks. Cut off the British soldiers might be, but this was something to be expected, and there seemed to be no reason why they could not hang on for a further day provided that their ammunition held out – and this was the crucial problem.

The first German intrusion that morning of 19 September took the shape of a headlong dash towards the British positions by some armoured cars, their guns blazing. The 6-pounder guns dealt effectively with them. Then began the shelling and the mortaring, and this was to continue all the day. SP guns and then tanks started to edge along the streets into the British positions, their movement covered by German infantry firing sometimes from houses next door to those occupied by the defenders. In a systematic manner the German armour smashed high-explosive or phosphorus shells into the British-held buildings, demolishing them or setting them ablaze, driving the defenders storey by storey down the blood-stained stairs, amid crashing masonry and blinding clouds of plaster dust.

Casualties now mounted steadily. By evening, of the fifty sappers in one of the houses on the eastern flank, four lay dead and twenty-seven had been wounded. In the stinking cellars the wounded were crammed so close together that the two doctors and few medical orderlies had difficulty in avoiding stepping upon them. The horrors were made worse by the lack of water. An offer, brought by a captured British soldier, for Frost to meet the German commander to discuss surrender terms was ignored, but by now Frost was even more worried, his concern about the failure of the other units of the division, which he knew were fighting nearby, to reach him aggravated by concern for the Polish battalions, due to drop during the day south of the bridge into an area still held by the enemy.

Later, after night fell, he discussed the future with Major Gough of the Recce Squadron as, through a gaping hole in the roof of one of the still-standing buildings, they watched Arnhem burn, the tall spires of the two great churches close at hand silhouetted against a vast pall of smoke. Their problem was intractable. If they continued to defend their present positions, the wounded would roast in the cellars; on the other hand, it was impossible to move to other positions, surrounded as they were by the Germans.

For the units striving to relieve 2 Para, it was to be a tragic day. Late on the previous evening, the South Staffordshires had managed to reach what was left of 1 Para near St Elizabeth Hospital, bringing with them some forty members of that battalion they had picked up on the way. Then, in the early hours of the third day, 11 Para arrived too. Lacking a commander, the three lieutenant-colonels were obliged to hatch a plan between them, and the result was that, at about 0400 hours, the South Staffordshires started to press forward further into Arnhem along the main road leading past the hospital; behind them followed 11 Para. At the same time 1 Para set off along the river road, and here the few survivors of the battalion encountered the remnants of 3 Para, who had made an independent and unsuccessful attempt earlier in the night to get through to the bridge on their own.

By 0630 hours on the 19th, the South Staffordshires had advanced only 400 yards to reach the Museum, and here they ran into even heavier opposition. Channelled into two narrow approach routes by the deep cutting of the railway yards and by the river, the four battalions had no room for manoeuvre. An attempt by 11 Para to strike round the left failed. In a dogged but hopeless fashion, the survivors of 1 Para pushed on to within 800 yards of Frost's position at the bridge; the final count showed thirty men still fighting. Of 3 Para, there were about the same number of survivors in all. What seemed to be conflicting orders which somehow arrived from Divisional Headquarters added to the confusion. Some German tanks forced the South Staffordshires to withdraw when their PIAT ammunition was exhausted, and others caught 11 Para as it was forming up to attack. All four of the commanding officers were killed or wounded during the morning; few other officers were left. A few demoralised survivors of these four battalions began to drift back in the direction of Oosterbeek, and it was fortunate that

Lieutenant-Colonel W.F.K. (Sheriff) Thompson of the Light Regiment, RA, met them as they came back down the road and managed to organise some 400 into a defensive position east of Oosterbeek Church, in front of his gun positions.

It might have been quite a different story if 1st Airborne Division had used the ferry at Westerbouwing to ship troops south of the river and so approach the bridges from the far side. Certainly there were few, if any, German troops between Driel and the southern end of the bridges during the early stages of the battle. A link between the villages around Driel and Oosterbeek, the ferry is said to have been still functioning on the Wednesday morning (20 September), with Dutch people crossing to Oosterbeek to buy bread. It is a mystery why its existence was not known to Urquhart's staff before the operation; if it had been, plans could have been made to attack the bridges from both ends on the first day. To compound the mischance, an officer of the Recce Squadron reported to Divisional Headquarters on the first evening that the ferry existed and was in working order, but the information was either lost or its importance was not appreciated by the staff officer who received it. But at least one Dutch civilian also pointed out the importance of the ferry to British staff officers. As it was, it was never used, and, at some time on the Wednesday, its moorings were cut and it drifted downstream, another opportunity lost.

Errors such as this might have been avoided if the British had brought themselves to make systematic use of the Dutch Resistance for gathering information. The means were there. Soon after the landing took place, a group of about twenty civilians offered their services to Divisional Headquarters. Their leader was a Dutch naval officer, Charles L.J.J. Douw van der Krap, who had been captured in 1940 and imprisoned at Colditz; from there he had escaped to reach Warsaw and fight with the Polish Resistance before returning to Holland by way of Germany. Christened the *Oranje-bataljon*, this party gathered a certain amount of information and helped also in collecting supplies, but its members were discouraged by the small use the British made of them. By Thursday 21 September, when it had become clear that all was far from well, the small group was disbanded for its own safety.

As the four battalions in Arnhem were making their final attempts to reach the bridge, 4 Parachute Brigade was starting on what was planned as the first stage of its advance towards the city. Ordering 156 Para to capture the high ground at Koepel, Hackett directed 10 Para to protect the flank of the advance by holding a firm base near the junction of the Arnhem-Ede road and the north end of the Dreijenseweg, the track where the leading company of 156 Para had hit 9th Panzer the previous evening. At first all went well. A company of 156 Para captured a small feature 200 yards short of the Dreijenseweg and made contact with the KOSB, who were discovered installed in the area of Johannahoeve, protecting the landing-zone for the glider-borne lift of the Polish Brigade, the arrival of which was expected at 1000 hours. What followed, however, had something in common with the fate of the four battalions in Arnhem. Without adequate covering fire, the other two companies of 156 Para assaulted the Lichtenbeek, the wooded area on the far side of the Dreijenseweg. Within minutes all five officers of the first of the two companies had been hit; only a handful of their soldiers even reached the track. The second suffered a similar fate. Fire from armoured cars, SP guns and infantry swept through the woods. Only on the left did 10 Para succeed in reaching its objective, having met much less opposition.

The two parachute brigades had both been asked to accomplish the impossible: to attack determined and well equipped troops without the benefit of surprise, and to do so without adequate support from artillery, armour or aircraft. This was something which had been continually glossed over during training. Short as they were of supporting weapons, the airborne troops had been encouraged to substitute dash and initiative for shells and bombs – 'gung-ho' or 'bash-on-regardless', as the more cynical put it. Such attacks would often succeed: if the enemy were sufficiently terrified, they would run away. This is possibly a simplification, but it demonstrates the essence of the problem. Time and again such attacks were to fail with grim losses. Few junior officers or NCOs survived the Arnhem battle unwounded – especially among the infantry battalions. One clear lesson which emerged from the fighting north of the Neder Rijn was that these lightly armed airborne troops were almost impossible to shift from their defensive positions, particularly when they were dug-in or barricaded among streets and houses, but that their fine *élan* led to their slaughter when they attacked firmly held positions.

This was only the first of the setbacks 4 Parachute Brigade was to suffer on the third day. Next, a squadron of Messerschmitt Bf109s swooped down out of the sun to attack both the Brigade Headquarters and the positions where 156 Para had been halted, killing a number of the survivors of the battalion's recent abortive attack. As had happened the day before, the first glimpses of fighters circling overhead had produced the happy cry of 'Spitfires', the generic name given by the untutored soldier to any Allied fighter. At last, or so it seemed, some sort of help had arrived from the outside world, and only at the last moment did men notice the black crosses and dive for cover. Again, it had occurred to no one that the aircraft could be anything but friendly.

It was fortunate indeed that the scheduled re-supply flights appeared several hours late, by which time the Germans fighters had departed. As the slow-moving Dakotas throbbed into view, German light flak hammered at them from the surrounding hills and woods, fire far more intense than anything seen on the Sunday or Monday. Far away, out of effective rifle or Bren-gun range, British soldiers could make out the German gunners, standing up to man their guns in the open. Without attempting to take evasive action, the massive aircraft flew straight into the circle of fire at a height of about 1,000 feet, making for their dropping-zone about a mile further on. Horrified, the soldiers watched as aircraft exploded in the air, and watched too as the supplies fell into the enemy lines. The men on the ground waved their yellow distinguishing scarves, fired Verey lights and spread parachutes out on the heather to try to attract the attention of the pilots, but in vain. One particular aircraft caught the eye of everyone. Although one wing was blazing, it made a second circle, its pilot clearly determined that his cargo should be delivered with precise accuracy. The khaki-clad despatchers were clearly visible, pushing their panniers through the open door, steadily doing their job regardless of the flames spreading towards them. Then the wing crumpled, the aircraft disappeared over the trees, and a ball of fire exploded into the sky as it hit the ground. The pilot, Flight Lieutenant David Lord of 217 Squadron, RAF, was later awarded a posthumous Victoria Cross. The supplies for British 1st Airborne Division had been delivered, but on to the DZ still in German possession. There had been no means of diverting the aircraft.

Early that morning, to the joy and relief of all, Urquhart had materialised at his headquarters, now operating in the Hartenstein Hotel at Oosterbeek. The SP gun which had been blocking the door of the house in which he had been forced to take refuge had moved when the South Staffordshires arrived in the vicinity of St Elizabeth Hospital during the night, so allowing him to escape. Borrowing a jeep from some nearby troops, he sped back to Oosterbeek, hastened on his way by a combination of enemy snipers covering the road and anxiety to get a grip on the battle once again. Had he been aware that the commanders of the South Staffordshires, 1 Para and 11 Para were co-ordinating their plans for the last attempt to reach the bridge only a hundred yards or so from the house in which he had hidden, he might well have delayed his departure. As it was, his first action when he arrived back at his headquarters was to despatch Colonel Hilary Barlow, the deputy commander of 1 Airlanding Brigade, into Arnhem to take control of the 1 Parachute Brigade sector of the battle. Barlow was never heard of again. Years later, his cigarette case was picked up near the St Elizabeth Hospital; it had been flattened, apparently by a heavy vehicle, an indication, perhaps, of how far he had got before he died.

Early that afternoon, Urquhart visited Hackett at the latter's headquarters. It was now obvious that there was no chance of 4 Parachute Brigade advancing further towards Koepel, but between Hackett's men and the rest of the division lay the railway line, its steep embankment impassable to vehicles except at two crossing places. The Germans held one of these crossings, at the southern end of the Dreijenseweg in Oosterbeek, and were threatening the other further to the west at Wolfheze, the loss of which would effectively trap the British brigade's jeeps and anti-tank guns north of the railway line. Because of this threat, Urquhart and Hackett decided that contingency plans should be made to withdraw the brigade south of the railway – plans not to be implemented until the order to do so was given.

At about 1500 hours, news reached Hackett from Divisional Headquarters that something was wrong in 1 Airlanding Brigade's area, south of Wolfheze. As a result he decided that the time had come for 10 Para to disengage and seize the Wolfheze crossing to avert the danger of his transport being trapped north of the railway. Although clear orders for the withdrawal had by now been issued all the way down the chain of command, things quickly went awry. First the companies of 10 Para discovered, as the withdrawal got under way, that the Germans were behind them, holding two of the places fixed as their rendezvous. Then the Germans started to follow up the withdrawal, and as the disengaging airborne troops began to cross the flat, open fields west of Johannahoeve, the landing-zone for the gliders carrying the Poles, due to arrive that morning but still awaited, they once again heard the throb of distant aircraft. Into view came the towing-aircraft and gliders, and earthwards the gliders swooped, down towards the retreating British troops. Again the German flak erupted. A glider disintegrated in the air, and men and a jeep tumbled towards the ground. Tracer bullets swept the area, and mortar bombs fell among those Poles who had landed safely and who were trying to unload their anti-tank guns and vehicles. From the edges of the landing-zone, the KOSB, still under Hackett's command, and 156 Parachute Battalion tried to engage those Germans within view; at the same time the frantic Poles, landing in the middle of the confused battle, shot at anything that moved, including some of the KOSB who were trying to help them unload their gliders.

As Polish survivors sought shelter in the surrounding woods, 156 Para received orders to move without delay to the Wolfheze area, and the KOSB were instructed to follow. The urgency was now such that there was no time to put into force the contingency orders so carefully prepared for the phased withdrawal, with companies and platoons covering one another as they pulled back. Pressed by German armoured cars and infantry as it moved along the north side of the railway line, 156 Para split into two parties; about three-quarters of what was left of the battalion made the hazardous crossing of the steep embankment under fire, but the rest kept straight on towards Wolfheze and were not seen again. That evening, in the woods south-east, of Wolfheze, 10 Para mustered 250 officers and men, 156 Para just twenty more. As for the KOSB, its commanding officer was later to write:

> It is against text-book teaching to break off an engagement and withdraw from the battlefield in broad daylight ... As a result, this fine Scottish Borderer Battalion ... was reduced, within the hour, to a third of its strength ...

This understandably bitter judgement is not altogether fair. A

127

night withdrawal is always preferable to one carried out by day, but the circumstances were such that there was no question of Hackett being able to postpone the move until nightfall. Rather the fault seems to have lain with the over-emphasis placed on the words 'without delay' in the orders which had reached battalions, so persuading the recipients that there was no time to put the prepared plans into operation. How this happened has never been discovered. Although by this second day of its battle 4 Parachute Brigade was running smoothly as a machine, somehow, somewhere in the chain of command the wrong emphasis had been placed upon a couple of words. Such errors happen only too easily in the stress of battle. It was all but a miracle that, despite everything, there was no panic, no disorder, just a steady and well disciplined move to the rear, the junior commanders in full control of their men.

Mystery also surrounds the report, received by 4 Parachute Brigade that afternoon, of trouble in 1 Airlanding Brigade's area. Somehow an inaccurate report had been received at Divisional Headquarters that Hick's brigade was under severe attack. The previous evening the Border Regiment had moved from the neighbourhood of the DZs and LZs to take up its planned position in the thickly wooded country between the railway line and the high ground at Westerbouwing, its sector of the planned twelve-mile position that the division was to have defended around Arnhem. To quote from the war diary of the Airlanding Brigade for the third day, Tuesday 19 September, it was not until 1900 hours that 'all coys of 1 Border were lightly attacked, the attacks being driven off without difficulty'. The battalion's account of the fighting bears this out. As the radios between division and the two brigades had functioned well throughout the day (the headquarters were quite close to one another), it is hard to understand how the misleading message about 1 Airlanding Brigade – a grievous error, and one that was to have such disastrous consequences for 4 Parachute Brigade – could have been originated.

In general, however, all was far from well at this time. Urquhart later described how, on the Tuesday, rumours spread without any basis of fact. At one point he was himself obliged to restrain an uncontrolled party of twenty men fleeing across the Hartenstein lawns in panic. Such incidents, he later reflected, were another consequence of not being able to 'blood' airborne troops gradually:

as soon as they landed, they were up to their necks in the battle.

English autumn weather had been responsible for the late arrival of the Tuesday airlift bringing both the gliders of 1 Polish Independent Parachute Brigade and the division's re-supply. Cloud and fog had again delayed take-off, and in the end only 655 troop-carrier aircraft and 431 gliders flew. Of these, 226 transports and 185 gliders failed to arrive at their destinations, forty transports and 112 gliders being listed as missing. The fighter escorts from Eighth Air Force and the Air Defence of Great Britain were to meet far stronger opposition on this third day of the battle, the Americans alone counting 425 Messerschmitt 109s and Focke-Wulf 190s. The Germans were now not only concentrating their ground forces to meet the Allied offensive, but were mustering their last reserves of aircraft as well. But for the lack of sound communications between the headquarters concerned on the Continent and in England, Allied fighter cover could have been more effective. News of the delay to the airlift never reached 83 Group, RAF, whose sorties flew as planned, several hours before the transport fleet appeared over the battlefield. So it was more than fortunate that, almost at the last minute, the drop of the three Polish parachute battalions had to be postponed to another day. To have dropped them south of the Arnhem bridges on the Tuesday, perhaps without adequate fighter support, would most likely have resulted in a débâcle similar to that which befell the Polish glider lift.

That night, a rough defensive perimeter began to develop around the Hartenstein Hotel. The Border Regiment, as we have seen, held most of the west flank, with some glider pilots and 21st Independent Parachute Company between the battalion and what remained of the KOSB, which, after its withdrawal from the Polish LZ, had occupied a position along the south of the railway line. On the east were some more glider pilots, the gun positions of the Light Regiment, RA, and the remnants of the four broken battalions which had failed to reach the bridge. Outside this perimeter, a mile or so to the north-west, was 4 Parachute Brigade, a reduced but still well organised force. Since Urquhart now planned to use this brigade on the next day, with its axis of advance south of the railway, in a fresh attempt to reach the bridge, it appeared to be arguable whether it was worth risking the possible confusion of a night move through the woods in order to bring the brigade into the Hartenstein area.

129

Hackett and Urquhart discussed the question at length, but in the end the latter decided to leave the brigade where it was for the night and move it at dawn. It was not to be a quiet night. As German armour rattled to and fro on the far side of the railway line, time and again infantry patrols attempted to push across the embankment and in among the 4 Parachute Brigade slit trenches.

The intensity of the fighting during the disastrous Tuesday is perhaps reflected in the two Victoria Crosses earned by members of the division that day, again both posthumously. Captain Lionel Queripel won his for his self-sacrifice during the withdrawal of 10 Para, and Sergeant J.D. Baskeyfield of the South Staffordshires for the way in which he fought his 6-pounder to the death against German tanks east of Oosterbeek church. Of the 5,500 or so glider and parachute infantrymen who had been flown into the battle north of the Neder Rijn more than 3,500 had already become casualties, and the proportion of officers and NCOs killed and wounded was much higher still. Everywhere the survivors seemed to be near the limit of their endurance.

CHAPTER THIRTEEN

'JIM, NEVER TRY TO FIGHT AN ENTIRE CORPS OFF ONE ROAD'

On the third day, as Frost's 500 men waited at the north end of the Arnhem bridge for what daylight might bring, the armoured cars of the Household Cavalry, followed closely by the tanks and infantry of the Grenadier Guards, were crossing the Wilhelmina Canal at Son, using the Bailey bridge which British sappers had spent the night building. The combination of the delay in capturing Eindhoven and the time lost in bridging this canal had played havoc with the planned programme for the advance of Guards Armoured Division. Forty hours had already passed, and the road bridge at Arnhem was still forty miles away. The operation was already thirty hours behind schedule, and it was now known that the bridges over the Waal river at Nijmegen were held by determined German troops.

Generals Browning and Gavin were waiting together at the Grave bridge over the Maas river to welcome the leading armoured cars, whose progress up the road between crowds of cheering Dutch and groups of waving American paratroops had been triumphal but uneventful. Bitterly disappointed though Browning was by the slow progress of the operation, the arrival of the Grenadier Guards tanks at about 1000 hours gave him double pleasure, for he himself was a Grenadier. To the regimental group he now gave the task of rushing the Nijmegen bridges, assisted by the 2nd Battalion of 505

Parachute Infantry, placed under command of the Grenadiers. And in order to strengthen 82nd Division, Browning also arranged for the Coldstream Guards group of armour and infantry, the next troops to arrive up the road, to be attached to Gavin. Spared thus far an attack by the German armour, the American general was both elated and reassured by the presence of the British tanks, and now felt capable of tackling anything that might come his way. His men shared his feelings.

The need for the leading units of Guards Armoured Division to divert south from Grave to cross the Maas-Waal Canal at Heumen, the bridge on the direct route at Honinghutje having been all but demolished, caused yet more delay, and it was mid-afternoon before the attacks on the Nijmegen bridges began. Both these initial assaults were to fail, although they hit the German defenders hard. That against the railway bridge, guided by members of the Dutch Resistance and with American paratroops riding on the British tanks, ran into trouble some 500 yards short of its objective. The leading tank was knocked out, and soon ammunition ran short. To the right, a second column succeeded in getting to within 300 yards of the highway bridge, but a log barricade across the street covered by 88-mm SP guns stopped this attack as well; in a short time another four tanks had been lost. A third column reached the Post Office, in which, according to Dutch sources, the Germans had installed the apparatus to blow the bridges, but this was found to be untrue; pushing on, the troops were then held up as they approached the road bridge by heavy fire coming from the direction of the Valkhof.

It had been a rushed, disjointed affair, complicated by the fact that the Grenadiers and the paratroops were strangers to each other. For all that, the British and the Americans had fought well together. The real trouble was that the Germans, about whom the Grenadiers had failed to obtain any reliable information before the attacks had begun, had proved to be top quality SS troops fighting from strong, well prepared positions. According to estimates produced a little later by Gavin's intelligence staff, some 500 Germans were defending the southern end of the highway bridge alone. The fighting on both this and the following day, Wednesday 20 September, was to be described by the historians of the Grenadier Guards as fiercer and more bitter than anything the regiment had so far experienced in the European campaign.

That night, buildings blazed in the neighbourhood of the bridges, set alight by the Germans to safeguard themselves from surprise attacks. In the wards of the Nijmegen hospital lay 600 wounded 82nd Division officers and men. 150 Americans were dead, and more were missing. Despondency had started to replace the elation with which the paratroops had welcomed the tanks that morning. Each time an attempt had been made to reach the bridges, the opposition had become tougher. And there were other reasons for unease. Over on the Groesbeek Heights, small parties of Germans were appearing out of the Reichswald and making nuisances of themselves, especially in the area held by 508 Parachute Infantry, around the Berg-en-Dal Hotel astride the road from Wyler to Nijmegen. A further blow had been the failure of 325 Glider Infantry to arrive as planned on that Tuesday, another victim of the breakdown in the weather. The shortage of supplies had also become acute: only about thirty C-47s had released their cargoes over the DZs that afternoon, and all of them at too great a height, with the result that only a negligible proportion was recovered. There were just not enough men or supplies for the job to be done, the outcome of the change in the weather combining with the single narrow road along which the vehicles of XXX Corps were edging, bumper to bumper, starting and stopping. As Horrocks put it to Gavin when the two generals met late that afternoon, 'Jim, never try to fight an entire Corps off one road'.

In Nijmegen, it was still far from clear what was happening eleven miles up the road in Arnhem. Following the telephone message received from the Dutch Resistance on the previous day about the German successes north of the Neder Rijn, a situation report from 1st Airborne Division did get through to Browning's headquarters at 0800 hours on the Tuesday (for a few minutes, radio contact had been made between the two headquarters), but it failed to provide an adequate account of what was happening. However, more Dutch reports passed over the public utility telephone network left no doubt that the Germans were fighting strongly in the Arnhem area, information which stimulated Browning to urge Gavin to get across the Waal, at the latest by the next day, 20 September. Such encouragement was in no way necessary: Gavin knew only too well that the success of the operation and the lives of his fellow airborne soldiers in the British division depended upon his taking the Nijmegen bridges.

Horrocks had now established his own tactical headquarters alongside that of Browning, in a schoolhouse between Mook and Nijmegen. The two generals were old friends, and from now on took decisions in concert, although it hardly seemed necessary that a total of four generals – Horrocks, Browning, Gavin and Major-General Allan Adair, the commander of Guards Armoured Division – should have been involved that evening in planning and organising a more powerful and better co-ordinated attempt to cross the river. The main problem, of course, was the near-inevitability of the Germans blowing the bridges as soon as the threat of their capture became acute; indeed, the four generals found it hard to understand why this had not already happened.

That day Gavin produced a startling proposal. To avoid pouring yet more American infantry and British tanks into a long and bloody battle in the streets of Nijmegen, perhaps only to see the Germans destroy the bridges at the last moment, his men would take the defenders in the rear by crossing the river about a mile downstream of the railway bridge. The snag, however, was that no boats were immediately available. But away in the rear, far down that crammed road, were vehicles carrying thirty-three canvas assault boats. Because there was no hope of bringing these flimsy craft up to Nijmegen before daybreak, yet more delays would occur, and the Americans would be faced with the task of crossing the river in broad daylight, two problems which could not be avoided. Gavin's idea was accepted, however, and two battalions of Tucker's 504 Parachute Infantry were relieved from protecting the Grave bridge in order to prepare for what seemed likely to be a perilous assault. While the crossing was in progress, the Grenadiers and the American battalion attached to them were to renew their attack on the southern end of the two bridges. For Tucker's men, their task was unexpected and appeared invidious: as paratroops they would rather have dropped on the far bank of the river in the first place than be faced with the task of paddling across the vast, 400-yard stretch of water in the face of German fire.

Although four generals were more than enough to organise an attack by five battalions, the total of senior officers in Nijmegen might have been even greater. General Ridgway, the commander of US XVIII Corps, whose headquarters had been given no more than some administrative functions to perform during the battle, had been bitterly disappointed at not being asked to command 'Market', a decision he had not anticipated given that two of the three airborne divisions employed were American. Unwilling to miss the excitement, both he and General Brereton had flown in B-17 bombers to watch the drop of 101st Division on the first day, and had encountered the heavy flak, Brereton's aircraft being hit in several places. Then, two days later, both generals flew to Antwerp, leaving any decisions that might need to be taken in England to their staffs, and started to make their way towards the battle-front by jeep. By dusk on Tuesday they had reached Eindhoven, where they only just escaped a German bomb during the course of an air raid. The extent to which Brereton, by acting in this way, severed connection with his command is made clear by an extract from a handwritten note he received, on Wednesday, from his chief of staff, the first direct information he had had about what was happening to his First Allied Airborne Army since he had left England on the 17th:

> Dear Boss,
> We had a helluva time yesterday 19 Sept. with weather. Fortunately about half couldn't clear and remained at bases ... British lost 18 out of 190 planes trying to drop resupply to 1st British A/B. The 1st British A/B are in a tight spot. Had been kicked off DZ and radio not working, so we dropped in German territory and got shot with flak for our pains. Have now establish-ed radio contact thru PRO channel and know their locations and where they want supplies dropped today. Also dropping Polish paras in area and asked for to help. The 1st British is in sight of, but do not hold bridge at Arnhem ...

One of the few accurate pieces of information in this message was the mention of the 'PRO channel'. This BBC set, operated from the Hartenstein, was at the time the sole link between 1st Airborne Division and the United Kingdom.

The German raid on Eindhoven in which Brereton and Ridgway had been caught had been carried out by a force of 120 Stukas and Junkers 88s. Damage had been inflicted on supply trains and ammunition dumps, roads had been blocked, and parts of the city had been left in flames, causing more delay to XXX Corps traffic moving along the tenuous artery to Arnhem. Civilian casualties were variously calculated at between 1,000 and 3,000, the cost of liberation to the Eindhoven townsfolk. The attack by the twin-engined Ju88s was the sole major strike in the west by long-range bombers during the autumn of 1944, a mark of the German determination to smash this Allied offensive.

Slow as the progress of XXX Corps had been, it would have been slower still but for the manner in which 101st Division had now begun to function. On the Tuesday this division was again to experience its most severe fighting around the Best crossing over the Wilhelmina Canal, a battle which sucked in a high proportion of Taylor's resources before the danger from the west flank could be eliminated. Help was to be provided by British armour, Horrocks having arranged to attach 15th/19th Hussars to 101st Division and the Sherwood Rangers Yeomanry to 82nd Division as soon as a link-up between XXX Corps and the airborne forces had been effected. Needless to say, the British regimental nomenclature at times puzzled the Americans.

Early that morning, the 2nd Battalion of 506 Parachute Infantry had made yet another unsuccessful attempt to reach the bridge over the Wilhelmina Canal at Best, and it was only after the attack had ground to a halt that the battalion commander learned from a patrol that his objective had been destroyed the day before. During the afternoon, the Americans tried once again to reach the canal, this time in a powerful and co-ordinated effort with two battalions of 506 Regiment and part of 327 Glider Infantry Regiment, which had landed the previous day, the whole being supported by a squadron of the 15th/19th Hussars and artillery fire from the XXX Corps guns, which were now within range. The tanks were too much for the now hard-pressed enemy infantry. First in small parties, then in hundreds, the Germans surrendered, even though a number who came out in the open with their hands in the air were mown down by their comrades in nearby positions.

When it was all over, the Americans counted 1,000 prisoners, 300 enemy dead, and fifteen 88-mm guns destroyed. Liberated were the few survivors of the platoon from 502 Regiment which had fought so doggedly for thirty-six hours near the bridge, and who had been captured after its demolition. Just before the end, PFC Joe E. Mann, four times wounded on the Monday, was sitting in his foxhole, his arms bandaged and useless. Feeling a German grenade fall behind him, he yelled a warning and lay back upon the bomb, taking the full force of the explosion himself, but saving the lives of the other men in the trench. His posthumous Congressional Medal of Honour* was the second to be awarded to a member of 101st Airborne Division. The first had been won by Lieutenant-Colonel Robert H. Cole for his gallantry in Normandy. He had been killed on the Monday while commanding the 3rd Battalion of 502 Regiment during the attempt to reach the bridge where Mann had died.

This heavy fighting around Best had drawn in large numbers of German as well as American troops, and this had resulted in the new bridge on the main highway at Son being made safe from attack from the western flank. Late on the same afternoon, however, a fresh threat developed from the east when German Panther tanks began shelling both the Son bridge and Taylor's command post nearby. His anti-tank guns, landed with the third lift only three hours before, knocked out a couple of the Panthers, encouraging the rest to withdraw, but the incident further delayed the packed column of vehicles crawling along the single thoroughfare. Elsewhere in Taylor's area sharp little actions had been fought both at St Oedenrode and Veghel to stave off more German attacks against this highway, and at Veghel the Americans were to identify their enemy as being paratroops, like themselves.

As with Gavin in the north, Taylor lacked the troops adequately to perform the immense task which he faced. The consequence was that his men were thin on the ground everywhere, and found themselves being rushed from point to point to deal with one new threat after another. The arrival of 101st Division's third lift should have helped, especially as Taylor had been allocated the larger part of the gliders at Gavin's expense, but in the end it brought only small relief to the now overstretched division. As already related, the weather on Tuesday 19 September had been disastrous – pilots afterwards remembered how, at times, they could see no more than three feet of tow rope through the dense cloud. As with the 82nd Division's glider infantry, the balance of 101st Airborne's 327 Glider Infantry, together with most of the division's artillery, should have landed that afternoon, but nearly half the gliders failed to reach the landing-zone: some tug pilots were forced to return to base,

---

*The highest United States award for gallantry in the field.

others were shot down or crashed, yet others were obliged to jettison their gliders, which then made forced landings, usually in enemy-held territory.

The pressure on 101st Division would have been that much the less if the two flanking corps of the British Second Army had succeeded in advancing rather more rapidly than they did. The reasons why this did not happen are the subject of controversy, and are likely to remain so. The intention had been that the two formations would protect the flanks of the advance of XXX Corps, with VIII Corps on the right moving through Weert against Helmond, just level with Eindhoven; on the left flank XII Corps was to advance to a line running roughly east and west through Turnhout, and then exploit to the River Maas, and possibly further. VIII Corps consisted of 11th Armoured and 3rd Infantry Divisions, and XII Corps of 7th Armoured Division, and 15th and 53rd Infantry Divisions.

At the root of the problem lay the fact the Montgomery was unable to give Second Army the administrative support necessary to allow it to deploy its full strength for the battle. Of Dempsey's nine divisions, he was able to use no more than four on 17 September. Throughout the battle, an infantry division was grounded, its transport used to supply other formations. Largely because of this general shortage of transport, XII Corps had been unable to do more than secure a single narrow bridgehead across the Meuse-Escaut Canal before 17 September. On the other flank, VIII Corps was unable to start moving its 3rd Division forward from the Seine until 16 September. The result was that the first troops of this formation did not succeed in crossing the Meuse-Escaut Canal until the early hours of 19 September, and the Class 40 bridge to carry the armour was not completed until 1930 hours that day, the time by when XXX Corps should have been in Arnhem. The comment in the Airborne Corps battle report that the flanking troops had 'made little progress' was only too true.

Whatever help Eisenhower and Bedell Smith may have promised Montgomery, what he received was in no way sufficient to provide the 'punch' necessary to counter resistance of the type Second Army was now meeting. Nor could Montgomery have postponed the start of 'Market Garden' to make time for the ground troops to be concentrated further forward for the start of the offensive, and for the necessary supplies to be accumulated. The longer he waited, the longer the Germans would have to bring forward their reinforcements. Perhaps if the advance of Patton's US Third Army in the south had been halted, Montgomery would have received a greater share of the supplies and transport. Perhaps not. A flood of conflicting statistics has managed to obscure the truth behind Second Army's supply problems.

One senior and very close observer of the battle has commented that the flanking formations did little more than 'lean on the enemy'. This was confirmed in a comment made years afterwards by the late Sir Richard O'Connor (then a lieutenant-general), the outstanding commander of VIII Corps, who remarked that he had received instructions not to press too hard on his flank. Certainly this appears to have been the case during the first few days of the battle, although before it had ended both flanking corps were to suffer very heavy casualties, as will be seen. Nearly all the senior British commanders were survivors of the slaughter on the Western Front of 1914-18, an experience that had taught them to be cautious of their men's lives. And, by September 1944, these lives were irreplaceable: Twenty-First Army Group had already been forced to break up and redistribute twenty-five infantry and armoured units, as well as a number of other formations including a complete infantry division, and still the front-line battalions and regiments could not be kept up to strength. The consequence was that, by this stage of the war, senior British commanders tended not to push their troops too hard unless they were forced to do so, especially now that the war in Europe was clearly drawing to an end. And Montgomery himself possessed a justly earned reputation for wasting 'metal not flesh'.

Needless to say, the outlook of the soldiers matched that of their commanders. Major-General Tony Jones, who played a prominent part in the Nijmegen fighting as a young Sapper officer in Guards Armoured Division, has written:

I remember talking to some Guardsmen in Nijmegen during the battle and finding that they had been transferred to the Grenadiers comparatively recently from the RAF Regiment and Anti-Aircraft Artillery and were not much liking their new rather more dangerous role. The thought uppermost in their minds was not to be the bravest soldiers in the British Army, just the oldest, and they were not alone in that. After all, hopes were still running high that we could finish it all in 1944. However, the Grenadiers certainly fought hard in Nijmegen ...

And so the Grenadiers did, as the Irish had done during the break-out from the Meuse-Escaut Canal. However, to some of the airborne officers, both British and American, who watched the Guards at work, they did give the impression of being deliberate and unflappable, as Guardsmen are expected to be, but possibly rather too much so at times. Much was to change during the harsh winter of 1944-45, when the war seemed as if it could well continue for ever. But, before that, the intoxicating successes of the late summer of 1944 had persuaded a lot of people to look towards the prospect of life in a post-war world.

CHAPTER FOURTEEN

'TOUCH THEM AND THEY REACT'

Seldom did the German generals display their innate professionalism to such good effect as they did in their reaction to the landing of Browning's Airborne Corps, and especially to that of the British 1st Airborne Division near Arnhem. It exemplified Brigadier Hackett's apt phrase, 'Touch them and they react', and he spoke with the benefit of experience, having seen how swift and violent German reaction could be when anything vital was threatened. Senior officers such as Generaloberst Student and Obergruppenfuehrer Bittrich may have been overcome with despondency at the sight of the second Allied airborne lift flying overhead on the Monday, delivering what appeared to be yet more divisions of troops into Holland, but that in no way influenced the speed and resolution with which they proceeded to scrape together men and weapons to throw into the critical areas of the battle.

On 17 September, the armoured reconnaissance unit of 9th SS Panzer Division had managed to slip across the Arnhem bridge and drive south into Nijmegen before Frost had seized the northern end of the bridge. But after that first evening there was only one way in which Bittrich could move his units from Arnhem to the crossings over the Waal, in order to control what he correctly saw as the place vital to halting the Allied advance, and to ensure the destruction of Urquhart's division. The ferry across the Neder Rijn at Pannerden, lying six miles south-east of the Arnhem bridge, was the key to Bittrich's problem.

When the first Allied lift had landed on the Sunday afternoon, Brigadefuehrer Heinz Harmel, the commander of 10th SS Panzer Division, was on his way back from Berlin where, on Bittrich's behalf, he had been arranging for reinforcements of men and vehicles. Late that evening he arrived at his headquarters, weary from the long journey. There he learned about the invasion, and was told that his division had been given the task of seizing and holding the bridges over the Waal at Nijmegen, and that his units were already on the move. Driving to Pannerden, he found the village crammed with his troops and equipment and discovered that one of his panzer grenadier battalion and an engineer company, some 500 men in all, had already been ferried across the river and were moving south towards Nijmegen. Arriving there later that night, they relieved 9th SS Panzer Division's reconnaissance unit, which then withdrew to Arnhem, and suffered such heavy losses to Frost's force as it drove bald-headed across the highway bridge the following morning – a disastrous move which demonstrated that German units, as well as British, could lose themselves in the fog of war.

Back at Pannerden, Harmel, watching his trucks being floated across the river on rubber rafts, realised that it could well take days for his engineers to build a heavy ferry capable of carrying 40-ton Tiger and Panther tanks, since the work would be confined to the night hours because of the ever-present threat of Allied air attack. In some way, therefore this aggravating small force of British paratroops which had inserted itself into the houses commanding the north end of the Arnhem road bridge had to be eliminated, so as to allow free passage over the river to 10th SS Panzer Division. Accordingly, Bittrich, as commander of II SS Panzer Corps, ordered 9th SS Panzer to carry out the removal of the source of aggravation.

To perform the task, Obersturmbannfuehrer Harzer proceeded to divide the available troops of 9th SS Panzer into two groups, the first, under Sturmbannfuehrer Brinkmann, to destroy Frost's force and capture the bridge. The second group, commanded by Sturmbannfeuhrer Spindler, was to form the backbone to the *Sperrlinie*, or blocking-line, which was being put together to prevent further reinforcements reaching the bridge from the direction of Oosterbeek. Brinkmann was, in fact, the commander of 10th SS Panzer's reconnaissance unit, which appears to have been exchanged for Harzer's equivalent battalion when the latter was rushed off towards Nijmegen on the 17th, and during that first night Brinkmann was to be reinforced by a panzer grenadier battalion and some ten obsolete tanks. Yet more infantry, tanks and SP guns were sent to reinforce Brinkmann as they became available, but the exact details of the German force which fought Frost at the bridge have never been unravelled. In the concluding stages of the battle there, both German divisions seem to have been involved in the fighting.

It was upon Spindler's *Sperrlinie* that British 1st Airborne Division smashed itself in its attempts to reach Frost. As has been described earlier, units of 9th SS Panzer were advancing through Arnhem towards Oosterbeek four hours after the first drop. First they had blocked the attempts of 1 and 3 Para to follow 2 Para towards the bridges, and on the next day, Monday 18 September, these small units had halted the efforts of the four British battalions to force their way past St Elizabeth Hospital. At the same time other Germans had established the line running south along the Dreijenseweg and through Oosterbeek; it was these troops which 4 Parachute Brigade hit on the Monday night, and which took such a heavy toll of 156 Para the following morning.

Kraft's SS Panzer Grenadier Training and Depot Battalion, which had succeeded so well in delaying 1 Parachute Brigade in the early stages of the battle, had on the Sunday evening withdrawn towards the north-east. Reinforced by a heterogeneous collection of marines and military police, this battalion was placed under Spindler's command on the Monday and ordered to advance south towards the Ede-Arnhem road, and at the same time to contact the units of 'Division von Tettau' approaching the battle from the east. And it was Kraft's battalion which, on the afternoon of Tuesday 19 September, had followed up the retreat of 10 Para across the fields below Johannahoeve on which the Polish gliders were blazing, and which had then harassed 4 Parachute Brigade that night in its positions south of the railway line. Kraft's unit had, in effect, become the lid of the box which the Germans were constructing to contain the forces still left to Urquhart around Oosterbeek, the base of this box being the river, its eastern side the *Sperrlinie*, and its western von Tettau's collection of administrative and training units. Day by day, as yet more German reinforcements arrived, this box was steadily to be strengthened.

It was US 82nd Airborne Division's misfortune that its soldiers should have encountered the troops of these two SS divisions during its initial attempts to reach the Nijmegen bridges, and again it was panzer grenadiers and engineers from 10th SS Panzer which had repulsed the combined attack by the Grenadier Guards and the Americans on the Tuesday afternoon. At this stage of the battle, it was, in fact, something of a coincidence that the two forces defending the Arnhem and the Nijmegen road bridges, one of them British and the other German, were of much the same size, each about 500 men strong. By Wednesday the 20th, however, still more of Harmel's troops had crossed the Pannerden ferry to reinforce the defences around the two Nijmegen bridges.

On the Groesbeek Heights, to the east of 82nd Division's area, the German units which had appeared out of the Reichswald on Monday and Tuesday to make a more-than-intermittent nuisance of themselves belonged to the Corps Feldt. Model's orders to this group had been very much a duplication of those he had given to Bittrich – namely, to destroy the airborne troops on the ground, to seize and hold the bridges, and to stand by for continued operations in a southerly direction. For such a makeshift formation it was all quite an undertaking, but the instructions were in keeping with the aggressive German doctrine of containing airborne troops after they had landed by attacking them without delay, and continuing to do so.

By Tuesday, Corps Feldt had succeeded in mustering only four battalions, each about 500 men strong, but these units managed to score a number of minor victories, either defending small but strong positions, or attacking Gavin's widely separated platoon or company posts. At times the fighting became intense, as in the battle for Hill 75.9, commanding the Wyler-Nijmegen road just east of the Berg-en-Dal Hotel: four times in twenty-four hours this isolated position was to change hands. These battles say a lot for the way a few junior German officers and NCOs could persuade troops such as this to fight in such a manner: some units did, of course, surrender after no more than a token resistance, but others showed themselves capable of taking on the very best Allied troops.

Further south, the Germans had moved with much the same speed and aggression. The two battalions of convalescent paratroops, all that Student could at first find to throw against Veghel and St Oedenrode, were no match for US 101st Airborne Division, but Taylor had not been able to repulse the remnants of the German 59th Division at Best until he had assembled a balanced force supported by heavy armour and artillery.

As all this was happening, further German reserves were being scraped together in every part of the Reich and moved by road and rail to help contain the narrow British salient. On the night of Tuesday 19 September, the first seven battalions of II Parachute Corps had arrived in the Reichswald opposite US 82nd Division. They were motley units in the main, but among them were two tough, although under-strength, parachute battalions. Further south, 107 Panzer Brigade and 208 Assault Gun Brigade were on their way from Aachen to join Student, and it was their leading tanks which had attacked Taylor's command post and the troops crossing the rebuilt Son bridge. Still more parachute units were continuing to arrive to reinforce Student, who now began to plan a concerted attack to sever the thin Allied line-of-communication, Horrocks's 'single road'. And Model had informed Bittrich that he could expect 506th Heavy Tank Battalion to arrive in the Arnhem area by about 22 September.

The Luftwaffe, urged on by frantic exhortations from Hitler, was also helping as best it could. One outcome of the Fuehrer's encouragement had been the bomber strike against Eindhoven on Tuesday night, and on the same day 300 fighter aircraft had been placed at Bittrich's disposal, a reversal of the former policy of sacrificing close support for the army so that everything available could be concentrated to defend the Reich against the unceasing American daylight bomber raids. For all that, the help the Luftwaffe could provide, either by attacking the troop-carrying and supply-dropping aircraft, or by strafing the British and American troops on the ground, was limited. By September 1944, because of lack of fuel, training and airfields, the Luftwaffe was all but a spent force on the western front.

The destruction of the Son bridge over the Wilhelmina Canal had delayed Guards Armoured Division for twelve hours, and to have bridged the vast width of either the Maas or the Waal would have been a very much more lengthy operation. So the Allied generals found it hard to understand why the Germans did not pull their men out of Nijmegen, back over the Waal, and then blow the bridges. Unknown to them, however, Model had prohibited the destruction of the bridges both at Arnhem and Nijmegen, because he was confident that they could be defended successfully (once Frost's party had been destroyed, of course), and that they would then be

145

needed for the subsequent German counter-offensive. Bittrich, however, disagreed with his commander. Fearful of the consequences of an Allied break-through, he had urged his Generalfeldmarschall time and again to permit the bridges to be blown. Model's decision was very much the mark of the aggressive confidence of the man. The Germans had certainly been 'touched' in their quiet backwater in eastern Holland, but now they were reacting as only they could.

CHAPTER FIFTEEN

'IT WAS THE OUTSTANDING INDEPENDENT PARACHUTE BATTALION ACTION OF THE WAR'

Dimly visible through the steady rain were the broken houses, still smouldering, roofless and with gaping holes in their walls. It was stand-to on Wednesday morning, 20 September 1944. For the survivors of Frost's force at Arnhem bridge, peering through bloodshot eyes at what, two days ago, had been busy offices and houses, there were still faint grounds for hope. Even though the troops of XXX Corps were eighteen hours overdue, the sound of the British tanks and guns would surely soon echo across the river.

Once again the bombs and shells started to crash down, and the German infantry and armour began to edge forward. During the early stages of the battle the solid houses had provided sound protection against light artillery and infantry weapons, but tanks and SP guns firing at point-blank range had now turned them into death-traps, to be abandoned for hastily dug slit-trenches in gardens and along the roadside verges.

Communications between the bridge and Divisional Headquarters at Hartenstein suddenly improved during the morning. First Gough, the commander of the Recce Squadron, managed to get through to

Urquhart on the civilian telephone, to the intense surprise of the latter. It was the General's first direct contact with the soldiers fighting at the bridge, and he now learned at first hand how desperate their prospects were. A little later a radio link was established. This continued to function for most of the day, and through it Frost's men learned that their chances of being relieved by their own division were slim. In the early afternoon, however, the information was relayed to them that XXX Corps had been delayed but should reach the south end of the Arnhem bridge by 1700 hours that day. With both Nijmegen bridges still in German hands, this was an oddly misleading message.

Early in the day Frost was wounded in the legs by a mortar bomb, and Gough assumed command of the force, consulting Frost when he could. By that afternoon the Germans had crushed all resistance in the houses and gardens near the river, and only around the now-blazing hulks of the buildings west of the ramp were the British still fighting. On the east side, Mackay had managed to move thirty or so of his wounded sappers out of the school, the upper storeys of which had been demolished by a Tiger tank and an SP gun. He then led his last ten men in the direction of the enemy but, after surprising and slaughtering a group of Germans gathered round a couple of tanks, only four of his soldiers remained on their feet; on Mackay's orders these last few men separated to try to find their way through the encircling enemy. Among the many who died that day was Lieutenant John Grayburn, already wounded three times and now killed as he faced an oncoming tank. For the manner in which he had inspired those around him, Grayburn was to be awarded a posthumous Victoria Cross.

With all the British anti-tank guns out of action and the PIAT ammunition finished, four or five enemy tanks had crossed the bridge from the south to join in the work of destruction. By the afternoon, no more than 140 airborne soldiers were still fighting around the cellars of the smashed houses, in which almost double that number of wounded had been crammed. Roughly bandaged, with only two doctors to succour them, many were dying or already lay dead. The Germans were close enough to be able to pitch phosphorus grenades through the holes in the walls to feed the flames of the already-burning houses; to avoid the wounded being burnt alive where they lay, Gough therefore decided that it was his duty to arrange a temporary cease-fire so that they could be evacuated. This he duly did. Knowing that he had been fighting SS troops and aware of the atrocities committed by such units on the Eastern Front and elsewhere, Frost was not alone in wondering what the outcome would be, but the British found their captors, who helped to carry them up from the cellars and save them from the flames, 'kind, chivalrous and even comforting', to quote Frost's words. Several Germans complimented their captured enemies on the way in which they had fought, grim confirmation of which was provided by the grey-clad dead littering the streets along which the wounded men were carried.

Once the wounded were out of the way, the fighting again started, but the position of the defenders, surrounded and with little ammunition left, was now hopeless. Fifty or sixty more British soldiers were to be killed or wounded during the night, but by 0900 hours the next morning it was all over. Gavin was to describe this battle fought by his British airborne comrades as 'the outstanding independent parachute battalion action of the war', praise indeed from the commander of the American 82nd Airborne Division. The Arnhem road bridge had been held, not for forty-eight hours as planned, but for three days and four nights, and not by a complete division but by a force of battalion strength, all that had managed to reach it. But now the bridge was once more in German hands.

That same Wednesday morning, Hackett had begun to move what remained of his 4 Parachute Brigade out of the woods south-east of Wolfheze to join the other units which Urquhart had collected around him at Oosterbeek. Although Hackett's two remaining battalions were at less than half strength (losses in officers were even higher, 156 Para having only eight left), morale in the brigade remained high and both units were tightly organised.

Leading the column and aiming for the Utrecthseweg west of Oosterbeek, 156 Para turned into the Breedelaan, one of the multiplicity of rides which intersected the dense woodland. Soon the battalion came under intense machine-gun fire, and each succeeding attempt to outflank the German positions around the right flank met even stronger opposition. Mortar bombs burst among the trees with deadly effect. One company got as far as the houses on the forward slope leading down to the Wolfhezerweg, but was held there by fire from SP guns. Rightly appreciating that he had run into a German force advancing towards Oosterbeek from the west, Hackett changed his axis and directed 10 Para towards the Valkenberglaan. The brigade, Hackett later recollected, was still 'handling beautifully'.

But then German tanks and SP guns appeared among the rides to surround and cut down the helpless men moving through the trees. In rapid succession all but one of the officers of Hackett's brigade staff were either killed or wounded, and both the commanding officer and the second-in-command of 156 Para were dead. At about this time there occurred an incident which has remained etched on the memories of those who observed it. Two jeeps with their trailers were parked alongside one another. One, loaded with ammunition, was blazing, and on the trailer of the other was strapped a stretcher on which lay a wounded officer, Lieutenant-Colonel Derek Heathcote-Armory,* a staff officer from a higher headquarters who had hitched a lift to Arnhem in order to see something of the war before it was all over. As those who saw what was about to happen hugged the ground, waiting for the explosion, a figure detached itself from the trees, ran to the wounded man's jeep, and drove it away. It was Hackett.

Despite the confusion and the slaughter, the brigade was still maintaining more than a measure of cohesion. Grabbing what remained of a company of 156 Para, Hackett ordered it to attack and clear a party of Germans out of a tree-ringed depression lying alongside the Valkenberglaan. Boldness succeeded, and in this hollow Hackett then rallied some 100 men and seven officers. There they fought for the rest of the day, holding off the encircling German infantry and the one or two enemy armoured vehicles which still hung about, the latter now rather wary of pushing their luck too far against the surviving airborne soldiers. With more and more men being hit, most of them by snipers or well placed automatic weapons, Hackett was again to demonstrate that boldness could pay. Gathering what was left of his brigade around him in a solid mass, he led the desperate party out of the depression in the direction of Oosterbeek, charging straight through the understandably terrified Germans. Only one or two of the British paratroops fell, and the rest pushed on without slackening their pace

* Later a Chancellor of the Exchequer in Macmillan's Government.

until they reached a company position of the Border Regiment, just to the east of the Hartenstein Hotel.

What remained of 10 Para had reached Oosterbeek some five hours before Hackett's group, and in a rather similar fashion. There Urquhart himself was to see the survivors. In his words

> The men were exhausted, filthy and bleeding, their discipline was immaculate ... Their commander, Lieutenant-Colonel Ken Smyth, his right arm bandaged where a bullet had struck, reported breathlessly: 'We have been heavily taken on, sir. I have sixty men left'.

For Urquhart, the virtual annihilation of 4 Parachute Brigade was a severe shock, destroying as it did his lingering hopes of relieving Frost at the bridge. All day his troops in Oosterbeek had been pressed hard, attacked by German infantry, SP guns and tanks, with some of the armour operating flame-throwers. Mortar and artillery fire had continued to harass the airborne men, steadily increasing the toll of casualties. On the eastern flank of what had now evolved into the Oosterbeek perimeter the situation had become both confused and dangerous, and Urquhart now decided to use the little that remained of Hackett's brigade to plug the gaps on this side.

The medical units of 1st Airborne Division had established dressing stations in two hotels on either side of the junction of the Utrechtseweg and the Stationsweg. How this came about, and the nightmare conditions in which the wounded suffered, is discussed later, but this road junction (afterwards known as the 'MDS crossroads', made famous in a painting by David Shepherd), had been the scene of a bloody battle on the morning of Wednesday the 20th. By the afternoon both dressing stations were in the hands of the Germans, although British casualties were still being received, and between the MDS crossroads and Divisional Headquarters at Hartenstein there were no British troops of any description except for a few glider pilots. Smyth, ordered by Urquhart to cover the crossroads, somehow managed to insert his few 10 Para men into a group of houses lying a little to the east of the hotels, even though both buildings were guarded by German troops. A little to the north, just west of the Stationsweg, two troops of the Recce Squadron were fighting on foot among the narrow streets of neat residential houses. Here Urquhart thickened the defences with 156 Para, its strength, after it had collected a handful of men found inside the perimeter, reduced to four officers and some sixty soldiers, much the same as that of its sister battalion, 10 Para.

Urquhart was now holding a small bridgehead based on the Neder Rijn about 2,000 yards deep and 1,000 wide, towards which XXX Corps could be diverted to build a bridge or bridges covered by the survivors of 1st Airborne Division on the north bank. It was by no means an ideal position for the airborne troops, the thick woods and narrow streets being difficult to defend with the limited number of men still left. At the south-western corner, the prominent 100-foot-high Westerbouwing hill overlooked not only the site of the Heveadorp ferry, the place where any crossing would have to be made, but also a large part of the British perimeter. Held for a time by a patrol of the Borders, the hill was now in German hands. If the perimeter had been shaped by design rather than the accident of battle, it might well have been centred upon this vital piece of ground, but such a position would have lain in even more thickly wooded country, still more difficult to defend.

CHAPTER SIXTEEN

'I'M PROUD TO MEET THE COMMANDER OF THE GREATEST DIVISION IN THE WORLD TO-DAY'

By Wednesday, General Horrocks had even greater cause to regret that he was being compelled to fight XXX Corps off that single road. The drivers of the vehicles moving up were displaying considerable caution, and understandably so. For the first five miles between the Meuse-Escaut Canal and Valkenswaard the highway was just wide enough to take two vehicles. A little north of the canal, alongside the wreckage of two 3-ton trucks, sappers had erected a notice reading 'DON'T LET THIS HAPPEN TO YOU. KEEP ON THE ROAD. VERGES NOT CLEARED OF MINES'. The drivers obeyed. Afterwards it was discovered that the Germans had laid a few mines at spots where they had fought delaying actions, but that the rest of the verges were clear and safe for overtaking and broken-down vehicles. As it was, whenever a single vehicle in a hurry tried to overtake the slow-moving columns, a traffic jam ensued.

To compound these early delays at the southern end of the highway, further problems lay ahead. The Tuesday night air-raid on Eindhoven had blocked the main streets for the next twenty-four hours, forcing the traffic to make a tortuous detour around the suburbs of the city. Then, at first light on Wednesday morning, 107 Panzer Brigade renewed its attack against the new Son bridge, effectively halting all movement across it for the next few hours. A battalion of 506 Parachute Infantry, helped by detachments from 327 Glider Infantry, managed to fend off two separate attempts by the German armour to reach the bridge, and in the end a squadron of 15th/19th Hussars arrived and drove off the enemy tanks.

Later that day, another battalion of 506 Regiment, supported by British tanks of 44th Royal Tank Regiment, now also under American command, made a wide sweep around the rear of the enemy and so regained the initiative. In a similar way, 501 Parachute Infantry mounted an attack against a body of Germans which was threatening Veghel from the north-west. Setting out in the morning from the village of Heeswijk, the American battalion adroitly encircled a complete German parachute battalion, killing forty of them, wounding forty more, and collecting a total of 418 prisoners. The American losses amounted to only four men killed and six wounded. Such actions were typical of the offensive manner in which General Taylor was to use his limited manpower to defend his fifteen-mile stretch of road – his 'Indian fighting', in which his troops were to seek out and destroy the successive bodies of Germans which threatened 'Hell's Highway'.

It has sometimes been said that, during the Second World War, the Americans tended to shine in the attack and the British in defence. As with most gross generalisations, this one possibly contains more than a grain of truth. Perhaps the characteristics had developed from the training and the traditions of the colonial wars which had engrossed the regular cadres of the two armies for so long during the previous century. The Americans skirmished offensively to protect the wagon-trains and railroads carving their way into Indian territory, and the British infantry formed squares to repel their particular savage enemies, or forced their punitive columns up the valleys of the North-West Frontier of India, laboriously picqueting the heights on either side of the slowly moving columns. Habits are easily formed.

Up the road in Nijmegen, the failure of the hastily organised attacks by the Grenadier Guards and US 82nd Division to carry the bridges over the Waal on Tuesday afternoon and evening emphasised the problem facing XXX Corps. In particular, it was

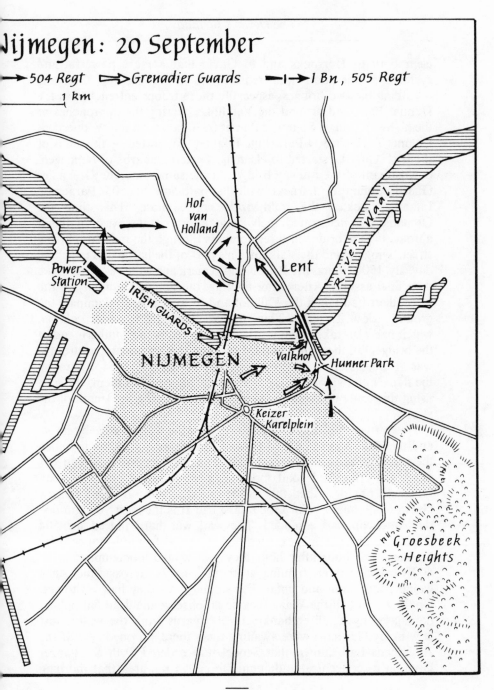

Nijmegen: 20 September

→ 504 Regt   ⇨ Grenadier Guards   ⊢→ I Bn, 505 Regt

|—| 1 km

Hof
van
Holland

Lent

River Waal

Power
Station

IRISH GUARDS

NIJMEGEN

Valkhof

Hunner Park

Keizer
Karelplein

Groesbeek
Heights

clear both to Horrocks and to Gavin that a more powerful and systematic operation was required to overcome the Germans defending the two bridges, especially those troops entrenched in the Hunner Park and around the Valkhof, covering the approaches to the highway bridge. So it was that at 0830 hours on the Wednesday, Colonel Tucker's 504 Parachute Infantry, supported by the tanks of the Irish Guards, started to clear the western suburbs of Nijmegen, downstream of the railway bridge. At the same time, the Grenadier Guards, again in harness with its battalion of 505 Parachute Infantry, tackled the road bridge once more. This time the Grenadiers concentrated their main effort on the western flank, aproaching the bridge in three columns through the maze of narrow streets lying behind the Valkhof. This part of the battle was to last all day. By 1500 hours, the British and Americans were ready to make their final assault. After bitter fighting, the King's Company of the Grenadiers had taken the Valkhof and so were able to dominate the ground below its walls. This success allowed the centre column, which had also taken heavy casualties, to reach the southern end of the bridge. On the right the third column, the American paratroops, was at times seen to be fighting its way across the roof-tops among the flames and smoke of the houses blazing beneath them, the men using this route to avoid the German fire sweeping the length of the streets.

Down river, 504 Regiment had reached the water's edge by noon, and there they were obliged to wait for the assault boats in which they were to cross the river. Delayed in the successive bottlenecks along the congested road, postponement followed postponement. Horrocks has described this as the one occasion on which he saw Gavin really angry: 'For God's sake try! It is the least you can do', the American had exploded. The wait was hard indeed for 504 Regiment, and Gavin's exasperation stemmed from his concern for his men. For hour after hour they had waited, contemplating the 400-yard-wide river, running at about 8 knots, across which they would paddle frail and unfamiliar assault craft they had yet to see. On the far side of the Waal, they could observe the dead flat polder, dominated by a tall embankment 500 yards from the water. Just how many Germans were awaiting them there, no one knew. If the Americans had known that Model had ordered 10th SS Panzer Division to concentrate additional forces in the area that morning for a counter-attack against Nijmegen, their distaste for the forthcoming operation would have been even more strongly expressed.

As 504 Regiment waited for their boats, a fresh threat developed away to the east. At about 1400 hours Gavin, who was down by the river, heard from his chief of staff that the Germans had overrun both Mook and Beek. Leaving Tucker to cope with the river crossing, Gavin jumped into his jeep and raced in the direction of this new danger. As he drove through his headquarters, he met General Ridgway, who had managed to make his way up the road to Nijmegen, so raising to three the strength of Allied lieutenant-generals in the Nijmegen area. Excusing himself from protracted conversation with his erstwhile boss on the grounds that he had a serious situation on his hands, Gavin continued towards the outskirts of Mook, where he found a lone GI covering the road with a bazooka; supporting him was a single tank of the Coldstream Guards. The tank then ran over an American-laid mine. There was nothing for Gavin to do but to thicken up the defences with one American general and a couple of members of his staff, and to send his jeep back to obtain more help from the Coldstream.

What had happened was that the newly arrived German II Parachute Corps had, with its seven mixed battalions, mounted two concentric attacks against Groesbeek. These German reinforcements were, however, faced by no more than five battle-weary American battalions, supported by the Coldstream Guards Group. Strung out across twelve miles of thickly wooded country, key villages were held by a platoon or so of Americans, against which the Germans were, in turn, able to concentrate more powerful forces. One after another, Wyler, Beek, Riethorst (just east of Mook) and Mook itself had fallen, the loss of the last-named threatening the axis of XXX Corps: just over a mile away lay the vital bridge across the Maas-Waal Canal at Heumen. It is a tribute to Gavin's leadership that by nightfall he had restored the situation. Neatly shifting his few troops from place to place and making excellent use of his limited artillery, he mounted a series of successful small counter-attacks. American casualties were high, but the Germans were pushed back.

If Gavin's 325 Glider Infantry had arrived on Wednesday, as planned, his task would have been rather less taxing, but the weather on that day had been worse than on Tuesday. In consequence, the staff officers concerned in the United Kingdom decided to despatch no reinforcements to Browning that day other than a company of US 101st Division's parachute artillery. In addition, 163 British and 286 American supply aircraft took off on the 20th, of which only one British and twenty-eight American planes failed to reach the supply DZs, a fine achievement by the aircrew in such conditions. The tragedy was that the British airborne troops at Oosterbeek, now hemmed inside their tiny perimeter, recovered only 13 per cent of the loads released; US 82nd Division picked up 80 per cent of its supplies, however, even though the dropping zones were being fought over for part of the day. In all, just fourteen supply-dropping aircraft were lost. Perhaps if Brereton, or Ridgway, or Browning, had been back in England in charge of events, then whoever it was might have taken the decision to risk despatching some part, if not all, of the so-badly needed Polish Parachute Brigade or Gavin's 325 Regiment. And if the aircraft to carry them had succeeded in taking off, there seems no reason why they should not have arrived as safely as did Taylor's artillery company and the supplies delivered to the two American divisions.

Gavin suffered, as did Taylor, because the American glider pilots lacked the skills of fighting infantrymen. Unlike their British opposite numbers, the Americans were Army Air Force pilots, untrained in ground fighting and not organised in units and sub-units. After Sicily, after Italy, and again after the invasion of Normandy, the American airborne divisional commanders had protested that the glider pilots should be organised and trained like the British, but their recommendations were ignored. In Holland, as the historians of 101st Division were to put it, the American glider pilots were 'the most uninhibited individualists in the Army ... Those who wanted to fight, fought like lions. Those who wanted to go back to Brussels managed to get there before anyone else'. In his report to US IX Troop Carrier Command, Gavin said much the same:

> Despite their individual willingness to help, I feel that they were definitely a liability to me. Many of them arrived without blankets, some without rations and water, and a few improperly armed and equipped ... they frequently became involved in small

unit actions to an extent that satisfied their passing curiosity, or simply left to visit nearby towns.

The 1,200 glider pilots of British 1st Airborne Division, organised into two wings, were to take a major part in the defence of the Oosterbeek perimeter. The number of pilots available to the Americans was smaller, but Gavin and Taylor would have given much for only a single unit of quality equal to the highly trained fighting soldiers of the British Glider Pilot Regiment, to thicken up their own defensive positions.

To return to Nijmegen and its river, Wednesday 20 September 1944. The final postponement of H-hour for the crossing by 504 Regiment had been to 1500 hours, and only half-an-hour earlier the thirty or so flimsy, paddle-powered canvas craft had been delivered to the river bank, enough to carry a little over two assault companies without their heavy support weapons. By then, Typhoons had already begun a planned programme of rocketing and machine-gunning the German positions on the north bank, and the preliminary pounding and smoke-laying by some hundred British and American artillery weapons was about to start. To thicken this heavy fire, two squadrons of Irish Guards tanks were lined up along the south side of the river, with the 504 Regiment reserve battalion.

Intense though this fire support was, it was not enough to stifle the German weapons. As Horrocks, Browning and Adair watched from the roof of the prominent power-station that overlooked the crossing-place, rather in the manner of 17th-century generals viewing the progress of a battle, the soldiers of Tucker's two leading companies heaved their twenty-six boats down to the river, pushed them out into the fast-flowing current, and scrambled aboard. Those who did not have paddles used their rifle butts to help propel the boats through the water but, unskilled as the paratroops were in watermanship, at times the frail craft spun around in circles. Soon the wind began to disperse the smoke-screen that the artillery was trying to thicken, and German machine-gun and rifle fire began to slash into the boats. Guns and mortars joined in. Some Americans collapsed over their paddles, dead or wounded; other frantically tried to plug bullet holes in the canvas with handkerchiefs, or to bail with their helmets. Boats sank, spilling the heavily laden soldiers into the river. Just half the assault craft made it to the far shore.

Exhausted, some of them vomiting, the men leapt out and began to run towards the high dyke, ignoring those who fell on either side of them. Battle-mad, they routed the Germans out of their trenches with bayonets and grenades. Few prisoners were taken. Meanwhile, the boats, now reduced to eleven in number, were crossing again and again with reinforcements. One American company eliminated the defenders of the ancient moat-encircled Hof van Holland. Another reached the village of Lent, about a mile back from the river, through which passed both the highway and railway between Nijmegen and Arnhem. Then, at about 1700 hours, as 504 Regiment's paratroops were closing in towards the north end of the railway bridge, the Germans started to crack. British observers on the south bank watched the enemy pouring out of Nijmegen, back across the bridge and straight into the cross fire of the Americans and the Irish Guards. Afterwards, 267 German corpses were to be counted on the railway bridge alone.

By now the Grenadier Guards and the battalion of 505 Parachute Infantry had between them wiped out what were left of the SS troops defending the southern end of the highway bridge, and, as the light started to fail, four Grenadier tanks, commanded by Sergeant Peter Robinson, began to roll across it. The crewmen well knew that at any moment a vast explosion might send their tanks hurtling down into the river, and Horrocks, from his vantage point, could hardly bear to watch them. It was, in the words of an American newsman, 'a very American-looking bridge – no quaint-looking arched-stone job, but a double-lane highway ...': if the bridge were to be blown it was a long way down to the water. But nothing happened. On across the bridge the tanks travelled and up the road towards Arnhem. Then, in rapid succession, two were hit. The other two, however, skidded through a road-block and smashed into the pair of anti-tank guns that had done the damage. For this distinguished feat of arms Robinson was awarded the DCM; two of his NCOs were decorated with the MM. A few minutes later, the survivors of Tucker's two leading companies joined the Grenadiers. It was 1910 hours on 20 September, and the crossing over the River Waal was safely in Allied hands. Over the years there has been some argument about who arrived first at the northern end of the bridge – British or Americans. It mattered little. The troops of the two countries had shown equal gallantry in what had been a joint victory.

Following the tanks over the bridge in a light recce car had been Captain Tony Jones, commanding a sapper troop. With the tanks safely across, he had summoned his Royal Engineers to join him, and they had then set to work, clambering around the enormous structure, cutting wires as they located them and removing the detonators from TNT charges they found fixed to the girders. As the work progressed, the sappers winkled out more and more of the German defenders, hiding in or alongside the pier compartments, most of them only too ready to surrender, although a few continued to snipe at the British from perches high among the girders. In all, the sappers captured eighty-one prisoners. As for the railway bridge, it was not to be taken until the following morning, when another column of Grenadiers swept over it without loss.

When Dempsey met Gavin a few days later, the Second Army commander greeted the American with the words 'I am proud to meet the commander of the greatest division in the world to-day'. It was a tribute which the ever-modest Gavin was to accept with reservations, but other British officers who saw US 82nd Airborne Division in action at Nijmegen accepted Dempsey's judgement.

At the time, no one could understand why the Germans had not destroyed these two great bridges over the Waal. Under increasing pressure from the Allies, Model had, in fact, changed his mind about demolishing them, but he waited until midnight on Wednesday before agreeing, and by then it was too late. The Allies were already across the river.

One of Model's subordinates had, however, attempted to destroy the Nijmegen bridges on his own initiative, but had failed to do so. Brigadefeuhrer Harmel, the commander of 10th SS Panzer Division, watched the battle from a bunker near Lent and saw the British tanks roll across the bridge. Realising that all was lost, Harmel disregarded Model's order and instructed his engineer, waiting by his side with the detonating mechanism, to press the plunger. Nothing happened. The reason why the charges failed to blow is still not known – perhaps Jones's sappers had already severed the vital wires. At one time it was believed that a gallant young Dutchman, Jan van Hoof, had cut the wires on Tuesday night, but the story was never corroborated, and is now thought to be unlikely. Perhaps the German firing mechanism failed. The practice of war can be

161

uncertain, much subject to human error, something which is often forgotten.

Harmel was to escape death or capture by no more than a narrow margin as Robinson's tanks drove on to join the American company at Lent. Soon afterwards, Captain the Lord Carrington (another future Cabinet Minister) crossed the bridge to reinforce Lent with the rest of the Grenadier squadron, to be followed by two companies of the Irish Guards who formed a close defensive perimeter around the village's northern end. Here they were found by Colonel Tucker (in later years to be described by Gavin as 'probably the best regimental commander of the war', praise indeed for him, and in that company). After what his 504 Regiment had endured that day, and the success it had won, Tucker had expected the British to race straight on through his men's positions to the Arnhem bridge. When Gavin met his tough, cigar-chewing colonel, he had never seen him so angry. 'What in the Hell are they doing?', Tucker demanded. 'We have been in this position for over twelve hours, and all they seem to be doing is brewing tea. Why in Hell don't they get on to Arnhem?'

Why indeed? At 0800 hours that morning Airborne Corps Headquarters had established radio communication with Oosterbeek, and had received a situation report from 1st Airborne Division which read 'Essential every effort is made to ensure earliest arrival Guards Division at Arnhem. Situation at bridge critical'. A second message, timed at 1510 hours that afternoon, was even more explicit:

> Enemy attacking main bridge in strength. Situation serious for 1 Para Brigade. Enemy also attacking position east from Heelsum and west from Arnhem. Situation serious but am forming close perimeter defence around Hartenstein with remainder of Div. Relief essential both areas earliest possible. Still retain ferry crossing Heveadorp.

Whether this second message reached Browning is uncertain, but the reports received over the public utility telephones from the Dutch Resistance about the strength of the Germans fighting in Arnhem must have underlined to him the seriousness of the situation.

Why then was no attempt made that Wednesday night to reach Arnhem, only eleven miles away, and where it was known that 1st Airborne Division was still fighting at the bridge? For the moment, of course, troops were scarce. After the fighting they had been through, both the Grenadier and the Irish Guards needed time to replenish their tanks with ammunition and petrol, and to snatch a little rest themselves, and the Coldstream were away on the Groesbeek Heights, fighting with US 82nd Division. On the other hand, despite the severity of the fighting, losses had been higher in armour than in men: since the start of the advance from the Meuse-Escaut Canal, the division had lost a total of only 130 men killed, wounded and missing. With the Germans disorganised after their defeat at Nijmegen, it is hard to understand why a small force was not put together to press forward up the road during the night. One of the problems seems to have been the rigidity, already mentioned, of the organisation of Guards Armoured Division, which made it all but impossible to split up one of the four armoured infantry groups, even temporarily. The delay at Nijmegen was very much a repetition of what had occurred south of Eindhoven on the first night of the battle.

XXX Corps' other source of troops was 43rd Infantry Division, commanded by Major-General G.I. Thomas. Only that morning had this division been able to start to cross the Meuse-Escaut Canal and move northwards, priority on the road having been given to what were possibly less vital groups of vehicles, such as the administrative tail of 1st Airborne Division, which had crossed by sea to the Continent. Although 43rd Division was then delayed when the German tanks caused trouble at the Son bridge over the Wilhelmina Canal, by the afternoon of the 20th its leading 130 Brigade had reached a point just south of the Grave bridge over the Maas. There it halted for the night, and there it remained, despite the dire need for troops a few miles up the road, north of Nijmegen.

A basic principle of warfare at every level is to ensure that a reserve is available at all times, either to restore a situation or to exploit an opportunity. Probably with some cause, the commanders of both Guards Armoured Division and XXX Corps have been criticised for not ensuring that such a reserve was available to exploit the success so hardly won by 504 Parachute Infantry and the Grenadier Guards that Wednesday in Nijmegen. An attempt to follow up that success might well have failed, but it was difficult indeed to explain to Tucker's paratroops why nothing at all was done, and easy to understand their anger.

During the day, Browning had received a message from Major-General E. Hakewill-Smith, the commander of 52nd (Lowland) Division – a formation just as anxious to get into action as 1st Airborne had been – offering to make one of his brigades immediately available to fly in by glider to help Urquhart. Browning's reply read 'Thanks for your message but offer not repeat not required as situation better than you think'. With the Poles standing by to jump and the situation obscure, there were good reasons for not committing the air-transportable 52nd Division at this juncture, but it is hard to understand Browning's reason for refusing the offer in the way he did. It was the second and last major decision he had the opportunity of making during the battle.

CHAPTER SEVENTEEN

'DER KESSEL'

At the same time as the frustrated Colonel Tucker was expressing his disgust at what he saw as the British failure to exploit the victory won at such cost by his 504 Parachute Infantry, the Germans had been striving to ferret Frost's last few surviving men out of their positions around the burning and wrecked houses north of the Arnhem bridge. Afterwards, German soldiers remembered with awe how two of the last British defenders fell, charging out of a house, one trying to draw the enemy fire as the other worked forward, fighting-knife in hand, all ammunition finished. Never received at Oosterbeek, but intercepted by the Germans, the final signal transmitted by a British radio operator at the bridge ended with the words 'God Save the King'.

On that morning of Thursday 21 September, as the flames died down and silence settled over the shattered area around the bridge, Urquhart was working out with his senior officers how Oosterbeek should be defended. Left to him were about 3,000 officers and men of his division, and these he divided into two forces, each commanded by one of his two surviving brigadiers*. Hicks's command on the north-west and west of the perimeter was by far the larger, and was much as it had been on the Tuesday night. Facing north was the KOSB, flanked on its right by two troops of the Recce

---

* Having been badly wounded on the 18th Brigadier Lathbury was by this time in German hands.

Squadron and on its left by 21st Independent Parachute Company, a squadron of glider pilots and the divisional engineers. South of the latter, stretching down through the wooded country to the Heaveadorp ferry, was the Border Regiment. Hackett, on the eastern flank facing Arnhem, had no more than the remnants of 156 and 10 Para Battalions, north and east of the MDS crossroads respectively, together with some more glider pilots, his Brigade Headquarters, and what was left of the four battalions which had been destroyed in Arnhem, the last-named now fighting as a formed body in and around the Oosterbeek church, 300 yards or so from the river bank. Behind the church were the gun positions of 1st Light Regiment, RA, soon to be in the thick of the fighting. A measure of the shallowness of the defences was the fact that Hackett's Brigade Headquarters with its attached men – cooks, clerks, signallers and the remnants of the defence platoon – some forty-strong all told and personally commanded by the brigadier, were the only fighting troops between Divisional Headquarters at Hartenstein and the Germans. His total command numbered only some 500 officers and men.

It was fortunate that the Wednesday night had been comparatively quiet, thus providing a little rest for the exhausted and now ravenous survivors of the division, few of whom had been able to snatch more than an hour or so of sleep during the desperate and near-continuous fighting of the previous three or four days. But with daylight, and with the defenders of the bridge eliminated, the Germans again began to plaster the area with artillery and mortar fire, a pattern which was to be repeated every morning. The most feared weapon was the Nebelwerfer, a six-barrelled mortar, its bombs heralded by the multiple thud of its firing, followed by the whine of the descending missiles which rose to a scream before they burst.

Around Hartenstein and the gun positions life was especially unpleasant. Everywhere casualties mounted: in one burst of mortar fire, Sheriff Thompson, the commanding officer of the Light Regiment, was hit in the stomach, Hackett was slightly wounded, and his new brigade major, a staff officer loaned from Divisional Headquarters and an old friend of the brigadier's from the Western Desert, was killed. The divisional ammunition dump was hit and exploded, and German snipers were starting to work their way

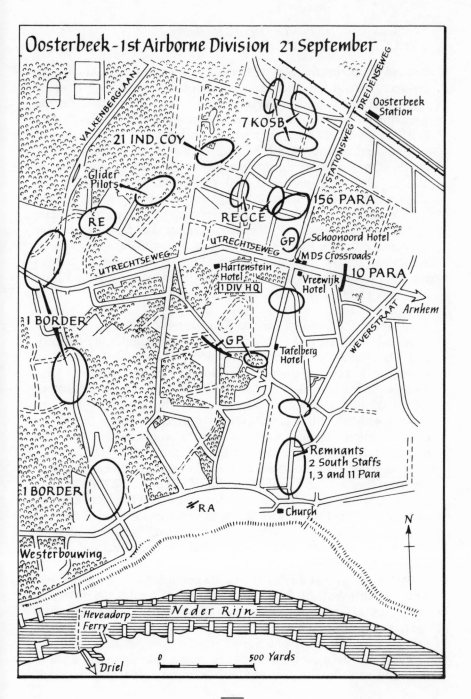

Oosterbeek – 1st Airborne Division 21 September

VALKENBERGLAAN
21 IND COY
7 KOSB
DREIJENSEWEG
STATIONSWEG
Oosterbeek Station
Glider Pilots
RE
RECCE
156 PARA
GP
Schoonoord Hotel
UTRECHTSEWEG
MDS Crossroads
UTRECHTSEWEG
Hartenstein Hotel
1 DIV HQ
Vreewijk Hotel
10 PARA
Arnhem
WEVERSTRAAT
1 BORDER
GP
Tafelberg Hotel
Remnants
2 South Staffs
1, 3 and 11 Para
1 BORDER
RA
Church
N
Westerbouwing
Neder Rijn
Heveadorp Ferry
Driel
0   500 Yards

167

through the perimeter. Mortar bombs burst among the 200 German prisoners herded into the tennis courts of the Hartenstein Hotel, a convenient compound; picks and shovels had to be found for the wretched prisoners to dig slit trenches for themselves. Hartenstein itself, an obvious target, was hardly an ideal site for a divisional headquarters. It had, of course, been chosen more by accident than anything, a temporary resting place on the way towards Arnhem, around which the perimeter had eventually developed. To this inferno, a place of shattered buildings and shattered trees, of broken vehicles and broken bodies, the Germans gave the name '*Der Kessel*' – 'The Cauldron' – a military term used to describe a pocket of encircled troops, but at Oosterbeek an accurate metaphor indeed. A German soldier who had fought at Arnhem was captured later in the war. Asked by his interrogators to tell them what it had been like, he described the battle as '*Das Teufels Geburtstag*' – 'The Devil's Birthday'.

At about 0900 hours on the Thursday morning, the Germans launched their first attack of the day into this 'Cauldron'. Infantry and Tiger tanks assaulted the Heveadorp ferry and drove off its defenders, a single platoon of the Borders, all it had been found possible to spare to defend this vital area. Later in the day, other troops of the regiment counter-attacked the area, but with no success, although three German tanks were destroyed in the course of the action. Similar German attacks continued around the perimeter throughout the day. In the afternoon, the KOSB fought hard to retain their positions and took heavy casualties, including twelve of their remaining officers killed or wounded. To the right, the Recce Squadron and Hackett's few troops held off the Germans, but in the end SP guns set alight the houses occupied by 10 Para, and what was left of the battalion was swamped, losing its last two officers, including its colonel, Ken Smyth, wounded the day before and now hit mortally.

By the end of that day's fighting the perimeter at Oosterbeek was a little smaller, but still firmly held. Writers have painted a picture of confusion, of small bodies of men desperately fighting with little control or distinction between units. Confusion there was, of course, for much of the time, but this is true of any battle. In general, however, the defenders were well organised, fighting as units under their few surviving officers and NCOs, minuscule though some of these units now were. And the now more-or-less static nature of the battle at least provided the opportunity to lay field-telephone lines, so enabling commanders to control the battle. Hazardous indeed was the work of the signal linesmen, continually risking the fire of snipers and mortar bombs to repair the lines, cut and cut again by fire every day. It was in this perimeter that a fifth Victoria Cross was won, by Major Robert Cain of the South Staffordshire Regiment, fighting near the church, the only VC of the battle not awarded posthumously.

The destruction of the defenders of the Arnhem bridge early that morning and the arrival of further reinforcements had provided the Germans with the resources they required to mount these attacks. It was a fresh unit, an NCO's school of the Hermann Goering Division, which had taken the Heveadorp ferry, and the bitterness of the resistance by the Border Regiment is shown in the losses suffered by the brave and enthusiastic German youths in this action – half their men and all but one officer. At about this time also (sources vary as to exactly when), the sixty *Koenigstiger* tanks of 506th Heavy Tank Battalion arrived in the Arnhem area, and with them another panzer grenadier battalion, thirty more flak guns, and several Luftwaffe and Dutch SS units, although the last-named were of small fighting value. As these new units arrived, they were placed under command of Obersturmbannfuehrer Harzer of 9th SS Panzer Division, now faced with the single task of eliminating the defenders of Oosterbeek.

Urquhart was not alone in wondering why the Germans did not launch one co-ordinated attack in strength against a single point on his perimeter, rather than a succession of dispersed thrusts, each supported by a few tanks or SP guns. Short of ammunition and heavy weapons as his men were, especially anti-tank guns, and with a number of wide gaps between his scattered units, it seemed to the divisional commander that the Germans should have been capable of driving a wedge through his positions whenever they wished to do so. It is supposition, but one possible explanation is that these hastily collected German units, not knowing one another and without experience of operating together, were just not capable of mounting a well organised, large-scale attack. If they had done so, they would certainly have crushed the British defenders, sturdily though the airborne troops were fighting.

Throughout the Thursday, there was still a widespread expectation of early relief, even though it was the fifth day of the battle and XXX Corps had not yet appeared. Inaccurate information sustained hope. At 1225 hours it was recorded in the diary of 1 Airlanding Brigade that news had been received that 43rd Infantry Division was being directed on Heveadorp ferry and might be expected to pass one battalion and ammunition across the river that night. Four hours later, XXX Corps was reported at Elst, only three miles from the river. And early that morning aid, both tangible and reassuring, had materialised. Urquhart's gunners made radio contact with Second Army's 64th Medium Regiment, RA, near Nijmegen. Suspicion greeted the first attempts by Lieutenant-Colonel Robert Loder-Simmonds, the Commander Royal Artillery of 1st Airborne Division, to identify himself. Knowing Loder-Simmonds well, the other gunner asked for the name of his airborne friend's wife. 'Merlin' was the reply. 'What is her favourite sport?' was the next question, and the answer 'falconry' settled any remaining doubts.

Two of 1st Airborne Division's most urgent needs were now to be satisfied. At last reliable radio communication was established with the troops south of the Neder Rijn, instead of the still uncertain link with Airborne Corps and the intermittent and roundabout channels through Phantom or the BBC in London. Secondly, effective and heavy fire support was now available. Henceforth, the 4.5-inch howitzers and 155-mm guns of 64th Medium Regiment, shooting from eleven miles away, were used to break up the German attacks, at times engaging targets only 100 yards ahead of the forward airborne troops. It was a fearful moment for those on the perimeter when the first shells roared over them to burst just ahead, unaware as they yet were that their own guns were within range. Within a few minutes, however, they realised that it was their own artillery reaching out to hit at the Germans, and that a measure of help had at last arrived from the outside world.

This gunner support was especially welcome in the absence of any help from the fighter-bombers of the Second Tactical Air Force, since the battle of Mareth, over eighteen months before, a battlefield weapon taken almost for granted by British soldiers. As Urquhart was to write:

Although I was naturally disturbed by the non-arrival of Horrocks's Corps, I was much more annoyed at the disappointingly meagre offensive air support we were receiving. The resupply boys' gallantry had been magnificent, but the fighters were rare friends. We needed the Typhoons and Tempests to carry out rocket attacks on the Germans' gun and mortar positions.

No air support of any type had been provided for the airborne troops at Arnhem since the initial landing on the first day of 'Market Garden'. It was a dismal story, the reasons behind it twofold. First, there was the restriction imposed by First Allied Airborne Army on Second TAF on the Continent, the latter force being scheduled to provide the close support. So as to avoid the fighter escorts to the transport columns getting mixed up with the close-support aircraft, Second TAF was prohibited from operating over the battle area when troops or supplies were being landed or dropped. This rule, combined with the poor weather, had the effect of limiting the possible flying hours to a very short period, usually in the evenings – it was a wretched quirk that the weather was often bad over Second TAF's airfields, when it was clear for the Luftwaffe east of the Rhine. This stultifying restriction might have been eased if a closer relationship had existed between the two headquarters concerned, which were separated by the Channel and without direct communications.

The second reason was the lack of communication between the troops on the ground and the supporting air formations. By 1944 air-support signal units provided detachments to work with ground formations, their purpose being to transmit requirements from the troops for air support and then to help direct the pilots on to their targets. Just before take-off, two American air-support parties had been allocated to each airborne division and one to Corps Headquarters, but the operators were new to their radio sets and had no experience of working with the troops they were supposed to be supporting. Each party had one SCR 193 netted to Second Army, through which requests were relayed to Second TAF Control Centre and from there to 83 Group, RAF; each also had a VHF SCR522 on which to talk to the pilots overhead. Neither of the two parties which landed with 1st Airborne Division ever made contact by

171

radio, and both were quickly knocked out by mortar fire. Given more time to plan 'Market Garden', better arrangements might perhaps have been made; one of Brereton's staff officers could have been located at Second TAF with direct and secure communications to First Allied Airborne Army, and more time would then have been available to marry up the air-support parties with the soldiers. It was not to be, however. With no heavy fire support until 64th Medium Regiment made contact, 1st Airborne was in trouble. As Urquhart was afterwards to complain, with considerable justification, a 'cab rank' of aircraft overhead, waiting to be called down when targets were met, could easily have turned the scale on the first afternoon and helped 1 Parachute Brigade to reach the bridge in strength.

A further failure was the absence of arrangements for interdiction aircraft to cover the countryside around the airborne landings and attack German troop and supply movements as they were observed, although the pilots of the escort aircraft carried out, on their own initiative, a great deal of impromptu harassing of such targets. This lack of interdiction strikes was something for which the enemy was to be grateful: one German post-battle report commented on their freedom to move troops as they wished during the drops because all the Allied aircraft were fully engaged in protecting the landing-sites.

Although Urquhart was to receive more encouraging news at 1715 hours that evening, Thursday 21 September, to the effect that the Polish Parachute Brigade had been dropped just east of Driel, near the southern end of the Heveadorp ferry, the reality of his situation was apparent to him. It was apparent also to his other senior officers, whom he consulted before sending a signal at 2144 hours to Airborne Corps Headquarters which made this abundantly clear. It read:

> No knowledge elements of Div in Arnhem for 24 hours. Balance of Div in very tight perimeter. Heavy mortaring and machine-gun fire followed by local attacks. Main nuisance SP guns. Our casualties heavy. Resources stretched to utmost. Relief within 24 hours vital.

Whether this message reached Browning is unrecorded, although there is no reason why it should not have arrived by one or other of the various radio links by then established. However, it is likely that it was received, since just before midnight, 1st Airborne Division heard from Corps Headquarters by radio that a number of the aircraft carrying the Poles had been obliged to turn back to base because of the weather.

CHAPTER EIGHTEEN

'MAJOR-GENERAL SOSABOWSKI PROVED HIMSELF TO BE EXTREMELY DIFFICULT TO WORK WITH'

For Major-General Sosabowski, as for the officers and men he commanded, it had been a trying week. Booked to land south of the Arnhem highway bridge on Tuesday 19 September, the three parachute battalions of 1 Polish Independent Parachute Brigade had fretted all that day on their airfields, waiting for the weather to clear, before learning at 1500 hours that there would be no flying. Sosabowski, who had been shocked to discover that radio communications between Urquhart and England appeared to be almost non-existent, could glean little more about what was happening in Arnhem than he could read in the morning papers. That evening, however, a report reached him that his glider lift, which had succeeded in taking off, had been destroyed on landing. The exaggeration was only marginal: just two of his anti-tank guns had, in fact, managed to reach the then evolving perimeter at Oosterbeek.

Early the following morning, Sosabowski was told that the plans for the use of his brigade had been changed. It was now to drop at Driel that day, south of Oosterbeek, and then cross the river by

174

means of the Heveadorp ferry to reinforce Urquhart. With the Polish units split between two airfields, there was time for no more than the sparsest of briefings, but it hardly mattered. As the first loaded aircraft began to taxi down the runways, they were halted. Another postponement had been ordered. That night, Sosabowski learned a little of what had been happening to 1st Airborne Division: he was also told that XXX Corps was 'bogged down and making little headway', as his British liaison officer, who brought him the news, expressed it. But it was all very vague, and the Polish general could not discover whether these reports were recent or outdated. Sosabowski was a hero to his men, and most of the British officers with whom he worked both liked and admired him. On the other hand, he was far from being an easy subordinate. Now fifty-one years of age, he had played a central role in the defence of Warsaw against the Germans in 1940, after which he had joined the Polish underground forces before escaping, first to France and then to England. The idea of raising a Polish parachute brigade had been his, and he had then formed and trained it, although not without what he saw as bureaucratic hindrance, both British and Polish. Short as the Poles were of reinforcements for their armed forces, General Casimir Sosnkowski, the Commander-in-Chief of the Polish Army that had been formed in Britain, had attempted to place restrictions on the use of this, his only parachute brigade, asking that it should be withdrawn from battle if its casualties reached 25 per cent, and that it should not be used in Western Europe if the opportunity arose for its employment in Poland. Montgomery tetchily refused to accept restrictions of this type, but this did not affect Sosabowski's determination to take his brigade to Warsaw to help liberate his beloved city if he could possibly do so: he seems to have viewed the fighting in the west as an aggravating interlude, in which he was ready to do his bit if asked, but not if it were to cost too many of his near-irreplaceable officers and men. In August 1944, the rising of General Bor-Komorowski's Home Army against the Germans in Warsaw had been the call for which every Pole had been waiting, but distances were such that there was no way of answering it. As everyone now knows, the rising had been premature, triggered by Bor-Komoroski's determination to gain control of the capital before the Soviet forces arrived. Cynically, the Russians had then halted their advance upon Warsaw in order to allow the Germans time to destroy the anti-communist Polish patriots.

Such were the stresses bearing on Sosabowski, a commander who was always ready to argue if he received an order which he thought to be unsound, and who would carry out such an order only when pressed hard to do so. He was a man with the potential to be a great leader, either military or political. During the planning for 'Comet' he had protested to Urquhart and Browning that he had been given an impossible task to achieve, and he had asked that his orders should be confirmed in writing. Later, when he received his instructions for 'Market Garden', he had told Urquhart that the divisional bridgehead around Arnhem was too large for the airborne force to hold, and he had expressed the fear that his DZ might not any longer be held by the British when his battalions dropped. Browning had rarely seen eye-to-eye with Sosabowski, so it was hardly surprising that, after 'Market Garden', the British general should have asked for his removal, complaining in his report to the Military Secretary at the War Office that the Polish commander was 'extremely difficult to work with'. Browning also criticised harshly the way in which the Polish brigade had been handled during the battle. It was an unhappy business.

During the night of Wednesday 20 September, the Polish airborne commander had time to mull over his fresh instructions for the drop at Driel. Appalled by the lack of information and of clear orders, he decided that he could not take his men into battle in such circumstances, apparently to reinforce defeat. The outcome of such a refusal was likely to be a court-martial and accusations of cowardice, but these he was ready to face. Things might have been solved if one of his seniors had been available to discuss the problems, but Ridgway was paying a hardly necessary visit to the Groesbeek Heights, while Brereton, after his escape from the bombing in Eindhoven, had flown to SHAEF to discuss a fresh request from Montgomery for an airborne operation against Walcheren.

At 0700 hours on Thursday morning, however, Sosabowski received the erroneous information that the Heveadorp ferry was safely in British hands, upon which he confirmed to First Allied Airborne Army that his brigade would take off at noon. But the early-morning mist persisted, to produce further nerve-racking delays until, quite suddenly, it cleared, and at last the aircraft could fly. At just after 1600 hours on the 21st, the Germans in Dunkirk reported the air armada overhead, thus giving their troops and fighters a full hour in which to prepare a reception. Flak batteries were alerted, as were one hundred or so fighter aircraft, but the Allied escorts succeeded in coping with their attackers, and did much to persuade the flak gunners to keep their heads down. Nevertheless, flak was bursting around the transport aircraft as they approached the DZ, and the Poles floated earthwards to fields swept by machine-guns and mortars, most of them firing from north of the Neder Rijn. For all that, casualties were surprisingly few, and the drop was in no way the holocaust described in some accounts of the battle. On the other hand, aircraft losses were high. Thirteen Dakotas were shot down, most of them after their passengers had jumped; another forty-one, carrying a complete Polish battalion, never arrived, forced by the weather to return to base.

The result was that Sosabowski mustered on the ground only two weak battalions, some 750 men in all. These he directed north towards the river, even though he had no idea what was happening, his radios having failed to contact the headquarters of 1st Airborne Division, only two miles distant. That evening, however, he learned from a woman member of the Dutch Resistance, and then from one of his own patrols, that the Germans and not the British controlled the Heveadorp ferry crossing place, and a little later he received dramatic confirmation of these two reports. Into his hedquarters, set up in a deserted farmhouse, appeared the naked, shivering and muddy figure of his liaison officer, who had landed with Urquhart. He had swum the river in the dark, bringing the news that the Heveadorp crossing had indeed been lost, but that an attempt would be made during the night to gather boats and rafts to ferry the Poles across to Oosterbeek. The Polish officer departed, to return by the way he had come, bearing Sosabowski's acknowledgement of Urquhart's instructions.

Nothing that had been hoped was to happen. The Poles waited near the river bank, listening to the Driel church clock chime the hours, but no one came. Failing to find any boats along the river, Urquhart's sappers had tried to improvise rafts from jeep trailers, but without success: three were built, but attempts to carry a line across the river by which the rafts could be towed over all failed.

Just before dawn, Sosabowski abandoned the vigil and marched his men back to Driel where they could dig in and wait, either for the means to cross the river or for the Germans to attack them.

Defeated at Nijmegen, 10th SS Panzer Division had retired towards Arnhem and was now waiting for XXX Corps' next move, and the drop of this fresh force of paratroops near Driel had given the German commanders cause for concern, posing as it did a double threat. Either the Poles might cross to reinforce the British at Oosterbeek, or, worse still, they could attack towards the southern end of the Arnhem bridge and so cut 10th SS Panzer's newly opened link to the area around Arnhem. With this latter danger in mind, Bittrich decided to direct the greater part of 506th Tank Battalion's sixty *Koenigstigers* south of the river to reinforce 10th SS Panzer; with them went a further company of Panther tanks and several miscellaneous infantry units, a sizeable force in all. Based on a line running north and south through Elst, this force was ordered to attack the Poles and keep the road to Arnhem open. It was fortunate for the Poles that the wet, ditch-bisected polderland south of the river (which its inhabitants called the Betuwe) was poor going for any sort of vehicle, and especially so for heavy tanks, which could not move off the narrow roads, and under whose weight the bridges tended to collapse.

Indirectly, then, the arrival of the Poles had brought considerable relief to Urquhart's troops. Although, for the time being, they had failed to find a means of crossing the Neder Rijn, their presence had forced the Germans to move armour and infantry south of the river, powerful units which might have made just the difference to the outcome of the Oosterbeek fighting.

CHAPTER NINETEEN

'I REGARD GENERAL SITUATION ON RIVERS AS NOW VERY SATISFACTORY'

Even before Bittrich moved these heavy tanks south of the Neder Rijn and into the Betuwe, 10th SS Panzer Division had made good use of the darkness to pull itself into shape and establish a blocking position around the small Allied bridgehead on the north bank of the Waal. It was 1100 hours on the morning of Thursday 21 September before the Irish Guards received orders to break through to the Arnhem bridge, where, so far as anyone knew, troops of British 1st Airborne Division were still fighting. But not until 1230 hours, nineteen hours after the road bridge at Nijmegen had been captured at such heavy cost, did the three squadrons of the Irish Guards start to drive forward in single file up the main road, with the infantry battalion, now reduced to only five platoons, sitting on the tanks of the rear two squadrons.

Waiting for them were the German infantry, by now well dug-in and supported by tanks and SP guns. Confined by the deep ditches edging the highway, the tanks of the Irish Guards could nowhere deploy off the high-banked road, on top of which they were silhouetted like shooting-range targets at a fairground. Twenty minutes after the Guards moved off, unseen guns opened fire and knocked out the three leading tanks, and when the infantry behind jumped off the ones in the rear to attack across the open polder, they came under intense artillery and mortar fire. It was not like the break-out from the Meuse-Escaut Canal five days before. Now artillery support for the Guards' attack was limited, and ammunition for the guns even more so. Added to that, radio communication to the 'cab-rank' of Typhoons waiting overhead failed, and there was no way of calling them in to attack the Germans holding up the advance. An attempt by the Welsh Guards to make a flanking movement round the enemy positions did no better, although they destroyed three German tanks. By nightfall it was evident that no further progress up this main axis was likely to be possible. Another day had been lost.

Joe Vandeleur, the commander of the Irish Guards Group, was among those who wondered why the orders for this advance had arrived so late, thus providing the Germans with the time to complete their preparations to block the main highway. There was, he remembers, a general lack of urgency. Horrocks, always generous in his readiness to admit an error, later confessed that he made a mistake in directing his troops up this main road, known by mid-morning to be strongly defended, instead of trying to make a wide sweep around the left, even though the minor roads there were thought to be difficult for tanks. Folklore has it, in fact, that the advance from Nijmegen to Arnhem had been a regular question set in pre-war Dutch Army promotion examinations: to take the direct route was to fail. Horrocks also blamed himself for not having insisted upon the attachment of a senior Dutch officer to his headquarters to provide local advice of this type.

Above all, Horrocks desperately required more infantry at this stage of the battle. The brigades of 43rd Infantry Division were sadly slow in arriving. In part this delay was due to the chaos along 'Hell's Highway', but this is not the full story. Although the German armour had halted traffic at Son on both the Tuesday and Wednesday mornings, US 101st Airborne Division had since then succeeded in keeping the road open 'without much difficulty', to quote the Airborne Corps' official report on the operation. Horrocks, in his account of the battle, stated that a German formation penetrated St Oedenrode and cut the road on Thursday, but this did not, in fact, occur until the following day. It was

Arnhem and its highway bridge, taken by a reconnaissance aircraft in September, before the operation.

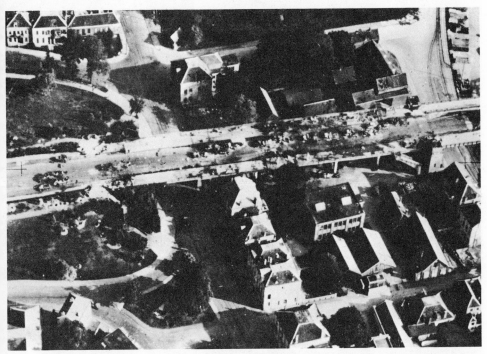

The north end of Arnhem highway bridge, taken by a PRU Spitfire on the morning of 18 September. The wreckage of 9th SS Panzer's reconnaissance squadron litters the roadway. The bridge (south) is to the right – the two 'pillbox-like structures' are clearly visible at right, as are the raised ramp and the houses from which Frost's men fought.

Frost's sketch map of the action at the north end of the bridge.
Lt-Col John Frost, who commanded 2 Para and other troops at the north end of Arnhem bridge – 'the outstanding independent parachute battalion action of the war', wrote Gavin.
A German photograph of the highway bridge, shortly after its recapture on the morning of 21 September. The wreckage has been bulldozed aside.

The school, east of the ramp at the north end of the bridge, defended by Captain Mackay and his sappers.
'The bravest and most patriotic people we had liberated' – Dutch civilian patients evacuating St Elizabeth Hospital, Arnhem, under a Red Cross flag, watched by the Germans.

British dead near the Municipal Museum, killed trying to reach Frost's position at the bridge about 2,000 yards away to the east. A German patrol in the mid-distance moves towards the bridge.

19 September. German soldiers climbing the fence beside the Municipal Museum in Arnhem. Four British battalions were destroyed in or near this area during that day, trying to reach the bridge where Frost was still holding out.

An SS corporal changing his socks near the railway line. Continual pressure from troops such as these forced Urquhart to give up the railway on the 19th, a decision made nearly disastrous by a tragic misunderstanding.

'Hell's Highway', 20 September – XXX Corps trucks burning while US and British troops take cover, waiting for Typhoons and armour to arrive and silence the German positions. 'Jim, never try to fight your corps off one road', said Horrocks.

The Hartenstein Hotel, Oosterbeek, Urquhart's Divisional HQ and a key position in the perimeter battle. By the end of the battle the lawn in front and the windows were swept by German sniper fire.

Men of the Border Regiment dug in near the Hartenstein on 20 September. It was here that the survivors of 156 Para fought their way into the perimeter, haggard, filthy and battle-weary after a successful withdrawal and counter-attack – to be told by a young Border captain to move on, lest 'the filthy shower' contaminate his men.

A PRU photograph of Nijmegen, taken on 18 September, two days before the road bridge was captured. Smoke from US 82nd Airborne's early assaults can be clearly seen. The final successful assault crossing by 504th Regiment was made downstream (left) of the railway bridge, out of the picture, while Sergeant Robinson's tanks stormed the road bridge at right, the Germans having failed to blow it.

Nijmegen road bridge on 21 September, the day after its capture, with Guards Armoured Division transport streaming north, past a shot-up Wehrmacht bus. But no attempt was made to reach Arnhem, 11 miles away, on the day before, and by the morning of the 21st the gallant defence of Arnhem bridge was ended.
A jeep from 325th Glider Infantry (US 82nd Airborne Division) carrying a badly wounded soldier in Nijmegen, after the bridge was captured.

Browning (left) and Dempsey, commander of British Second Army visit Gavin at his HQ near Groesbeek. By 19 September there were four generals in Nijmegen, and they were joined by Ridgway.

XXX Corps transport in Valkenswaard, about 5 miles south of Eindhoven, on 21 September. In Arnhem the bridge is once more in German hands, and the remains of 1st Airborne are fighting desperately in the perimeter.

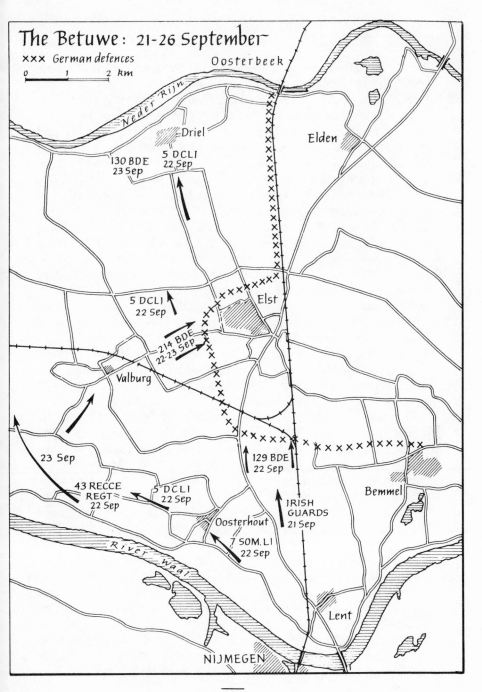

The Betuwe: 21-26 September

××× German defences

0   1   2 km

Oosterbeek

Nede r Rijn

Driel

Elden

130 BDE
23 Sep

5 DCLI
22 Sep

5 DCLI
22 Sep

214 BDE
22-23 Sep

Elst

Valburg

23 Sep

43 RECCE
REGT
22 Sep

5 DCLI
22 Sep

129 BDE
22 Sep

Bemmel

Oosterhout

IRISH
GUARDS
21 Sep

7 SOM. LI
22 Sep

River Waal

Lent

NIJMEGEN

181

Wednesday afternoon when the leading formation of 43rd Division, 130 Infantry Brigade, arrived south of Grave; it was to spend Thursday in guarding the Grave and Honinghutje bridges, the latter by then in use again, and in searching Nijmegen for German troops, none of whom were found. By the evening a single battalion had occupied a close perimeter around the north end of the two Nijmegen bridges. Earlier that day, the second formation to arrive, 214 Infantry Brigade, had concentrated six miles south of Nijmegen, where its commander, Brigadier Hubert Essame, received orders to cross the river by the railway bridge and advance towards Arnhem around the west flank of the Guards. This brigade, after being delayed overnight in Eindhoven where it had taken a wrong turning into the vast Phillips factory (the result of the absence of traffic police), again ran into difficulties as it started to move forward through Nijmegen. Impeded by a combination of sporadic German shelling and excited townspeople, garlanding their liberators and pressing apples into their pockets, a part of the brigade again went astray, being directed to the road bridge (reserved for the Guards) rather than the railway bridge. Such mistakes are all too possible when 20,000 troops have to be moved along a single narrow road under continual threat of enemy attack, but they were especially unfortunate at this particular time.

The failure to push 130 Brigade forward from Grave on the Wednesday evening, after the Grenadier Guards and US 82nd Division had between them captured the Nijmegen road bridge, has already been touched upon. When, on the next day, Major-General Thomas, the commander of 43rd Divison, gave Essame his orders for the advance towards Arnhem, he took pains to emphasise the desperate situation of British 1st Airborne Division, something well known to everyone by then, and the need for the utmost speed. This emphasis hardly matched the cautious step-by-step approach so far demonstrated, nor the use of 130 Brigade on Thursday (the day Thomas gave these orders to Essame) to guard the bridges and clear Nijmegen of non-existent Germans.

Over the years Thomas has been harshly censured for his division's part in the battle. Among his critics has been the American reporter and historian Chester Wilmot, an eyewitness to the advance of XXX Corps, whose authoritative study *The Struggle for Europe* has largely stood the test of time. In that book Wilmot described Thomas as 'By nature ... cautious and methodical and his troops followed his example'; it has been said that the American may have been influenced by his personal dislike for Thomas, and this could be so. The general lacked human qualities, and his acerbic manner did not endear him to everyone, something that may have prevented his later being given command of a corps, for his reputation was high indeed by the end of the war in North-West Europe.

Be that as it may, Thomas had been chosen for command of 43rd Division because of his reputation as a 'pusher', and the decision to use the leading 130 Brigade to clear Nijmegen must have been made by Horrocks or with his knowledge, for Thomas had been in close touch with his corps commander ever since he had arrived in the area on Wednesday 20 September, D-plus-3. To what extent, then, was the methodical behaviour of 43rd Division due to Horrocks himself?

Something of a question-mark does perhaps hang over Horrocks's conduct of this battle. He had displayed to his assembled commanders, before the operation began, his usual confident optimism, despite the doubts that seem to have troubled him. But several people who were in contact with him during the battle have commented that he seemed far from fit. Was he perhaps suffering from one of his periodic bouts of illness, the legacy of his North African wounds? He had been laid low for several days at the end of August 1944; on 28 December, three months after 'Market Garden', Montgomery was to send him home on leave because, as he signalled the CIGS, 'During the past ten days he has been nervy and difficult with his staff and has attempted to act foolishly with his corps.' It is hard to offer any explanation other than ill-health for Horrocks's failure to exercise greater pressure on his divisions at such a time of crisis. He had, after all, proved himself in Africa as possibly the most brilliant and thrusting corps commander produced by the British Army during the war, a general who Montgomery insisted on bringing back into the battle in Europe, even though he was aware of Horrocks's uncertain state of health. Do we then find here the reason why no effort was made to exploit beyond Valkenswaard on the first day of the battle, why the limited objectives given to Guards Armoured Division bore little relation to the problem of reaching Arnhem in forty-eight hours, and why

183

XXX Corps halted for nineteen hours after the Waal at Nijmegen had been crossed?

Montgomery's own behaviour at this time was hardly characteristic. To keep in touch with a battle, it was his habit to site his tactical headquarters level with the headquarters of his immediate subordinates, and to pay regular visits 'two down' – that is, as an army commander to divisional headquarters, and when in charge of an army group, at least to his corps commanders. Brigadier Bill Williams, one of Montgomery's closest associates during his years with Eighth Army and Twenty-First Army Group, has said that the Field-Marshal commanded his armies like corps, never having learned to be an army group commander: as the American generals often complained, he found it difficult not to interfere. Although it was not possible for Montgomery to reach Horrocks after the second day of the operation, why did he not visit his XXX Corps commander in the early stages, and why did he not see Dempsey until Saturday 23 September? As Williams has also remarked, Montgomery would normally 'have been breathing down Horrocks's neck'. For although the Twenty-First Army Group commander was involved at the time with Eisenhower in the continuing arguments over the 'broad' and 'narrow' front strategies, the opening of Antwerp, and the question of who should have command of the land battle, it is strange how remote he remained from 'Market Garden', upon which so much had been staked. This remoteness is perhaps exemplified in the signal he despatched to the CIGS on Thursday 21 September:

> 1 Para ... rounded up. We shall now advance and if Germans destroy main bridge we shall cross the river at the place where 1AB is located using them as a secure bridgehead. It will not matter greatly if Germans destroy bridge since we have now plenty of bridging material and the river is no greater obstacle than Seine which was quite easily bridged. I regard general situation on rivers as now very satisfactory.

Very satisfactory! Not one to admit that a plan had gone amiss, Montgomery may or may not have believed what he wrote. If he did, he was very out of touch.

Elsewhere in the 'Garden' area, Thursday was the quietest day of the battle. On the Groesbeek Heights, the Germans appeared to have shot their bolt after the tough little battles of the previous day. Only around Beek had there been some troublesome fighting, but by that evening 508 Parachute Infantry had finally repulsed their opponents. Further south, around Mook, all was peaceful and the Heumen bridge was now safe – not that it mattered so much any more, with traffic flowing across the newly opened bridge at Honinghutje. Further south still the situation was much the same. With the enemy comparatively inactive, the two northernmost regiments of US 101st Airborne Division had made good use of the opportunity to push out and give more depth to their positions. Impressed by the success of the classic manoeuvre performed by the battalion of 501 Parachute Infantry near Veghel on the previous day, and aware from Dutch civilian reports that German forces were concentrating south of Schijndel, Colonel Howard R. Johnson and Colonel Michaelis of 501 and 502 Regiments together planned a similar but larger-scale operation, with two of Johnson's battalions sweeping up from the south to trap and destroy the Germans. By midnight, the first phase had been successfully completed, an unreconnoitred night attack against Schijndel, one of the battalions employed being the same unit that had trapped the German force the day before. This aggressive manner of defending the long line of communications was a measure of the tough endurance and confidence of Taylor's airborne soldiers.

CHAPTER TWENTY

'THOU SHALT NOT BE AFRAID FOR ANY TERROR BY NIGHT: NOR FOR THE ARROW THAT FLIETH BY DAY'

By Friday, the sufferings of the wounded men in the Oosterbeek perimeter had become severe indeed, both for them and for the medical staff who were attempting to bring them some relief. Day by day the number to be cared for had increased. Even by Monday afternoon, the Airlanding Brigade's 181st Field Ambulance was looking after a hundred wounded men at Wolfheze, and all the time more were being brought in on foot, in jeeps and on stretchers. A few, however, had arrived in a less orthodox manner: one on a horse and cart, accompanied by a Dutch nurse, and another in pyjamas from the guest room of a house where he had spent the night. The other medical unit which had landed on the first day of the battle, 16th Field Ambulance, had on the Sunday afternoon moved directly into Arnhem behind its 1 Parachute Brigade; unlike the fighting battalions, however, it managed by an odd quirk of fortune to slip around the German defenders. That night it was functioning and caring for its wounded in St Elizabeth Hospital. On the following day, Monday, during the bitter attempts by 1 and 3 Para to reach the bridge, the Germans overran the hospital and removed as prisoners all the British medical staff, other than the two surgical teams. These were allowed to stay and carry on with their work in what a Dutch observer described as a 'gentleman's agreement' between the two enemies, whose doctors managed to establish a professional relationship with one another that at times bordered on the friendly.

On the Monday morning, 181st Field Ambulance was ordered to move forward and set up at the Hotel Schoonoord, at what was soon to be known as the MDS crossroads, with its surgical unit based at the Hotel Tafelberg, half way between the crossroads and Oosterbeek church. When 133rd Field Ambulance arrived on the Tuesday with 4 Parachute Brigade, the two medical units combined as the wounded poured in, taking over yet more houses and hotels, including the Hotel Vreewijk opposite the Schoonoord. By the morning of Wednesday 20 September, the two field ambulances were already coping with 400 casualties, and more were arriving all the time, some of them hit outside the very doors of the dressing stations.

It was disastrous that the area chosen for the care of the wounded in the early stages of the battle should have evolved into the eastern flank of the Oosterbeek defensive perimeter, the scene of the most bitter fighting of the week. Round and about the buildings the battle flared; again and again, mortar bombs and shells crashed in and about them, jagged shards of metal flying through the makeshift wards. Although some of the wounded men were moved from the outside rooms into the corridors, there was no place of refuge from the shells of the SP guns which punctured the walls, to burst among the stretchers. Men were killed where they lay, or were wounded yet again. Doctors and medical orderlies themselves became casualties. Jeeps crammed with more wounded, festooned though they were with Red Cross flags, were hit as they ran the gauntlet of cross-fire. Time and again buildings changed hands, and German wounded lay alongside the British. Some of the medical staff were removed as prisoners, but most were left to care as best they could for the patients. Short of nearly every type of medical supply, the surgeons performed one operation after another. In the dark and stinking corridors and rooms pain-racked men lay side by side, cold and hungry, often on bare boards with hardly space between them for orderlies to pick their way. Others lay in cellars in outlying houses,

187

bandaged and splinted, treated as best they could be by the few regimental medical officers still surviving.

Here and there Dutch nurses materialised to lend their help, and other civilians also did what they could. Among these was Mrs Kate ter Horst, whose house near the church was taken over by the medical officer of the Light Regiment. When she emerged on Wednesday morning from the cellar in which four Dutch adults and five young children were sheltering, she found every inch of her house – stairs, cupboards and lavatory – crammed with wounded men, lying so close together that it was difficult to move those who had died. Every pane of glass had been smashed, and her furniture lay outside where it had been thrown to make more space for the wounded. Over everything was the stench of blood, excreta and death. In the garden, awaiting burial, was a row of bodies, tangled hair hanging over muddied faces; when Mrs ter Horst returned to her home after the war, the graves of fifty-seven airborne soldiers were found in her garden. In the evenings, after consoling her terrified children with songs and stories, she moved around the rooms above them, doing what she could and fortifying the wounded men with the words of King David's Ninety-First Psalm: 'Thou shalt not be afraid for any terror by night: nor for the arrow that flieth by day'. But men were afraid. As shells tore gaping holes in the walls, killing the wounded and orderlies, and wounding the solitary doctor, the men who lay there fighting their pain needed even more courage to sustain them than those fighting from their trenches outside.

In one important respect this pattern of the fighting in Oosterbeek followed that at the Arnhem bridge. In the early stages, when German tanks and SP guns had yet to appear in force, the German infantry had been held off from barricaded positions in buildings, usually in upstair rooms: these provided fields of fire, a measure of protection and often the cover to shield movement between buildings. The arrival of the enemy armour in strength was to change all this. With nearly all the British 6- and 17-pounder anti-tank guns destroyed, the German armoured vehicles were able to stand off, out of range of the PIATs, and methodically smash each building in turn, thus compelling the defenders to fight from slit-trenches dug in gardens or along roadside verges. For all that, the airborne soldiers managed to hold the armour at bay, using their few PIATs and Gammon bombs.* Men stalked Tiger tanks around the backs of the houses, Gammon bombs in their hands, or waited in slit-trenches until tanks were all but on top of them before firing their PIATs. It was in this type of grim defensive fighting that the British excelled.

During Thursday night Urquhart had adjusted his defences, withdrawing the KOSB a little further to the south, and moving 21st Independent Parachute Company over from the west side of the perimeter to a position astride the MDS crossroads, to fill the gap in Hackett's area. Further south still, a few of the Divisional Royal Army Service Corps were brought in to thicken Hackett's line – for line it was. At no point was there any adequate depth to the British defences. After five days of continuous battle, men could do little more than fight where they stood or lay, or sometimes make a quick sally to hunt a sniper or trap a tank. When the enemy mortaring slackened and the grey-clad figures once more began to edge forward with their flamethrowers and grenades, it was as much as most of the airborne troops could do to raise their heads over the edge of the parapet and begin to shoot. Rarely now could the determination be found to counter-attack to recover a lost house or trench, and those attempts which were made often ended in the loss of yet more of the few remaining officers and NCOs.

It was inevitable that some men could cope no longer. The Germans watched two individuals leap from their trenches and run towards them, hands in the air. Some of the men sought refuge in cellars, putting at risk their lives of their Dutch occupants; one such soldier died redeeming himself, shielding a woman with his body when the Germans found his hiding-place and tossed in a grenade. Other men huddled in a row of the Hartenstein buildings, for some time escaping anyone's notice, until at last they were found and sent to join their units, where most then fought as well as anybody. Ammunition was almost finished: on the Thursday a small amount

---

* The No. 82 Gammon bomb was a bag fitted with a contact fuse and filled with putty-like plastic explosive. Thrown against a tank, the fuse detonated the charge on contact, carving the inside of the vehicle into lethal splinters. The Americans coveted the Gammon bomb, as they did the PIAT, a more effective weapon than their Rocket Launcher M1, the bazooka. Their light M1 carbine, easily jammed by a few grains of sand, was another undependable weapon – like the British Sten gun, for that matter.

had been recovered from the supply drop, together with a little food and some medical stores, but no supply aircraft were to fly on the Friday. Not that the food reached everyone – some units received none from the start of the battle to its end.

On Thursday night Urquhart became so concerned that Horrocks and Browning could in no way comprehend the parlous condition of the survivors of his division, that he decided to send Lieutenant-Colonel Charles Mackenzie, his senior staff officer, back across the river to try to reach the advancing troops, and to explain at first hand how serious the situation was. Faced also with the immediate problem of arranging for Sosabowski's battalions and urgently required supplies to be ferried over the river, Urquhart ordered Lieutenant-Colonel 'Eddie' Myers, his senior engineer, to accompany Mackenzie on what was likely to prove an exacting mission.

Their daylight journey over the Neder Rijn was hazardous enough. First the two officers had to carry a two-man rubber dinghy across a broad stretch of open polderland, and then paddle it over the 200-yard wide river. Although the early morning mist had lifted, there was still a slight haze to hide them from German machine-gunners firing sporadic bursts across the water. Possibly the enemy were not as alert as they might have been, for the two men reached the far side unhurt, and found there guides with bicycles waiting to take them to Sosabowski.

Mackenzie and Myers had arrived in the middle of a battle. During that morning, Friday 22 September, the Poles were to continue to fight off attacks by German infantry and tanks, but the enemy did not press them too hard. All that day, however, the Polish troops were to lose men to shells ariving from the direction of both Oosterbeek and Elst. Sosabowski toured his units on a commandeered bicycle, and visited his surgeons struggling to save lives in the school being used as a dressing station, pondering as he did so how he was to get his men across the river without either boats or rafts.

With the Polish Brigade, the two British officers found two troops of the Household Cavalry. The first reconnaissance armoured cars of XXX Corps had reached the Neder Rijn. They had crossed the Nijmegen road bridge before dawn, edging around the side roads west of Elst under cover of the early mist and joining the Poles without their crews having seen a single German. For the time being, however, no one was to follow them. During the morning, these two troops were to make themselves generally useful, helping the Poles hold off the enemy armour and shooting-up a German steamer and three barges on the river.

Mackenzie was now able to use the armoured car radio net to pass to Headquarters XXX Corps exact details of what was happening in Oosterbeek. But he could offer Sosabowski no more than four of the small rubber boats, similar to the one which he and Myers had used that morning, all that 1st Airborne Division possessed, and little enough in which to pass half a brigade across the Neder Rijn. At the very best, it was unlikely that more than 200 men could succeed in crossing in them during the night. But that evening, as Myers was starting to make the best preparations he could for the ferrying to start, a column of tanks and infantry was reported approaching. A short exchange of fire ensued before the Poles realised that the new arrivals were not German but British, although it was too late to avoid one of the tanks being knocked out by a Polish-laid mine. The newcomers were the 5th Duke of Cornwall's Light Infantry supported by a squadron of tanks of the 4th/7th Dragoon Guards. Together they had followed the route taken early that morning by the Household Cavalry, solid affirmation of the approach of 43rd Infantry Division. With these troops were two DUKWs – large amphibious vehicles – loaded with supplies for 1st Airborne Division.

The river crossing that Friday night was hardly a success, even though German fire from the far bank did little damage. A dozen battle-weary sappers had been pulled out of the firing-line at Oosterbeek to organise everything, and David Storrs, a tough field engineer subaltern, made the double crossing twenty-three times to ferry just twenty-three Poles over, an extraordinary physical feat at such a time, and one for which he was to be awarded a well merited Military Cross. By dawn, no more than fifty Poles had crossed the Neder Rijn. As for the DUKWs, the vehicles that might have tipped the balance, both had run off the slippery approach road on the south bank and bogged down. For the British in Oosterbeek, the disappointment could not have been more grievous, uplifted as they had been all day by the prospect of a large-scale crossing by 1 Polish Independent Parachute Brigade that night.

191

Of these fifty Poles, thirty-five were sent to reinforce the Border Regiment, but, as the Airlanding Brigade report put it, 'as they were not battle inoculated they did not dig satisfactory slit trenches and were quickly reduced to half by shelling'. Ever since the Poles had come under Browning's command in June, Sosabowski had represented that his brigade was only half-trained and not yet ready for action, protests that some British staff officers thought exaggerated, the consequence of Polish reluctance to become involved in costly fighting in Western Europe. It now seemed that Sosabowski's warning had been made with good cause.

CHAPTER TWENTY-ONE

'ABOUT THE BLACKEST MOMENT OF MY LIFE'

The arrival on Friday evening of 5th Duke of Cornwall's Light Infantry and the squadron of 4th/7th Dragoon Guards tanks in the area held by the Poles at Driel, encouraging as it was to everyone, concluded what had been for Horrocks two depressing days. 5th DCLI was a part of Essame's 214 Infantry Brigade, the leading unit of which, 7th Somerset Light Infantry, had failed to find its way to the railway bridge on the previous evening, lost in the traffic chaos of Nijmegen. This was a bitter disappointment to the senior officers of the brigade, who had hoped to see the flanking move around the west of Guards Armoured Division's line of advance start on Thursday. As it was, the Somersets did not begin to move across the Waal until dawn on Friday, following well behind the Household Cavalry, who had slipped off towards Driel under cover of the early morning mist.

The Somersets were not so fortunate. As the battalion approached the village of Oosterhout, one-and-a-half miles north-west of the Nijmegen railway bridge, enemy anti-tank and automatic fire pinned down its vehicles, strung out as they were in single file along the high bund, sitting targets, unable to turn around or drive off the embankment. The commander of the leading company was killed as he planned what next to do; unsuccessful attempts were then made to probe through the banks and ditches surrounding the village, which effectively concealed the German positions from the British troops. It was rather like being back once more in the thick Normandy *bocage*. Time slipped away, and it was only at midday that Essame decided that a deliberate attack was required in order to crush the enemy resistance. With the support of a medium regiment and a heavy battery of artillery, two troops of tanks, some heavy mortars, and the entire divisional artillery, the Somersets then captured Oosterhout at a cost of nineteen men wounded. In the smashed ruins of the village, 130 SS men were discovered, anxious to surrender, with a single SP gun and three tanks, one undamaged. By then it was 1630 hours.

This eventual success was brilliantly exploited, as has already been touched upon. Waiting behind the Somersets was 5th DCLI, ready to move. With the leading infantry companies travelling on top of the squadron of 4th/7th Dragoon Guards tanks and in the battalion's own armoured carriers, the ten miles to the Neder Rijn were covered in just thirty minutes. Lieutenant-Colonel George Taylor, the incisive commanding officer of the DCLI, had been surprised that the brigade had not begun to move forward towards Driel on Thursday evening, and had suggested the advance along the side roads as a possible manoeuvre to Horrocks when the two had met that same day. On Friday afternoon, 'tracks clanking, motors roaring' (as Taylor described the action), the vehicles drove through the mass of minor roads, the tank drivers finding the going in no way difficult. Watched by the cheering and shouting people of Valburg and the other villages through which they passed, the twin dangers of ambush and mines were ignored in the rapidly fading light. Except for a couple of German tanks about 1,000 yards away, to which Taylor turned a blind eye, no Germans were seen.

But, as the leading vehicles reached Driel, their occupants could hear the sound of battle behind them. Way back in the column of vehicles the British found themselves using the same road as five German Tiger tanks probing out of Elst. Fortunately the enemy tank crews were as disconcerted as Taylor's men, and did little damage to the column. The British company commander at the rear then correctly appreciated that the tanks were likely to return to Elst by the way they had come, and laid an ambush for them with mines and PIATs at a crossroads only 1,000 yards west of the enemy-held village. What followed was an object lesson in the vulnerability of tanks in the dark to determined infantry. Three of the Tigers were knocked out, and the other two ditched, to be abandoned by their crews. Boldness and cunning had been the mark of the DCLI's work that night, a tribute to their commander.

Colonel Taylor's first thought when he reached the Polish position was to turn east and make for the south end of the Arnhem road bridge. Mackenzie, however, discouraged him from doing so, explaining that there was now little, if any, hope that any part of 1st Airborne Division could still be fighting there. Without any boats, therefore, there was nothing for Taylor to do but to wait, a frustrating situation with the Allied troops around Driel now approaching in strength the numbers still fighting in Oosterbeek. Even more units of 43rd Division were on the way. By 2000 hours that night Essame's reserve battalion, the 1st Worcestershire Regiment, travelling in DUKWs behind the DCLI, had reached Valburg after a certain amount of confused fighting; over towards the south-east, 129 Infantry Brigade had also crossed the Waal during the late morning, although it had made no better progress up the main road than had the Guards, being short of artillery support, all of which had been concentrated for the attack by the Somersets. The brigade was, however, at least helping to keep the German defenders occupied.

There were, of course, DUKWs in plenty, which might have been used to ferry troops across the river. As well as those in which the Worcesters were travelling, more were in use carrying supplies forward to the DCLI, but these amphibious vehicles had their limitations. Besides being troublesome to manoeuvre on the narrow roads, they were also extremely difficult to drive across country, down to the river to be launched.

For three days now, the dogged resistance of Brigadefuehrer Harmel's SS troops, fighting in the Betuwe between Nijmegen and Arnhem, had slowed the pace of the British advance. From Friday onwards, the Germans further south were to display similar resilience. On the day before, Generalfeldmarschall Model had issued fresh orders to Generaloberst Student, instructing him to use his First Parachute Army to sever the Allied corridor at Veghel. To accomplish this, Student had the two Kampfgruppen. That to the west was under Major Huber and consisted of a regiment of 59th Infantry Division supported by some guns and Panther tanks; on

195

the east was Kampfgruppe Walther, completely reorganised and now lacking 6 Parachute Regiment, but including 107 Panzer Brigade with some extra infantry battalions and artillery.

General Maxwell Taylor's wisdom in encouraging the Dutch Resistance now produced further and valuable results. Successive reports from local civilians provided him with information about these two German troop concentrations, and he rightly surmised that their purpose was to cut 'Hell's Highway' somewhere in the region of Veghel or Uden, the former occupied on the Friday morning by only the reserve battalion of Colonel Johnson's 501 Parachute Infantry, and the latter quite bare of American troops. To counter the threat, Taylor had already ordered 506 Parachute Infantry to move to Uden from Son, where it was no longer needed because of the increasing pressure that British VIII and XII Corps were exercising on Student's army. The American troops were only just in time. At 1100 hours on Friday morning, the advance party of 506 Regiment, some 150 men, reached Uden, having driven through Veghel. A few minutes later the leading unit of Kampfgruppe Walther arrived in Uden as well. As the small body of men from 506 Regiment dodged from one house to another, displaying a façade of opposition so as to deter the attacking Germans in Uden, the main thrust of the Kampfgruppe crashed into Veghel. Fighting doggedly, the single battalion of 501 Regiment defending the village deflected this initial German attack, causing the tanks to sheer off to the north. There they cut the road south of Uden and then turned down the line of the highway back towards Veghel, destroying as they did so the halted British supply vehicles that lined the road.

More American troops were on the way. First into Veghel was the leading battalion of 506 Regiment, en route to Uden but destined to get no further for the time being, and close behind it came a battalion of 327 Glider Infantry. And, by a lucky chance, the artillery commander of 101st Airborne Division, Brigadier-General Anthony C. McAuliffe, was at hand, reconnoitring a new site for the Divisional Headquarters. As each unit arrived, some marching, others ferried in whatever trucks could be grabbed, McAuliffe seized them and thrust them into position. Weary as they were after five or six days of near continuous combat, the speed with which these troops reached Veghel on foot demonstrated both their physical toughness and their determination.

As the leading German Panther tanks edged back down the main road into Veghel from the direction of Uden, rounds from two American anti-tank guns smashed into them, discouraging the others for the time being, but at 1400 hours Kampfgruppe Huber swept in from the west to seize the bridge over the Willems Canal. As the Germans appeared, however, so did a squadron of 44th Royal Tanks and a company of 506 Regiment, which between them drove the enemy off. When other units of Kampfgruppe Huber swung down to cut the main road south of Veghel, they were quickly repelled by the other two battalions of 327 Glider Infantry Regiment coming up from the south. If Huber's Kampfgruppe had joined battle simultaneously with that of Walther, the outcome of this action might have been very different, but early that morning Huber's troops had hit the other two battalions of 501 Regiment as they drove through Schijndel, with the result that they were then compelled to take a circuitous route to Veghel and so lost valuable time.

It was fortuitous that these two battalions of 501 Regiment were in Schijndel, having completed at midnight the first phase of the pincer movement planned with 502 Regiment the day before to trap the Germans operating in the vicinity. With both the Americans and the Germans on the offensive together, it was hardly surprising that the fighting around Schijndel was just about as complicated as anything that had so far occurred in an extremely complicated battle. It began when one of Huber's battalions fought its way into the village at first light, but two hours later it had been ejected and the American pincer movement was able to continue. All went well until 1430 hours, when Colonel Johnson heard what was happening in Veghel, the place his regiment had been charged with defending. Abruptly abandoning his sweep, as difficult a military manoeuvre as can be conceived, he withdrew his two battalions towards Veghel, encumbered though they were with their own wounded and 250 German prisoners, not to mention 170 German wounded whom they were now compelled to abandon. With his force Johnson also took a number of the inhabitants of Schijndel who had given him assistance, and who could not be now abandoned to the SS troops. At about the same time, the two battalions of 502 Regiment, also hearing news of the German offensive against 'Hell's Highway', fell back towards St Oedenrode,

197

but only after losing Colonel Michaelis and several of his staff officers, all hit by splinters from a tree-burst. To calculate the profit-and-loss of this ambitious little action is not easy. The Americans lost some men, but the Germans far more. Possibly too few American troops were left to garrison Veghel, but, set against this, the thrust by Kampfgruppe Huber had been badly upset by the battle being fought in its rear.

The fighting around Veghel continued all day, but by nightfall the village and the road south of it were secure, with McAuliffe holding Veghel with a total force of six infantry battalions and two squadrons of British tanks; to the south-west, Johnson was occupying two other villages as outposts. In some way the successful fight for Veghel had been a rehearsal for 101st Airborne Division's defence of Bastogne three months later, a battle which was to make McAuliffe, temporarily in command of the division at the time, a household name in Britain as well as in America. To the north of Veghel, however, XXX Corps' main axis of advance was to stay cut, even though the small party of 506 Regiment in Uden succeeded in holding its own.

This gap in the artery of his corps, through which had to flow all the supplies and reinforcements needed for the battle ahead, threatened Horrocks's remaining hopes of relieving 1st Airborne Division and of forming a bridgehead across the Neder Rijn. Even more worrying, it endangered the very existence of the other three Allied divisions fighting north of the Maas, which had now been joined by 69 Infantry Brigade from 50th (Northumbrian) Division. A major disaster was impending. The severing of his supply line, allied to the desperate straits of 1st Airborne Division, the slow progress of 43rd Infantry Division, and the apparent daily arrival of fresh German reinforcements, made this, as Horrocks was to record, 'about the blackest moment of my life'. He was finding it hard to sleep, and he knew only too well that a commander who failed to do so soon became incapable of carrying out his job.

It was fortunate therefore that, on the Friday, German pressure against 82nd Airborne Division from the direction of the Reichswald had, at last slackened. Because of this, Horrocks was able to turn the Grenadier and Coldstream Groups of Guards Armoured Division around, directing their tanks and infantry back by the way they had come to open the road between Veghel and Nijmegen. For the luckless Grenadiers, who had been scouring Nijmegen for billets in which to recover and refit after the battering they had received on Tuesday and Wednesday, everything suddenly seemed to have gone sour (as their regimental historians put it) when they received these orders to drive straight back down the road up which they had laboured so hard. On the left of the Grenadiers, the Coldstream, relieved of their task of supporting 82nd Division on the Groesbeek Heights, were given as their objective the village of Volkel, lying a couple of miles south-east of Uden. Arriving too late to make a deliberate attack that night, the Guards took up positions ready to assault at first light. A little distance away, the Grenadiers had found Uden to be clear of Germans, but one of their patrols, scouting south towards Veghel, had run into trouble. Uden was an odd sight. Besides the detachment of 506 Regiment which had arrived in the nick of time to avert the village's capture, there were Allied supply lorries, trapped by the German activity, parked in every street. And a number of staff officers sat mournfully in their cars; to quote the Grenadier historians again, 'If they had been passengers on a Tube train stuck between two stations this odd assortment of stragglers from the British and American Armies could hardly have looked more annoyed.'

CHAPTER TWENTY-TWO

'HE WAS CERTAIN IN HIS OWN MIND THAT NO REINFORCEMENT COULD ARRIVE IN TIME ...'

On the morning of Saturday 23 September, using a pincer movement similar to the one they had employed the day before, the Germans made yet another attempt to capture Veghel and thereby strengthen their hold on XXX Corps' axis. 6 Parachute Regiment formed the western jaw of the pincers, replacing Kampfgruppe Huber, badly battered the previous day. However, this new German formation was thrust into the fighting weary after two days on the march, and, as its regimental commander was to complain, one of its battalions was a 'rotten apple', poorly led and disciplined. The other enemy formation involved in the attack also had problems. Even though the panzer brigade of Kampfgruppe Walther had been fighting and moving without respite ever since it had first attacked the highway at Son on Monday, it was obliged to form the eastern jaw of the pincer. Furthermore, Walther was now fighting with one eye looking over his shoulder: British VIII Corps had crossed the Willems Canal on Friday and was threatening his rear.

The result was that neither German attack was pushed very hard. The two outpost battalions of 501 Parachute Infantry in Veghel halted the attack from the west, and Walther broke off his eastern assault at about midday. For all that, fighting in places was savage, and US 101st Airborne Division both took and inflicted heavy casualties. By 1300 hours, however, it had become clear to Brigadier-General McAuliffe in Veghel that he had won the initiative, and he thereupon despatched two battalions of 506 Parachute Infantry to link up with the Grenadier Guards Group, which had begun to attack down the main road from the direction of Uden. Two hours later the Allies met, and traffic on the road started to flow once more. The disruption, which had lasted for twenty-four hours, was at an end. Somehow the enemy had just melted away, and the road had been opened, at a cost to the Grenadiers of ten men wounded in a patrol action to the east of the highway.

General Taylor, as was his way, had hoped for more than the opening of the road. During the morning he had despatched his reconnaissance unit on a hazardous journey through German-frequented country. The unit was to contact the Guards and suggest to their commanders a plan for trapping the Germans on the eastern flank between the American infantry and an encircling movement by the Guards. Afterwards, Taylor claimed that he had spent hours urging the officer in charge of his patrol to get the British moving and that, when they did so, they were painfully slow and declined to budge from the highway, thereby missing a great opportunity by failing to put his plan into effect. His judgement was perhaps a little harsh. The Coldstream, who were best able to carry out such a manoeuvre, being placed to the east of the Grenadiers, were to experience a hard day's fighting, and their infantry battalion, as with so many British units, was only two companies strong. Attacking towards Volkel on that Saturday morning, the Coldstream lost a number of tanks, and one of the infantry companies its two last surviving officers. It was to be afternoon before this village and its surrounding woods had been cleared of the enemy, by which time the Germans threatening the road had melted away.

More reinforcements for Browning's Airborne Corps were to arrive in Holland that Saturday. The weather, bad for four days (no supply or transport aircraft at all had been despatched for 'Market Garden' on Friday), now improved and 654 troop-carriers with 490 gliders flew in by the southern route. In yet another attempt to supply 1st Airborne Division, one in ten of the British aircraft were lost over the battle area, and the troops in Oosterbeek hardly

201

recovered anything at all. But against the twelve supply aircraft lost north of the Neder Rijn, the missions elsewhere were uniformly successful, only a single American C-47 being destroyed. Sosabowski's third Polish battalion, forced back to England by the weather on Thursday, dropped south of Nijmegen, a landing at Driel now being thought impracticable because of the fighting in the area. Gliders delivered the rest of 327 Glider Infantry, and the balance of the division's field artillery to 101st Airborne, and 82nd Airborne Division received its long-awaited 325 Glider Infantry. This regiment, so badly needed in the early stages of the battle, was even now a welcome reinforcement for Gavin's battle-weary troops, who, that afternoon, consolidated the eastern flank of Nijmegen by occupying the polderland lying between the hills at Beek and the River Waal.

That day, Saturday 23 September, opportunity had arisen to fly in and land either badly needed supplies or further reinforcements. Standing by in England was the British Airborne Forward Delivery Airfield Group (AFDAG), its task first to prepare and then to operate captured airstrips or airfields on which troop-carrying aircraft could land. Two miles north-west of Grave, at Oud Keent, a suitable grass airfield had been captured, and at 1025 hours on the 23rd Second Army had given Airborne Corps permission to use it for the landing of supplies, a far more efficient means of delivery than pushing the stores in bundles out of aircraft doors, or dropping them in containers by parachute. Nothing was to happen, however, even though XXX Corps had made a light anti-aircraft regiment available for the defence of the airfield. By then, Brereton had returned to his headquarters in England, where he was at hand for decisions such as this, but the AFDAG was not to be flown into Oud Keent until 26 September, the day 'Market Garden' was abandoned.

At Driel in the meantime, Mackenzie and Myers had been fully occupied, first in discovering just what was happening south of the Neder Rijn, and second in trying to ensure that Horrocks and Browning were left in no doubt as to the true situation at Oosterbeek. On the previous day they had found no means of reaching Nijmegen, but this problem was solved on the Saturday by the Household Cavalry, one of the two troop commanders offering to drive them from Driel back to Nijmegen by the way he had come, once again making full use of the cover provided by the early-morning mist. Soon after setting out, the small column of two scout and two armoured cars ran into a German half-track, an encounter that resulted in Mackenzie's armoured car toppling over into a ditch and the column of vehicles splitting; he and the crew were then to play hide-and-seek with the Germans in a turnip field before being rescued by a tank of the 4th/7th Dragoon Guards, the firing having been heard in Driel. When Mackenzie eventually caught up with Myers at Browning's headquarters, he was so weary, wet and shivering that a hot bath was produced to thaw him out before business could be discussed. But the visit seemed to Mackenzie to accomplish little. He doubted whether he had succeeded in persuading either of the two corps commanders of the seriousness of the plight of 1st Airborne Division – after all, messengers bearing ill tidings are usually thought to overstate their case. Worse, Urquhart's two officers were both disenchanted by what, rightly or wrongly, they saw as a lack of urgency both at XXX Corps Headquarters, and at 43rd Division, which they visited subsequently.

At the time, the problems facing 43rd Division were twofold: first a continuing shortage of assault boats, and secondly the strength of the German positions around Elst. As with Guards Armoured Division on the Thursday, 129 Infantry Brigade had failed to shift these SS troops outside Elst, and although the infantry were supported by the 13th/18th Hussars, the latter's tanks were unable to move off the road. As a result, Thomas decided to slip his reserve, 130 Infantry Brigade, around the side roads to Driel, thus releasing 214 Brigade to attack Elst from the east and eliminate this aggravating enemy presence. But it was late afternoon before 130 Brigade completed its move. The unwieldy DUKWs in which the troops were travelling slipped off the narrow embanked roads at sharp corners, and the Germans in Elst harried the column with artillery and tank fire, forcing the British battalions to deploy their mortars to put down a smoke screen, and their 6-pounders to neutralise the fire from the tanks. Only when the Valburg crossroads were clear of 130 Brigade's vehicles could 214 Brigade start to deploy its heavy weapons to support the attack on Elst. The subsequent and confused fighting among the village houses was to continue throughout that Saturday night and the Sunday as well.

130 Brigade had with it only some dozen assault boats, and in these the Poles were faced with the task of trying to get more of their troops

across the river into Oosterbeek, after the almost abortive attempt with the rubber recce boats on the night before. Stout-hearted the Poles may have been, but they were not easy to control, and General Sosabowski himself, to quote the 43rd Division historian, was 'the reverse of cooperative'. Myers, who had returned from Nijmegen late in the morning to assume charge of the crossing, was to have yet another busy night. A burning building lit the river, and German shelling and mortaring took their toll of the Poles trying to cross, but most accounts of the intensity of the enemy opposition have been somewhat highly coloured. Muddle rather than the Germans was the main enemy. By dawn, some 200 Poles in total had succeeded in crossing the river into Oosterbeek, but most of those assault boats still undamaged were then abandoned on the south bank of the river, where enemy fire destroyed the larger part on the next day. To control events had been beyond the power even of Myers. Given a few sappers, or even infantry, properly trained in watermanship to paddle the boats, it should have been possible to have got both Polish battalions across that night.

In Oosterbeek the agony had continued. Almost everywhere in the perimeter, Saturday was to prove to be the hardest day to bear. The weight of metal poured into the small area by the German mortars and guns seemed to be heavier than ever, and there were few anti-tank weapons of any type left to halt the German armour. During Friday night, Urquhart had wisely abandoned plans that had been made for the Border Regiment to attempt to retake the high ground at Westerbouwing. Everywhere men now crouched in their slit-trenches, their ears straining above the noise of the shelling for the German tanks, clanking towards them unrelentingly, the sound echoing ever nearer through the woods and the narrow suburban streets. Sometimes the German infantry would be behind the tank, sometimes ahead to be cut down by Bren and rifle fire just before the gross armoured monster juddered into sight, its long gun spitting smoke and flame as its gunner spotted the British position. Worse still was the sheet of burning liquid belched from a flame-throwing tank, the most terrifying weapon of all, and against which few men could bring themselves to stand firm.

But men did hold on, most now fatalistic. Their closest friends were dead, and death now seemed a certainty for them too. After a week, talk of relief by XXX Corps had degenerated into bitter mockery. Hope might have gone, but few contemplated the possibility of either surrender or retreat, and, in any case, there was nowhere to retreat to. For the majority it was sheer stubborn bloody-mindedness. They fought on as men do when faced by an enemy known to give no quarter, even though those who gave thought to the matter understood that most of the Germans were holding to the Geneva Convention and taking prisoners, SS troops though they might be.

More and more holes were torn in the thinly held perimeter as sections or platoons were annihilated, and through these gaps enemy snipers wormed their way, hiding in trees and attics to compound the dangers of the mortar fire for those whose duties forced them to move around in the open. Finding themselves surrounded, or nearly so, small bodies of soldiers turned themselves into hedgehogs, bristling in every direction, grim little centres of resistance between which no sizeable body of German troops ever succeeded in penetrating.

That day the Germans were to concentrate their greatest effort against the north of the perimeter. Here, in a rough half-circle, fought a company of the Borders, a detachment of glider pilots, the KOSB, a composite force based on the survivors of 156 Para and the Recce Squadron, and, last, 21st Independent Parachute Company. By nightfall, these units had hardly moved, despite repeated attacks. If, instead of hammering at the 'nail' of the thumb-shaped perimeter, the Germans had cut the 'thumb' off from its base by driving inwards from both flanks along the river bank, they would have succeeded in severing all contact between British 1st Airborne Division and the troops south of the river, tenuous though that contact was.

A very rough measure of the intensity of the fighting in Oosterbeek is given by a count of British soldiers who died there. It was not in the battalions of 1 Parachute Brigade, as might have been expected, that the greater number of men were killed, but in the units whose fighting was confined largely to the perimeter battle. The Border Regiment and the Glider Pilot Wings suffered the highest proportion of such losses; hard hit also was the Recce Squadron, of whose members one in five died, much the same as among the glider pilots. 4 Parachute Brigade, although it suffered its greatest casualties before it reached the perimeter, also had more men killed than its sister brigade.

Before Myers had left XXX Corps Headquarters on Saturday morning to return to Driel, he had been given to understand that if a large enough part of the Polish Brigade failed to get over the river during the night, the whole of 43rd Division would cross on the following one. Mackenzie had his doubts. That night, as Myers tried vainly for the second time to exercise control over the Polish crossing, Mackenzie was paddled back to Oosterbeek to report to his general. Urquhart described their conversation:

> He was torn between telling me what Horrocks and Thomas thought was going to happen, and the contrary view he held as a result of what he had seen and heard. He was certain in his own mind now that no reinforcement of any consequence could possibly arrive in time, and he chose to gloss over this interpretation and to give me the official picture which was rosier. It was not until years afterwards that I learned of Mackenzie's dilemma.

At 2020 hours that Saturday evening, a signal was received at Browning's headquarters from Second Army, giving permission for 1st Airborne Division to be withdrawn from Oosterbeek if the situation warranted; twenty minutes later a further message stated that 52nd (Lowland) Division would not be flown in without reference to Dempsey. Mackenzie's instinct, his doubts about a 43rd Division crossing, had indeed been sound, although no one in Nijmegen that morning had mentioned to him the possibility of his division being withdrawn. Except for the reopening of XXX Corps' main axis to traffic in the afternoon, nothing had happened that day to lighten the gloom around the various Allied headquarters grouped in the neighbourhood of Nijmegen. And, as we shall see, the road was not to remain open to traffic for long.

It was a time of sadness and frustration for Browning, powerless as he was to influence the battle in any way. US 101st Airborne Division had been under command of XXX Corps since it had arrived, there was nothing he could do to help Urquhart in Oosterbeek, and the Polish Brigade had been placed under command of 43rd Division, a logical decision, but one correctly foreseen by Mackenzie as likely to result in trouble between Sosabowski and Thomas. All Browning had left was US 82nd Airborne Division, effectively commanded by Gavin and now cut off from the main battle. Browning had, in fact, not been called upon to make any decision of consequence since Wednesday afternoon, D-plus-3, when he had rejected the offer from the commander of

52nd Division to fly in a brigade by glider to assist 1st Airborne Division.

As for Brereton, back in his headquarters after his trip to Europe, his ignorance of what was happening in Holland seemed to be near complete, if the entries in his diary are to be believed. On Friday he had been 'encouraged', so he wrote, by the copy of Browning's signal to 52nd Division, sent two days earlier, rejecting the offer of help. According to Cornelius Ryan, Brereton then signalled Eisenhower to the effect that the situation was showing much improvement. The next day, another entry in the diary recorded that *'Troops* [author's italics] and supplies were sent to hard-pressed 'Red Devils' ...'

CHAPTER TWENTY-THREE

'THE POSITION HELD BY THE AIRBORNE DIVISION HAD NO MILITARY VALUE'

By 24 September, the second Sunday of the battle, the Germans in Oosterbeek appeared much less inclined to brave the fire of the remains of 1st Airborne Division, although in several places round the perimeter, especially in the north, there was little let-up. Elsewhere, however, the effective fire-support from the medium guns on the south bank, now at Urquhart's call, was doing much to discourage the Germans. As Obersturmbannfuehrer Harzer, the commander of 9th SS Panzer Division, afterwards wrote, 'The more the perimeter shrank, the more stubbornly the British troops defended every heap of ruins and every inch of ground'.

Particularly inept, more of an amusement than an annoyance, were German attempts at psychological warfare. From the direction of their lines disembodied voices broadcast appeals to the 'Tommies' to surrender, dwelling upon the misery of their wives and families awaiting news of them, and the quality of the British rations dropped in the wrong place and now being enjoyed by their German recipients. Current songs, such as 'In the Mood' and 'One More River to Cross' lent light relief. As Harzer admitted, the appeals to surrender were met only by heavy artillery fire.

208

Rocket-firing Typhoons were at last helping to take some of the pressure off 1st Airborne Division. With the better weather, one or two had appeared over Oosterbeek on Saturday, and, with only a single small supply drop scheduled for Sunday, the opportunities for close-support aircraft to fly had been increased. In the absence of contact cars, the channels for calling for the support were, to say the least of it, involved, requests being channelled from 1st Airborne Division through 64th Medium Regiment, RA to Airborne Corps, and thence to Second Army, Second TAF and 83 Group, RAF. Then, without direct communications between the troops on the ground and the pilots, the support which the Typhoons could provide was limited, reluctant as the RAF was to engage area targets, tactics wasteful in resources and hazardous to friendly troops. However, the presence of these aircraft over the battlefield was still of inestimable value. Not only were the German mortarmen and gunners reluctant to man their weapons when the aircraft – fearsome-looking, with shark's head and jaws painted on the machine's nose – were overhead, but the effect on the morale of the airborne soldiers, given even a temporary respite from bombardment, was tremendous, especially so when they could observe and admire the precision of the pilots. But it was a tragedy that so many requests for support either failed to get through or were rejected when they did so. Close support for the Airborne Corps was provided on only five days – ninety-seven sorties being flown for US 82nd Division on the first Monday, 119 for US 101st Division on the Friday, the odd few for British 1st Airborne Division on the Saturday, followed by twenty-two sorties on the second Sunday and eighty-one on the Monday.

The news that only some 200 Poles, and not the whole brigade, had managed to cross the river and reach Oosterbeek was a further and cruel blow. Urquhart allocated most of the few who did arrive to Hackett, in order to strengthen the defences around the MDS crossroads, but as the brigadier was making arrangements for the Poles to be put into position, he was hit once more by mortar fire, this time in the stomach and leg, and seriously. Again, this had occurred as Hackett was moving about in the open, to all appearances unaware of the German fire, a habit which both aggravated and inspired those of his subordinates who found themselves in his company.

The evening before he was hit, Hackett had become involved in face-to-face negotiations with the Germans. An enemy officer appeared in a half-track under a Red Cross flag, to insist that, unless the British defending the area of the MDS crossroads moved back some 800 yards, the locality would be heavily mortared. This was a strange threat, since the crossroads had been under as heavy fire as anywhere else ever since the battle had started, but, confronted by what he saw as a direct threat to the hundreds of wounded packed into the Schoonoord and Vreewijk Hotels, Hackett felt bound to agree. He compromised, however, over the distance and withdrew only about 100 yards: to have pulled back the full 800 would have involved a retirement to the west of Divisional Headquarters at Hartenstein, a point he did not explain to the German.

Shortly after Hackett was hit, Colonel Graeme Warrack, the division's senior medical officer, advised Urquhart that an attempt should be made to persuade the Germans to evacuate the British wounded from Oosterbeek to hospitals in Arnhem and elsewhere. Early that morning, during the regular 'hate', a dressing-station had been set on fire and its 150 wounded occupants moved out, to sit or lie in the drenching rain, the bombs and shells bursting around them, tearing at their already overstretched nerves. In few of the dressing-stations was there any water; in some men lacked even a single blanket to cover them. More wounded were being hit again where they lay; more were dying despite the devotion of the weary doctors, orderlies and Dutch helpers. Three days before, Warrack had calculated that his men were trying to care for 1,200 wounded; by this second Sunday, the perimeter held two wounded men for every three still fit to fight. In the Schoonoord Hotel a German doctor told his British opposite number that he had served in almost every theatre, including Russia, but that this battle exceeded in ferocity anything he had known.

Protected by a Red Cross flag, and accompanied by Lieutenant-Commander Wolters, Urquhart's Dutch liaison officer (who wisely changed his name to Johnson for the trip), Warrack went down to the Schoonoord and explained to the young German doctor in charge, a Major Skalka, that he wanted to arrange for the wounded to be evacuated, and for the shelling and mortaring to be stopped while this was happening. Sympathetic to Warrack's suggestion, Skalka offered to drive the two men into Arnhem to discuss the proposal with his own commander. Without blindfolds, Warrack and Wolters were then driven down the Utrechtseweg, through the German positions, the road a two-mile stretch of smashed vehicles and bodies, broken houses and trailing wires.

Arriving at the enemy headquarters, Warrack received a warm welcome from the German staff officers. Soon Bittrich himself appeared, to agree straight away to the British proposals, at the same time offering what were, by this stage of the war, almost routine expressions of regret that British and Germans should be fighting one another. A drink was offered, but refused by Warrack on the grounds that it would make him drunk on an empty stomach, a remark that produced amusement, a plate of sandwiches, and a bottle of *eau-de-vie*. The two men were also able to fill their pockets with captured British morphia. Allowed to visit St Elizabeth Hospital on the return journey to Oosterbeek, Warrack was relieved to discover it intact; the British wounded were lying in beds between sheets, being cared for by Dutch nurses, and the British surgical teams were operating in proper conditions alongside the Germans and the Dutch.

Soon the evacuation of the wounded was under way, and the Germans slackened their fire while it was happening. There were, of course, misunderstandings: as soon as he returned, Warrack himself became a prisoner for a time when the Tafelberg group of buildings was invested by a company of German infantry. It also proved difficult to discourage the Poles at the MDS crossroads from shooting whenever they had a German in their sights. Soon, however, some 500 wounded men had been removed in what Urquhart described as 'a strange afternoon of not quite total war', and the following day many more were to be taken away to comparative safety. Among those evacuated was Hackett, his life to be saved in an operation carried out by a British surgeon. A German doctor advised that it would be a waste of time to do so: euthanasia was his answer to a head or stomach wound.

On Sunday 24 September, some of the hardest fighting was to occur forty miles south of Arnhem. There, at the hamlet of Koevering, just to the north of St Oedenrode, the Germans cut the road once again, only twenty-four hours after traffic had once more started to flow along it. The action began early in the morning when about 200 Germans with five tanks attacked the battalion of 501

Parachute Infantry holding the village of Eerde, just south of Veghel. A squadron of 44th RTR, sent forward to help the Americans, lost three of its tanks in rapid succession, and bloody infantry fighting among the sand-dunes, much of it hand-to-hand, lasted most of the morning. Although the German attack in this area was halted, just before nightfall a fresh and fanatical Jungwirth battalion established itself astride the road to the south of Koevering. Two companies of 502 Parachute Infantry, rushed up from St Oedenrode, were beaten back, and some more British tanks were destroyed. Despite heavy pounding by British and American artillery, the enemy's 6 Parachute Regiment fed in more infantry, tanks and SP guns during the night. It was the most serious assault on the highway to date, the German prizes twofold. Success would not only cut off the large British forces to the north of the gap in the road, but would also re-open the line of retreat of German Fifteenth Army from western Holland towards the Reich.

Model had reshaped his command on the day before, making Student responsible for all operations on the east flank of the Allied advance and Fifteenth Army for everything on the west. This change, combined with the steady pressure British VIII Corps was now exercising north of the Zuid Willems Canal in the general direction of Nijmegen, was the reason why 6 Parachute Regiment's attack had not been supported by a similar movement from an easterly direction, the threat to Kampfgruppe Walther's rear now being serious and its commander further concerned by an inaccurate report that fresh Allied paratroops had dropped at Uden on Saturday. On the Allied side, control of operations in this area was now much simpler: VIII Corps had been made responsible for the protection of the whole of 'Hell's Highway' as far north as Grave, and under its command were now both 101st Airborne Division and 50th (Northumbrian) Division, the latter with one of its two remaining brigades (69 Infantry Brigade had been detached to Nijmegen) south-east of St Oedenrode and the other moving forward to take over the area south-east of Veghel.

Among those who had been trapped south of Veghel by the latest German attack on the highway was Horrocks, summoned on the Sunday morning to meet General Dempsey, his army commander, at St Oedenrode. Before setting out, Horrocks had examined the battleground north of the Neder Rijn from the exposed vantage

Maj-Gen Stanislaw Sosabowski, commanding Polish Independent Parachute Brigade. 'A hero to his men, and most of the British officers with whom he worked both liked and admired him. On the other hand, he was far from being an easy subordinate.'

The Polish Parachute Brigade parades with its colours. For all that it suffered at Arnhem, the brigade was never to see Warsaw, as its commander had so ardently hoped, and was disbanded after the war.

British armour on a Dutch road, 22 September. Even now it might have been possible to link up with 1st Airborne, and transfer troops across the Neder Rijn into the Arnhem bridgehead. The vehicle at right is an SP gun on a Sherman chassis.

Air re-supply to 1st Airborne was a nightmare of shattered hopes – most of the material fell into the enemy's hands, and many aircraft were damaged or lost. Stirling bombers photographed from Arnhem.

Sometimes supplies got through to the perimeter. Men from 1st Airborne carrying ammunition, with one of the supply baskets in the background.

In the perimeter, the men made desperate attempts to attract the supply pilots' attention. British paratroops waving their celanese identification panels just west of the Hartenstein.

By 22 September, there was at last help from outside for the airborne soldiers. 64th Medium Regiment, RA, in action in support of 1st Airborne from its position near Nijmegen. This unit's accurate shelling did much to break up German attacks on the perimeter.

A 6-pounder anti-tank gun in action in the perimeter. By now, most of the anti-tank guns had been destroyed, and PIAT ammunition was virtually exhausted – still the German armour was held at bay.

One of 1st Airborne's air-transportable 75-mm howitzers in action. Sheriff Thompson's men and guns formed a vital part of the perimeter defence.

The Hartenstein Hotel, 23 September. British troops taking advantage of a lull to clean weapons and brew up. In the background are the tennis courts where the German prisoners were kept.

'Thou shalt not be afraid for the terror by night . . .' A wounded paratroop is carried off for attention, the perimeter, 24 September. The wounded man's face has been scratched off the photograph by the Official Censor.

'. . . Nor for the arrow that flieth by day'. German soldiers and SPs attacking along the Utrechtseweg towards Oosterbeek.

Outside the Vreewijk Hotel at the MDS crossroads, early in the battle, where German and British medical teams laboured together, and buildings changed hands all the time. Captured British glider pilots and paratroops with a German SP gun.

The end for many men from 1st Airborne Division – haggard, dirty, exhausted, 'withdrawn but undefeated'. The Germans, said Frost, 'were kind, chivalrous and even comforting'.
Some of the lucky ones – 1st Airborne soldiers who escaped across the Neder Rijn on the night of 25 September. Of 10,000 or so men of the division who had flown into battle, 1,400 were dead and more than 6,000 were prisoners.

The unofficial monument to British 1st Airborne Division, set up near Oosterbeek after the liberation of Holland. It is made from shell-cases, supply canisters, helmets, rifles, and a 6-pounder anti-tank gun.

'A tale you will tell your grandchildren . . .' The commemorative ceremony in Oosterbeek, September 1946. The tradition of children laying flowers upon the graves was revived in 1981, after a break of about 10 years.

'We have no regrets' – the concluding words of General Urquhart's report on British 1st Airborne Division's battle for Arnhem. Taken as Urquhart landed in England after 'Market Garden'.

point of the Driel church tower. With him had been General Thomas, George Taylor, the commanding officer of the DCLI, and Myers, 1st Airborne Division's senior sapper. Both the British lieutenant-colonels remember how very weary Horrocks appeared, and Myers has described his own bitter disappointment when he learned that, far from the whole of 43rd Infantry Division crossing to Oosterbeek that night, only a single brigade was to be sent to the assistance of 1st Airborne Division; later that day, he discovered that the force had been whittled down to but one battalion of British troops, and the rest of the Polish Brigade.

Horrocks has described the orders he issued to Thomas and Sosabowski that morning before he left the Betuwe. At least one battalion of 43rd Division would cross the river, as would the Poles, and as much as possible in the way of stores, especially ammunition, would be taken. At the same time Thomas's forces were to reconnoitre further to the west with a view to side-slipping his division across the Neder Rijn if the night crossing went well; having achieved this, 43rd Division would carry out a left hook against the Germans in the direction of the western side of the airborne perimeter. Writing his account of the events twenty-five years earlier than Horrocks, Major-General Essame, the 43rd Division historian and the commander of 214 Brigade at the time, remembered differently:

> Lieut.-General Horrocks faced the facts. The position held by the airborne division had no military value. It was merely a nebulous area ... He [Horrocks] therefore instructed 43 Division to carry out the evacuation ... The final decision was reached at a conference at headquarters, 43 Division, on the morning of the 24th.

Essame then discusses how the object of the crossing that night had been to obtain a firmer grip on the far bank in order to facilitate the withdrawal.

Later that day Thomas gave Myers, who was to cross the river with the Poles that night, a letter for Urquhart, a copy of which he entrusted to one of the company commanders of the 4th Dorsetshire Regiment, the battalion chosen for the assault crossing. The letter explained that Second Army had decided that a bridgehead was not now to be formed west of Arnhem, and that Urquhart's division was to be withdrawn at a date to be agreed between him and Thomas. The code-word for the planned withdrawal, 'Berlin', might perhaps have been better chosen.

It does appear that, after the lapse of time, Horrocks's memory of events may have been faulty. Thomas is unlikely to have misunderstood his instructions about such a vital matter: he was a particularly precise officer, one whose career was to culminate in the post of Quartermaster-General to the Army.

The atmosphere at Horrocks's orders group at Driel that morning had hardly been cordial. Sosabowski, whose 1st Battalion was to reach him that day from Nijmegen, took the greatest exception to Thomas detailing it by name to cross the river that night, the same mistake that Hicks had made with Hackett six days earlier. Within his rights, and knowing as he did the condition and positions of his units, Sosabowski retorted 'Excuse me General, but *one* of my battalions selected by *me* will go there'. Thomas's subsequent snubbing of the Polish general was hardly conducive to happy Allied relations. Matters deteriorated even further when Sosabowski declared, after hearing the plan, 'I am General Sosabowski. I command the Polish Parachute Brigade. I do as I like.' To this Horrocks retorted, 'You are under my command. You will do as I bloody well tell you.' Sosabowski, meeting his match, capitulated gracefully with the words 'All right. I command the Polish Parachute Brigade and I do as you bloody well say'. He was not a person to bear malice, but this little affray did not discourage him from complaining forcefully to Browning, whom he visited at Nijmegen later in the day, that, if ambulances could reach Driel to evacuate the wounded, so could adequate river-crossing equipment.

The attempt to get help to 1st Airborne Division that night was to prove a costly failure. All that could go wrong did. Two lorries carrying assault boats took the wrong turning into the enemy lines at Valburg, and two more slipped off the muddy road into a ditch. The fifth, when it did arrive, was found to contain nine boats but no paddles. With so few boats now available, the crossing by the Poles was cancelled, and the few of their craft that had survived from the previous night were transferred to the Dorsets. As a result, it was 0100 hours on the morning of Monday 25 September before the Dorsets were able, at long last, to pick up their boats and start to hump them down through the mud to the water's edge. Despite a steady pounding by every British gun and mortar available, the Germans managed to reply in kind. Some boats were sunk; more were swept downstream by the rapid current. Embarked in successive waves were 350 men, but only seventeen officers and 298 other ranks reached the far bank. Those who managed to do so were faced by the high, wooded Westerbouwing escarpment, down which the Germans pitched grenades on top of them. A handful only reached the airborne perimeter, the rest being scattered in the thick woods. Equally unsuccessful was the attempt to get six supply-laden DUKWs over the river. Only three of them managed to enter the water, and these stuck in the mud on the north bank of the river. It had all been very gallant, but quite useless. Another infantry battalion had been destroyed, with nothing gained.

But even if boats and bridging material had been available to get more men and weapons across the Neder Rijn, it would have been to no avail. The entire Allied force in the sixty-mile-deep salient stretching north from the Meuse-Escaut Canal was now engaged with the enemy. Half of Guards Armoured Division, backed by 69 Infantry Brigade, was protecting the east flank in the Betuwe and still endeavouring to capture Bemmel village, only two miles north-east of Nijmegen. Around Elst, 129 Infantry Brigade was still butting the southernmost defences of the village, in which 214 Infantry Brigade was fighting a grim house-to-house battle, one which was to last until Monday afternoon and which had already cost the lives of two company commanders. South of the Waal, the Grenadier and the Coldstream Groups were still fully employed. During the Monday, the Grenadiers were to parry yet another threat to the road, this time from the direction of s'Hertogenbosch: in a hard two-day battle for Heesch, seven miles north-west of Uden, they were to destroy a German battalion, capturing 300 prisoners, but it was to cost their already depleted infantry yet another fifty-four casualties. And it was to take the most sizeable effort to date to open the road at Koevering, further to the south. 506 Parachute Infantry, which had reached Uden only on Sunday evening, was turned round and began to march south again at 0300 hours on the Monday, in the pouring rain. Directed by 50th Division, a borrowed brigade of 7th Armoured Division was moved up from Eindhoven in two columns, one directed on Schijndel and one along the main road. Although 506 Regiment was supported by the ubiquitous 44th RTR, its advance was halted by well directed fire from infantry, artillery and dug-in tanks. By dark on Monday, however, the pressure from the British moving in from the south began to be felt, and the Germans pulled out. They had gone by dawn on the following day, leaving the road heavily mined, but it was much later on Tuesday before traffic began to move. By then, however, an alternative route had been opened to the east of the main highway, along which a column of 500 vehicles of XXX Corps was passed during the day.

Throughout western Holland, the Germans had, in fact, demonstrated how well they could react to any major threat upon a battlefield.

CHAPTER TWENTY-FOUR

'THE NIGHT WAS MADE FOR CLANDESTINE EXITS'

Among those swept downstream with the Dorsets on Sunday night was Myers, in the pocket of his airborne smock the letter General Thomas had addressed to Urquhart. Myers arrived at the north bank eventually, but to reach the airborne perimeter he had to splash through the water in the lee of the river bank, a hazardous and exhausting journey for an already weary man. Just before dawn, however, he was handing the letter to his divisional commander. With it was another from Browning, given to Myers on Saturday before he left Nijmegen for Driel. Part of it read:

> You can rest assured that XXX Corps are doing their maximum under the most appalling difficulties to relieve you ... the road has been cut between us and the main body for 24 hours, which does not help matters much. It is now through again, and the Army is pouring to your assistance but, as you will appreciate better than I, very late in the day ...
>
> I naturally feel, not so tired and frustrated as you do, but probably almost worse about the whole thing than you do ...
>
> ...
>
> It may amuse you to know that my front faces in all directions, but I am only in close contact with the enemy for about 8000

yards to the south-east, which is quite enough in present circumstances.

The ever-reticent General Urquhart has not revealed the extent of his amusement.

Two hours after Myers arrived, Urquhart signalled Thomas to confirm that Operation 'Berlin' would take place that night. Urquhart could ask no more of his men. There was no point in doing so anyway now it had become clear that XXX Corps was not capable of crossing the river in strength. By 1030 hours on Monday 25 September, Urquhart had explained how the withdrawal was to be carried out to his senior officers, some of whom had reached his headquarters only after an alarming daylight sprint across the by-then sniper-dominated lawns of the Hartenstein Hotel.

Confusion still reigns as to the timing of the decision to withdraw 1st Airborne Division. Horrocks has described how the decision was made at 1000 hours on Monday 25 September, in consultation with Browning, after he had completed the dangerous cross-country journey back to his tactical headquarters in Nijmegen from St Oedenrode, escorted by a carrier platoon of the Durham Light Infantry. This matches the entry in Dempsey's War Diary for Sunday 24 September which read:

> Met Cmdr 30 Corps at St Oedenrode. Contact with 1st Airborne Div. Depending on next 24 hours 30 Corps on night 25/26th will either; (a) Pass complete Bde. of 43 Div across river, West of Arnhem, and build a bridge, and establish bridgehead; (b) Withdraw 1st Airborne Div. South of Rhine and give up bridgehead.

Montgomery was also in the dark as to what was happening. That same Sunday evening, 24 September, he had signalled the CIGS:

> If we suffer heavy casualties tonight in trying to get across (tricky business because we have not a wide front or sufficient troops) I shall probably give it up and withdraw 1 AB. Decision will be taken to-morrow morning. It may well be that we can attain our object equally if not better by developing thrust from lines eastwards and we shall have greater resources for these if we abandon attempt to cross the Neder Rijn west of Arnhem.

Assuming that Thomas did not misinterpret the instructions he had received from Horrocks at Driel on the Sunday morning, the fact that he and Urquhart had been instructed to decide between them when 1st Airborne Divison should withdraw (the basis of Thomas's letter to Urquhart sent on Sunday) would seem either to have been forgotten or ignored.

It was somewhat ironic that, just as the senior British commanders were finally admitting defeat, Model was reporting to his senior, von Rundstedt, that in a continually deteriorating situation he had for the past week been able to do no more than delay the enemy; he needed, at the very least, a minimum reinforcement of an infantry and a panzer division, a panzer brigade, two assault gun battalions, together with ammunition and infantry replacements.

Promotion examinations can have their value. When, as a young officer, Urquhart had been faced with his, he had studied the classic withdrawal from Gallipoli. Early on Monday morning, as he pondered upon his plan for the delicate and chancy operation facing his division, the details of the 1915 withdrawal down from the hills and across the beaches to the boats came back to him. The quiet thinning-out of the forward positions, the façade of resistance maintained until the very end, the elaborate care taken to organise the move: these were the principles which had succeeded against the Turks at Gallipoli, and which were now to guide him. Much, however, might happen during the coming day to upset what could only be an extremely complicated plan.

It was fortunate that the scale of the German attacks lessened a little during Monday. For all that, the gun positions were penetrated during the morning, clearly in an attempt to cut the British off from the river, but the Germans were pushed back with the help of the remaining 75-mm pieces, manhandled to fire over open sights at ranges down to fifty yards. In the north, the mixed bag of units based on the remains of 156 Para, harassed by SP guns and finding that both flanks were in the air, was given permission to pull back to the line of houses north of the Utrechtseweg. Elsewhere, snipers continued to infiltrate and establish themselves within the perimeter, and a larger party of enemy managed to set up a machine-gun in the woods some 300 yards south of the Hartenstein, so placed that it severed one of Urquhart's planned withdrawal routes. This German post was, however, eliminated by the medium artillery, firing at a range of 15,000 yards, and directed from a high roof on the north side of the target, just about as bold and as accurate a shoot as the Royal Regiment can ever have attempted. Scrappy fighting still continued everywhere. In one house there might be a few British soldiers; next door they would suddenly discover a party of Germans, Sometimes a PIAT fired through a window would settle the matter, but grenade and submachine-gun were the usual weapons in these bloody little struggles, most of them unrecorded.

All the time enemy mortar and shell fire smashed into the perimeter, filling once again the spaces in the dressing-stations made empty by the removal of the wounded into Arnhem. As Harzer later recalled, by this second Monday Model was still insisting on the liquidation of *Der Kessel*, but so as to limit German losses the Generalfeldmarschall had agreed that heavy artillery fire should be used to provide the coup-de-grâce for what had been a crack British division, the survivors of which were still resisting so doggedly.

South of the river, the staff of 43rd Infantry Division were making equally thorough preparations for the success of the coming operation. In one respect, however, they were working in the dark, for nothing was known of the fate of the Dorsets, all communications having failed. But the promised craft had arrived, sixteen assault and twenty-one storm boats for each of the two crossing sites, the former manned by two divisional field companies of the Royal Engineers, and the latter by Canadian sappers. Routes down to the river were taped, matching those Urquhart's men had laid out through the Hartenstein grounds. Thomas hoped that the weight of his fire support – all the guns of XXX Corps, as well as his own artillery and machine-guns – would mislead the Germans into thinking that a further and larger attempt was being made to reinforce Oosterbeek, rather than that British 1st Airborne Division was being withdrawn. To compound this hoped-for deception, a motley column of armoured and unarmoured vehicles, including some bridging lorries, was ordered to simulate, as dusk approached, preparations for a river-crossing just east of Renkum. Here the river bank was held by the Reconnaissance Regiment of 43rd Division, and not by an armoured brigade, as stated by some authorities, an error that suggests the presence of more powerful forces near the Neder Rijn than were in fact there.

As Urquhart remembered, 'The night was made for clandestine exits', dark with an inky sky, strong winds and persistent rain. It was the first stroke of good fortune the airborne division had experienced. To deceive the enemy further, wounded men, unable to walk, transmitted spurious radio traffic or fired their weapons from otherwise deserted positions. Helped by the weather, the ruses succeeded. Although the Germans heard the outboard motors of the storm boats, it was not until midnight, three hours after the crossing had started, that they realised that the British were abandoning their bridgehead.

At 0230 hours on Tuesday morning, the last few men left their posts and started down towards the river. These were military police, who had volunteered to stay until the end to ensure that the prisoners remained confined within their tennis-court compound, to prevent them from giving the game away to their fellow Germans. At the same time the small quantity of ammunition still remaining was blown up, and the gunners removed their breech-blocks and sights to dump them in the river.

The medical staff stayed behind. When Warrack had reported to Urquhart at 0800 hours on the Monday morning to give his general the latest news on the evacuation of the wounded, he learned that the division was to pull out that night, but that his own officers and men would stay, as would the chaplains. With hundreds of wounded men still lying within the perimeter, many in dire need of proper treatment, there was no alternative. That night, as they went about their work, the doctors, orderlies and chaplains listened to the din of the withdrawal, aware that some at least of their friends were on their way to safety.

As dawn broke over the Neder Rijn, some hundred men were still waiting on the north bank of the river, they and their boats now exposed to the full force of aimed enemy fire. A young Canadian officer made the last two crossings, carrying loads of lifebelts. On the first of the journeys, five of his passengers were wounded. On the second, everyone in the boat was hit, some fatally. There was no more to be done.

Among the 2,398 officers and men who were ferried across or who swam the river that night were 160 Poles and seventy-five Dorsets; 1,741 were members of 1st Airborne Division and 422 were glider pilots. Of the 10,000 or so officers and men who had been flown into the battle, 1,400 were dead and over 6,000 were prisoners of war, about one third of them wounded, although no accurate count was ever made. Many of those brought out were also wounded, some hit as they made their way to the boats. Each of the two parachute brigades had returned about a company strong; the Airlanding Brigade numbered less than a weak battalion.

At the end of his after-action report on 'Market Garden', Urquhart wrote 'We have no regrets'. Forty years have passed, but the author has met no one who fought there who disagrees with his general's verdict.

CHAPTER TWENTY-FIVE

'IN THE YEARS TO COME ... NO ONE WILL REMEMBER THAT TWO AMERICANS DIVISIONS FOUGHT THEIR HEARTS OUT IN THE DUTCH CANAL COUNTRY'

Immaculate as ever, 'Boy' Browning addressed the survivors of 1st Airborne Division in their Nijmegen billets on the afternoon of 27 September, the day after they had arrived in the city. The turn-out of Browning's audience almost approached that of their commander. Their boots had been polished, their cap-badges gleamed, and they wore their best battle-dress, which had travelled in their transport by sea and road to meet them.* Except for their treasured airborne smocks, the filthy and often blood-stained garments in which they had fought had been thrown away.

---

* To the aggravation of the drivers, this transport and its contents was ordered to remain in Holland for the use of other units. For some of these men who had driven their vehicles up 'Hell's Highway', the temptation was too much. To the Nijmegen people the stores were priceless, and not a few of the drivers managed to conclude advantageous bargains, so making a small contribution to the rehabilitation of the Netherlands.

Browning, almost broken by the failure, had confided to a member of his staff that he could hardly face the task of speaking to his men. Nevertheless, he could talk to soldiers in language they could understand, and no trace of his anguish at the destruction of the division he had raised and trained was apparent when he told them, in a few plain words, what they wanted to hear, above all that they were to be flown back to the United Kingdom without delay. They would not have been altogether surprised if they had been pitched straight back into the battle. They had flown into Holland convinced that the capture of Arnhem would be no more than the first stage of a lengthy campaign; it had happened to airborne troops in Tunisia and again in Normandy, and there was no reason why the pattern should not be repeated. But, hardly able to believe their good fortune, by the Saturday night, 30 September, the survivors were back in England, starting on the grim task of compiling the casualty lists and coping with the fearful wives, mothers and girl-friends who knocked on the billet doors or telephoned, pleading for news. The decision to bring the remnants of the division back to England had been wise: Urquhart was not alone in remembering 'the incredible lassitude' which he shared with others, and which was to persist for weeks to come.

The Poles were not quite so fortunate, the Americans much less so. The former, who had lost one in four, were marched back the fourteen miles to Nijmegen, at first under mortar fire, and were then used for guard duties and patrolling for ten days. They too then returned to England. 1 Polish Independent Parachute Brigade was never to see Warsaw.

As always there was a shortage of infantry, with the result that the two American airborne divisions stayed. US 82nd Airborne Division had already lost 1,432 men during the course of 'Market Garden', and 101st Airborne Division even more, a total of 2,100 casualties. Before the two divisions were finally withdrawn from the battle in the second half of November, these figures had been doubled; among those killed was Colonel Howard R. Johnson, who had led 501 Parachute Infantry ever since it was formed. With such a vast salient carved out of Holland, one that was too large for the entire British Second Army to hold securely, it was understandable that Montgomery clung on to these two fine American divisions for as long as he could. Thus, for two months, they fought on under

British command and ate British rations – an unhappy combination in their view, although the American distaste for the solid British 'compo' was equalled by the dislike of their allies for the American rations. Huddled in trenches into which the water seeped if they dug down more than three feet, the American airborne soldiers experienced the routine misery and danger of infantry divisions in the line. It had happened to them before in Normandy, but there they had not stayed so long and the weather had been better. Hardest of all was life in 504 Parachute Infantry, where Tucker prohibited cooking fires and greatcoats in the front-line foxholes.

Within a week of 1st Airborne Division's return, Brereton was recording in his diary his grave concern at Twenty-First Army Group's retention of his two divisions. He protested to Eisenhower, and Eisenhower protested to Montgomery, but the Supreme Commander did not press his ally too hard, aware as he was of British manpower shortages and the need to secure the seaward approaches of Antwerp so that the port could be brought into use, now the primary task of Montgomery's Twenty-First Army Group. Only when that job had been completed, and the convoys had begun to sail up the Scheldt, were these two American divisions released to rest and refit for their next airborne role.

American resentment at the retention of the two airborne divisions in Holland was aggravated by the lack of publicity given to their share in 'Market Garden'. With British newsmen typing their copy in slit-trenches around Hartenstein and passing their stories back by way of the BBC radio, the British press and wireless had been able to carry magnificent first-hand descriptions of the feats of 1st Airborne Division, stories repeated by the American press without any mention of US 82nd and 101st Divisions. Some American officers blamed the British, accusing Montgomery of deliberately playing down the American side of the battle in his attempt to present Arnhem as a victory, a charge which has yet to be proved. It was an unhappy business. 82nd Airborne Division in particular was to look back on Nijmegen as its most difficult battle of the war, and Gavin has complained, and with some justice, that 'there has been lasting discontent over the historical record of the Americans in "Market Garden".' As Brereton forecast, with almost complete accuracy:

In the years to come everyone will remember Arnhem, but no one will remember that two American divisions fought their hearts out in the Dutch canal country and whipped hell out of the Germans.

As the German tanks moved into Oosterbeek on Tuesday morning, their crews took few chances, slamming shells into any building which they feared might still contain their enemy, to the terror of the British wounded lying in the aid posts and dressing-stations. Then into the chaos of wrecked jeeps and guns, of shattered buildings and sprawling corpses, came the German infantry and with them Colonel Warrack, coolly searching for wounded men among the debris, explaining his presence when challenged by surprised German soldiers, and arranging for the evacuation of the hundreds of wounded still remaining in the perimeter. Thirty-six ambulances were produced by the Germans to remove the injured to a barracks in Apeldoorn. Here, three days earlier, captured British medical staff had started to organise a hospital; short as the Germans were of food and medical supplies, even for their own wounded, they did what they could to help.

Hiding in the woods and cellars in and around Arnhem and Oosterbeek were over 200 airborne officers and men; some of them, for one reason or another, had been separated from their units during the fighting, some of them were wounded who had managed to escape from German-held hospitals. A few of these evaders hoped to be rescued by advancing Allied troops, but most realised that their main hope of freedom lay in crossing the Neder Rijn and finding their way back to the Allied lines. To chronicle the adventures of these men is beyond the scope of this book, but a few should be mentioned. Brigadier Lathbury, recovering from temporary paralysis, just walked out of St Elizabeth Hospital on the night that the remnants of 1st Airborne withdrew. Making his way to the ruins of Johannahoeve, he then joined others whom Dutch people were feeding and sheltering. Brigadier Hackett, recovering from his abdominal operation in the same hospital (where Lathbury had been told that his colleague's chances of survival were 50 per cent), was taken to a waiting car by members of the Dutch Resistance, his bandages hidden under civilian clothes, and removed in broad daylight to a house in Ede where four Dutch ladies, three of them elderly, were to nurse him back to near health. Warrack, deciding that he was free to escape when less than 100 wounded men still remained in the Apeldoorn hospital (the rest having been removed to prisoner-of-war camps in Germany), hid himself for fourteen days in the cupboard of his room, from which in due course he slipped away, also to find refuge with a Dutch family. Another evader was Major Tony Deane-Drummond of the Signal Regiment. Finding himself with 1 Para, after the final attempt by that battalion to reach the bridge, he had hidden himself with four other men in the lavatory of a German-occupied house. He then swam the Neder Rijn, but was captured and held in a large house near Velp; there he also concealed himself in a cupboard, in which he stood for thirteen days before escaping into the care of yet another gallant Dutch family. It was not the first time he had done this sort of thing: taken prisoner after the parachute raid in February 1941 against the Tragino aqueduct in southern Italy, he had managed to escape back to England through Switzerland.

To those who spent the war in the armed forces, the cold courage of these Dutch people (and of those of so many other people in other countries) who succoured Allied troops in this way is beyond understanding. If discovered, they risked not only certain death and probable torture themselves, but also the lives of their families. Often they fed their guests on the little food they had to keep their wives and children alive. Perhaps only those who have experienced a brutal occupation can understand what sustains such heroism.

There was then a double incentive to rescue these airborne soldiers from occupied Holland: a number of highly skilled individuals would be recovered, and an intolerable burden would be removed from their Dutch hosts. To accomplish this task, members of MI9, the British organisation responsible for the rescue of evaders, were parachuted into Holland to work with members of the Dutch Resistance, now a better co-ordinated and more effective organisation than it had been earlier in the war. Helping also was the Belgian SAS party that had parachuted in before 'Market Garden' had started. On 22 October, the first group of 138 British soldiers and four American airmen, among them Brigadier Lathbury, was brought back across the river. Although it was a well disciplined body, led by competent officers, the three-mile approach march to the river posed problems, following as it did a circuitous route through thick woods in order to avoid the German positions.

227

Hitches there were, and serious ones, but in the end storm boats manned by Colonel Sink's 506 Parachute Infantry ferried the men back to safety. It had been a chancy operation. In Lathbury's pocket was Hackett's detailed report on the operation, recommendations for gallantry awards, and his personal mail, some of it to officers of his brigade whom he had somehow learned had survived the battle.

A second party, a month later, was not so fortunate. The earlier success had received too much publicity, and the Germans were anticipating another attempt. The numbers were much the same, but the circumstances were very different. Because the Germans had strengthened their riverside defences, the by-now unfit men faced a sixteen-mile approach march; the party also contained a larger number of aircrew than before, and several Dutch Resistance workers, including women. It was a heterogeneous body with which to undertake a night operation that would have taxed the best-trained infantry company. German patrols intercepted the party, a number were killed and only seven escaped over the river. It had been a disaster, although the attempt had been necessary. Warrack was among those who evaded capture, one of the few who managed to do so. In the company of Hackett, he finally succeeded in getting away in February. For the brigadier, it involved a journey by bicycle and canoe half-way round Holland, an arduous undertaking for a man still far from fit.

Life had been hard enough for the Gelderland Dutch even before the Allied invasion. After it was over, the German need for strong defences along the Neder Rijn to counter any further Allied thrust accorded well with their zest to revenge themselves on a people who had welcomed their seeming liberators with such enthusiasm and help. Many of the inhabitants of Arnhem and Oosterbeek had left their homes in the early days of the battle, but on 23 September the Germans ordered everyone out of the area, young and old, sick and maimed. When Mrs ter Horst emerged from her cellar on the morning of Tuesday 26 September, the Germans were starting to clear her house of British wounded. After spreading a waterproof cape over the naked body of a soldier lying just outside her door, she brought her children up and loaded a few possessions on to a hand-cart. Then, with her baby and two smaller children tucked among the bundles, she walked away, the two older ones by her side, to join the long, sad and weary column of refugees trailing out into the countryside, wet, cold and hungry. Within thirty-six hours, 100,000 wretched people had left their homes, most of them walking in the direction of Apeldoorn.

The Germans then proceeded to divide the city and its suburbs into areas and loot them systematically, one lorry collecting sewing-machines, another radios, and yet another household linen. The goods were then carried away to be allocated to the inhabitants of bombed German cities, mainly in the Ruhr. Anything too cumbersome to move was destroyed. Strong-boxes and safes were rifled. Most of the younger Dutchmen who had failed to evade conscription were already working as slave-labourers in Germany, but all remaining men aged between sixteen and twenty-five were now put to work on building defence positions. Doors, floor-boards and roof timbers were used to reinforce dug-outs, and furnishings were taken to embellish them. Forced labour brought in from Rotterdam and elsewhere took a hand in the looting when opportunity arose. The refugees whose homes were being destroyed sheltered where they might, some with relatives, some with friends, and some with total strangers. Money supplied by the more affluent helped to feed them, as did raids conducted by the Resistance on ration offices to steal food coupons.

That season in Holland was to be remembered as the 'Hunger Winter', and as it dragged on, food became still scarcer. In September, the daily ration had been 1,500 calories, just over half that of the British civilian ration, but enough upon which to exist. By the end of the winter it had fallen to less than 500 calories – two slices of bread, two small potatoes and half a sugar-beet each day. Dogs and cats were eaten when they could be found. Those who were children at the time have never forgotten the disgusting taste of tulip bulbs and sugar beet. A black market existed, but on it a loaf of bread cost a man half his month's wages. Weak from starvation and disease, people from the cities trudged out into the countryside to barter their few remaining possessions with the farmers for food. There was neither gas nor electricity, nothing to heat the houses. Wood blocks from the roads, scrub or timber from ruined buildings were used to cook what little food there was.

During this 'Hunger Winter', 18,000 Dutch people died of starvation, but these were only a small part of the men, women and children of the Netherlands who lost their lives during the war. Of the 120,000 Dutch Jews shipped to Germany, no more than 16,000 returned, and another 5,000 Dutch men and women died in the concentration camps. Killed in air-raids were 23,000 men, women and children; 6,000 soldiers, sailors and airmen died in battle. Nearly 3,000 men and women were executed by the Germans, and of the 550,000 men deported to Germany for slave labour, 30,000 never came back. Probably a further 48,000 people died through lack of proper medical care. The total of deaths from all these causes numbered 237,000, one in thirty-one of the population of the Netherlands.

The Dutch had chosen to starve. Despite the frequent execution of recalcitrant railwaymen, the countrywide railway strike, called on 17 September, was to last until the end of the war. The Germans retaliated by placing an embargo upon all inland shipping; and, without either railways or barges, it was impossible to move food from the agricultural east into the starving industrial cities of the west. But the strike had become the national symbol of resistance to the hated *moffen*, the Dutch term of abuse for the oppressors they loathed. Most of Holland had been denied the opportunity of taking a direct part in the defeat of Nazi Germany, and this was the one way in which the Dutch could retaliate.

For all that, few Dutchmen or women could understand why they were being left to rot and die that winter, why the Allies did not liberate that large part of their country still occupied by the Germans. One crucial factor, hard to comprehend, was that their liberation would do nothing to speed the ending of the war. The German garrison numbered 120,000, and the Allied commanders had every reason to believe that they would resist just as doggedly as their comrades were doing elsewhere in Europe.

There was, however, another and equally critical reason why the Allies did not invade. It was not only a question of strategy. By the end of the war, one-eighth of Holland was flooded, a third of that by sea water. The sea flooding was largely the consequence of the Allied bombing of the dykes during the fighting to open the Scheldt estuary, but the greater part of the inundations had been carried out by the German forces, in order to strengthen their defences. Explosive charges had been placed in still more of the dykes, ready to bring about even more widespread flooding. A full-scale invasion of the country would probably have resulted, not only in the inundation of most of the Netherlands, but also in the emptying of the canals: if the banks and beds of these had dried out, the entire system of waterways upon which the life of the country depended would have been rendered useless for years to come. The loss of Dutch lives, both during and after the invasion, would have been countless.

The consequence was that the Allies did not move against Holland until the first week in April 1945. By then the Rhine had been crossed, and the British and American armies were streaming across the North German Plain. On 12 April, 49th (West Riding) Division, as part of I Canadian Corps, crossed the Ijssel; two days later the Yorkshiremen had fought their way into the deserted and burning shell of Arnhem.

In May, the first of that city's refugees were permitted to return to their ruined and despoiled houses, and a start was made on repairing them. Of the 8,000 doors that had been removed from Oosterbeek alone to provide overhead cover for German trenches, as many as possible were recovered; glass from greenhouses was brought into the city to mend windows. Short though everything was in Holland, household goods were collected throughout the country to help give the people a fresh start. Slowly life began to pulse through the city once again. Such was the industry of her inhabitants that, six years later, it was hard to detect signs of the damage the war had inflicted upon Arnhem.

Today there is still less sign of the ordeal Arnhem and Oosterbeek underwent, other than the many war memorials and the quiet cemetery lying just outside what had been the perimeter. In the woods, an observant eye may notice the outline of a bomb or shell crater. On the larger trees a saucer-sized ring reveals the presence of a metal shard: to use a chain-saw in the woods around Oosterbeek can be hazardous. Here and there a building is pock-marked. But what does remain after forty years is the friendship and kindness shown by the people of Arnhem and Oosterbeek to the survivors of the troops whose arrival promised them or their parents so much, but which was to bring only misery. Such a response often puzzles those who meet it.

CHAPTER TWENTY-SIX

'OPERATION "MARKET" WAS A BRILLIANT SUCCESS'

With the war still in progress, it was not surprising that some of the early reports on the results achieved by 'Market Garden' were meretricious. One example was Churchill's reply to Field-Marshal Smuts, who had ventured to express his grief and sympathy at what he saw as a failure. The British Prime Minister was brazen:

> As regards Arnhem, I think that you have got the position a little out of focus. The battle was a decided victory, but the leading division, asking, quite rightly, for more, was given a chop. I have not been afflicted by any feeling of disappointment over this an am glad our commanders are capable of running this kind of risk.

Montgomery was to claim 90 per cent success for the battle on the spurious grounds that the advancing troops had covered 90 per cent of the allotted distance. Generaloberst Student, hardly an impartial witness, airborne enthusiast as he was, agreed with his enemy, judging the battle to have been a 'great success' for the Allies: his grounds were that it had left them with vital bridges and valuable territory, and that the capture of Nijmegen had created a good jumping-off board for the offensive that contributed towards ending the war.

The truth, of course, was that the aims of the operation had not been attained: the flank of the West Wall had not been turned, the German Fifteenth Army had not been isolated, and the Ruhr had not been encircled. Above all, the hoped-for collapse of the German armies, not specified as a formal objective but implicit in the plan, had not happened. Instead the Allies had been left with a sixty-mile salient into Holland in which a succession of unhappy divisions were to spend a frigid winter, some of them fighting a web-footed war in the flooded Betuwe. The eight-day battle had cost Browning's Airborne Corps over 11,000 casualties, as many as the total American and British losses on the first day of the Normandy invasion. Few would disagree with Brigadier's Hackett's verdict on 'Market Garden'. 'If you did not get all the bridges', he wrote, 'it was not worth going at all'.

In his report to Generals Marshall and Arnold, Brereton commented as follows:

> Despite the failure of the 2nd Army to get through to Arnhem and establish a permanent bridgehead over the Lower Rhine, Operation 'Market' was a brilliant success. The 101st Division took all its objectives as planned; the 82nd Division dominated the southern end of the bridge at Nijmegen until noon of D-plus-1, by which time it had been planned for the Guards Armoured to be there; the 1st British Division similarly dominated the Arnhem bridge from its northern end until noon of D-plus-3, 24 hours later than the time set for the arrival of the 2nd Army. Hence the airborne troops accomplished what was expected of them. It was the breakdown of the 2nd Army's timetable on the first day – their failure to reach Eindhoven in 6 to 8 hours as planned – that caused the delay in the taking of the Nijmegen bridge and the failure at Arnhem.

It is a sad catalogue of half-truths. The 101st Division did take 'all its objectives as planned', but it failed to prevent the Son bridge from being blown; it was the morning of D-plus-2 before that structure had been replaced, by which time XXX Corps should have been approaching Arnhem. At no time did US 82nd Division 'dominate' any part of the Nijmegen bridges until Guards Armoured arrived to help in their capture, and this was not accomplished until the evening of D-plus-3. 'The breakdown of the 2nd Army's timetable on the first day' did contribute towards the delay in crossing the

Waal, but it was certainly not the major factor. In describing 'Market' as a 'brilliant success', Brereton was speaking as an airman rather than as the joint commander of air and ground formations. The delivery of the three divisions into battle could in no way have been bettered. The first major Allied daylight airborne operation of the war had been carried out with precision, and with no more than marginal losses to aircraft and their crews. It had been shown that strong supporting air formations could either eliminate or neutralise flak, so allowing safe passage to the vulnerable transport fleets. The extent to which the execution of the air plan matched the needs of the passengers was quite another matter, and one upon which Brereton failed to comment. Gavin afterwards reflected 'There was no failure at Arnhem'. In a limited but vital sense this was true. The northern end of the Arnhem bridge had been held, not for forty-eight but for seventy-two hours, thus denying the Germans the use of it, and it had been held, not by a complete division as planned, but by Frost's battalion-sized force. Brereton's report would have been rather less removed from the truth if he had described Frost's battle as a 'brilliant success' and 'Market' as the utter failure it was.

Brereton was a general whose fellow-countrymen seem to have had even less to say in his favour than had his allies. Bradley criticised him for being neither sincere nor energetic, enthusiastic nor co-operative, and the American historian Russell Weigley has described him as being perpetually discontented and querulous. Granted that the concept of a joint commander to take charge of both ground and air forces was new in 1944, and that senior officers had been neither trained nor prepared mentally for such responsibilities, Brereton was an odd choice to head an inter-Allied command so complicated as First Allied Airborne Army. He can hardly be said to have measured up in any way to the challenge.

Errors compounded by ill fortune produced the failure of 'Market Garden', a strategic defeat despite the individual tactical successes gained during the eight-day battle. Luck, as Napoleon insisted, is an essential ingredient of successful generalship, but luck was conspicuously absent during this operation. What could go wrong did, except for the German failure to blow one or all of the three major bridges, and this was an important failure indeed on the part of the enemy. If just one thing fewer in the planning and execution of 'Market Garden' had gone wrong then the outcome might have been very different. How was it, though, that, at this stage of the war, so many errors could be made by commanders and staff officers who were experienced, highly trained and of proven ability?

Few would argue that the major mistake in the plan was to land British 1st Airborne Division so far distant from the centre of Arnhem. This was the prime cause of the virtual destruction of the three brigades of the division in their various attempts to force their way through to reach the vital bridge across the river. The plan as produced effectively negated Brereton's admonition that the bridges must be grabbed with 'thunderclap surprise'. If Frost could succeed in holding the north end of the Arnhem bridge with his small force for three days, there is small doubt that two parachute brigades, preceded by a glider-borne *coup-de-main* party, could have seized and held the bridge until XXX Corps arrived, one of the brigades landing immediately to the south of the bridge and one as near as possible to the northern end.

The story was much the same at Nijmegen. There US 82nd Airborne Division was faced with problems very similar to those of British 1st Airborne Division – DZs and LZs many miles distant from the bridges over the Waal, the need to defend those DZs and LZs for the arrival of the second lift, and a consequent long approach march through closely wooded and built-up country.

As it was, DZs and LZs were chosen that offered small chance of success unless the German opposition proved to be derisory. Success might still have been gained, however, if two sorties had been flown on the first day. With his whole division in action on the Sunday, less the Polish Brigade, Urquhart could hardly have failed to reach Frost with a force large enough to hold the Arnhem bridge for a week. In the same way, if Gavin had been able to land his fourth regiment on the Sunday evening, he would have had the extra troops required to capture the bridge over the Waal as well as that over the Maas at Grave.

In a file of miscellaneous Cabinet papers lodged in the Public Record Office is a diary kept by a senior RAF staff officer concerned with the planning of airborne operations. His name is illegible and his appointment nowhere revealed. His summing up of 'Market Garden' concludes with the following words:

The Air Plan was bad. All experience and common sense pointed to landing all 3 Airborne Divisions in the minimum period of time, so that they could form up and collect themselves before the Germans reacted. All 3 Divisions could have been landed in the space of 12 hours or so, but F.A.A.A. [First Allied Airborne Army] insisted on a plan which resulted in the second lift (with half the heavy equipment) arriving more than 24 hours after the Germans had been alerted.

As the RAF was afterwards to admit, the flak intelligence proved to have been inaccurate. Furthermore, the escorting fighters showed themselves well capable of coping with what flak there was. With the intelligence such as it was, however, it is hard to blame the air forces for not dropping 1st Airborne Division closer to Arnhem – after all, 40 per cent losses had been forecast even if the defences around Deelen, Arnhem, Nijmegen and Eindhoven were avoided. So far as is known, the possibility of landing US 82nd Division closer to Nijmegen was not even considered. Nor, from a strictly air standpoint, was the American refusal to fly the double sortie on the first day unsound in theory, given their limited resources for aircraft maintenance. With more time to press his case, however, Browning might surely have persuaded Brereton to act with greater decision and question Major-General Williams's advice, especially as Air Vice-Marshal Hollinghurst was willing to fly the double sortie.

If this extra time had been available for careful thought and discussion, Brereton might also have been persuaded to examine the basis for the flak intelligence and to ask for the aircraft loss estimates to be justified. And, even if Brereton had done nothing, it is all but certain that Montgomery himself would have intervened to ensure that a realistic plan for the operation was produced. As it was, his staff did not see the 'Market Garden' plan until two days before take-off. By then, it was far too late to make major changes, although the Field-Marshal did attempt to persuade Brereton to produce a double sortie for British 1st Airborne Division. The wide separation of the many headquarters, combined with often inadequate communications, did not make for speedy consultation and quick decision. Montgomery was to admit afterwards that 'The airborne forces at Arnhem were dropped too far away from the vital objective – the bridge. It was some hours before they reached it. I take the blame for this mistake.' It was a rare example of the

Field-Marshal confessing to error – an error which would hardly have happened if time had been available to consider the full implications of the decision.

It is simple now to stroll across the hills above Nijmegen, and to judge at leisure and with hindsight that the city and its bridges could have been defended from the Germans by holding a smaller area of ground, thus making troops available to tackle the Nijmegen bridge with the despatch which attended the capture of the one across the Maas at Grave. At the time, however, Browning and Gavin were making their plans from maps and air photographs, and hours not days were at their disposal for considering the problem and making these plans. Nevertheless (and this is a subject upon which strong divisions of opinion exist), if Browning had given Gavin the task of defending a closer perimeter around Nijmegen, and had insisted also that the immediate priority of US 82nd Division was to seize and hold a crossing over the Waal, it is all but certain that the Nijmegen highway bridge could have been secured straight away. The flak around the city could then have been silenced, and the second and subsequent lifts landed in the flat country nearby, thus eliminating the need to hold the LZs and DZs on the Groesbeek Heights. With the Nijmegen bridge in American hands when Guards Armoured Division (late though it already was) arrived in the city about midday on the Tuesday, 19 September, the chances of reaching Frost before he was overwhelmed would have been that much the greater, given that 10th SS Panzer Division was then only starting to build up its strength in the Betuwe.

Too much has perhaps been made of the failure to provide the airborne divisions, before the operation, with an accurate and up-to-date summary of the available intelligence about enemy strengths and possible intentions in eastern Holland. The dramatic details of the tale has caught the public imagination: suppression of information, whether by incompetence or design, is excellent material for headline or filmscript. What are the facts? The intelligence summary issued for the abortive Operation 'Comet' (produced without the benefit of the subsequent Ultra information regarding the movement into the area of 9th and 10th SS Panzer Divisions) forecast one broken panzer division resting and refitting north of Arnhem. That for 'Market Garden' predicted about fifty to one hundred tanks in the whole of Holland; and, at about the same time as the intelligence summary was issued, Browning told Urquhart to expect nothing more than a German brigade group supported by a few tanks. In the event, the strength of each of these two so-called panzer divisions equated to about a brigade group, and, at the start of the battle, each possessed a few tanks, 9th SS Panzer having about a company's worth of twenty or so Mark V Panthers. The fact that the information about the presence of these two broken divisions in the Arnhem area was not passed to the airborne divisional commanders, and that it probably did not reach Browning either, made hardly any difference, adding as it did little to what those concerned already knew about the size of the enemy forces they were likely to meet. With the greater part of 10th SS Panzer directed towards Nijmegen as soon as the battle began, the estimate of enemy strength passed to Urquhart was not too wide of the mark. Whether or not Browning did suppress some of the information he had received from his intelligence staff about the presence of German tanks near Arnhem is hardly material to the issue. In any case, the need to protect Ultra as a source could well have debarred everyone involved from being told the exact designations of the two German formations.

Over the years, Montgomery has been criticised for the risk he took with the airborne divisions, aware as he was of the presence of enemy armour in the area. The stakes for which he had been playing could, however, hardly have been higher – the end of the war in Europe in 1944. On 15 September, two days before 'Market Garden' started, Eisenhower had written to his army group commanders: 'We shall soon, I hope ... be in possession of the Ruhr, the Saar and the Frankfurt area ... Clearly, Berlin is the main prize.' Given such a prize, the risking of the lives of a few thousand airborne soldiers was justifiable. Such risks involve harsh decisions, but they lie at the root of a senior commander's responsibilities. There was, indeed, another and similar example. In March 1944 Major-General Orde Wingate (as he had then become) learned, immediately prior to taking-off on his second deep penetration into Burma, that one of his glider landing-grounds had been obstructed with tree trunks. He was certain that the operation had been betrayed, and therefore urged his commander, General Bill Slim, to cancel it. Slim, however, decided that the assault should go in, making use of the other two landing-grounds, but later he spoke of 'the weight of responsibility crushing in on me with an almost physical pressure ... a burden a commander himself must bear.'

Although he recognised both the prize and the responsibility, it is strange that Montgomery, having staked so much on 'Market Garden', remained so uncharacteristically remote from its actual execution, once the operation had been launched. Bill Williams recollects that the normal tension of battle was absent at the time, perhaps because of the summer euphoria, and that he observed 'a lack of grip surprising in Montgomery'; he also noticed how the army group commander appeared to let things go their own way. If this was so, it is possible that the attitude spread further down the chain of command, and that this could be one of the reasons why XXX Corps did not move with the speed expected.

Despite the difficulties of moving a complete corps along a single vulnerable artery, and the delay and confusion caused by German attacks against that artery, Horrocks could well have succeeded in covering the sixty-four miles to Arnhem on schedule, thanks in great measure to the work of Taylor's 101st Airborne Division in helping to keep the road open. If the Guards had not halted on the first night at Valkenswaard, a quicker start could have been made in replacing the bridge at Son, and if the bridge over the Waal at Nijmegen had been seized with similar despatch to that over the Maas, XXX Corps could have reached the Betuwe in thirty-six hours. It could then have tackled the final stage of the journey before 10th SS Panzer had brought sufficient men and armour across the Pannerden ferry to stop the British advance.

As Urquhart, however, commented twenty years ago, with much justification, '... it is possible that for once Horrocks's enthusiasm was not transmitted adequately to those who served under him, and it may have been that some of his more junior officers and NCOs did not fully comprehend the problem and the importance of speed.' Undoubtedly this same criticism can also be levelled at some of Horrocks's more senior commanders. Guards Armoured Division was slow in exploiting success, not only at Valkenswaard, but also after the crossing of the Waal. It is equally difficult to justify the performance of 43rd Infantry Division. As with the Guards, this division had recently absorbed large drafts of reinforcements to replace casualties, and its units had been resting and refitting for nearly three weeks after their successful crossing of the Seine. This had been a peaceful interlude, one that perhaps persuaded them, as it did others, that the war was all but over. Nevertheless, it is hard to believe that the division would not have moved with greater speed if it had been led with a vigour similar to that displayed by the commanding officer of the DCLI in that battalion's dash to Driel on the evening of Friday 22 September. In the Reichswald and beyond during the coming winter, after the euphoria promised by easy victory had evaporated, this tough line division was again to show its formidable fighting qualities.

If the two British corps flanking the advance of XXX Corps had moved more quickly, the task of US 101st Airborne Division in keeping the main artery open would have been much less difficult. The commanders concerned may not have pushed their men too hard in the early stages of the battle, but given more time to concentrate VIII Corps along the Meuse-Escaut Canal, and to accumulate the supplies to provide a proper punch, the story might have been different. What should be noted is that the fighting in which these two corps were engaged was a great deal more severe than has sometimes been represented. During the eight days of 'Market Garden', VIII and XIII Corps between them lost 3,874 officers and men; by comparison, XXX Corps suffered 1,480 casualties during the same period. In aggregate, the two British flanking corps lost as many men during 'Market Garden' as did the two American airborne divisions. 15th (Scottish) Division was part of the left-hand corps, and the account of its fight to retain its bridgehead over the Meuse-Escaut Canal is revealing:

> The long ordeal of the Aast bridgehead was over. What had been endured by all in it can never adequately be described. Packed together in that tiny patch of ground barely four hundred yards in depth, pounded by a ceaseless bombardment, and assaulted by swiftly recurring counter-attacks pushed with fanatical courage, the 44th Brigade and then the 227th Brigade in its turn had known no respite in this inferno. They had lost over 700 men in six days.

Between 13 and 21 September this line division suffered 924 casualties, and in the fighting around Best during the subsequent ten days a further 925 names were added to its casualty lists.

In the nature of things, Browning's part in the battle was limited, and it is not easy to justify the use of a battalion-sized glider lift to land his headquarters on the Groesbeek Heights on the first day. If he had remained with his main headquarters in England, he would have been able to provide, if nothing else, help and encouragement to Sosabowski. With 1st Airborne Division's communications with England functioning better than those with the Nijmegen area, he would also have been better placed to control the use of the available reserves waiting to fly in on the subsequent lifts. As it was, he was faced with no major decision until the afternoon of Monday, D-plus-1. That decision was whether to allow Gavin to tackle the Nijmegen bridges again in strength on the same afternoon. Why Browning should have refused to do so, after 82nd Division's second lift had arrived safely, and after it had become for the time being apparent that the reports of German armour in the Reichswald were untrue, is hard to explain. Nevertheless, Montgomery retained his confidence in Browning's ability as a commander in battle, informing the CIGS when it was all over that he would like to have Browning as a corps commander if a vacancy occurred – high praise indeed.

The outcome of the battle to reach the Arnhem bridge might have been different if the radios of 1st Airborne Division had worked better, and if, as a result, Urquhart had not been cut off from his headquarters at a vital stage of the battle. For the state of the communications, Urquhart must take his share of the blame. As he has admitted, 'signal failures were no new phenomenon', and like all else in his division, this particular buck stopped with him; signal officers can be sacked if they do not produce the expected results. But it was not just a question of inexpertly handled or malfunctioning sets. Better sets were needed, and this was a matter for Browning's headquarters and for the War Office. The problems which would arise when operating over extended distances in enclosed country had been foreseen, and time and again the division's requests for more powerful radios had been rejected. When, both for 'Comet' and for 'Market Garden', such conditions had to be faced, there was no way of obtaining new, more powerful sets at short notice, or of packing and loading them if they had been available. There was just not time for such changes.

Other errors can and have been blamed on Urquhart, among them the failure to appreciate the importance of the Heveadorp ferry for tackling the Arnhem bridges from their southern end, and his mistake in not informing Hackett that Hicks would assume command of the division in the event of both Lathbury and himself becoming casualties. In making criticisms of this kind, however, it is important to remember that the most complex activity known to man is modern warfare. Errors are inevitable, but success more often than not attends the commander who commits the smaller number. If Urquhart had been an American general, he might well have been fired afterwards *pour encourager les autres*, an expedient that has virtues at times. Instead, he was rightly appointed a Commander of the Order of the Bath, and recommended by Montgomery, again to the CIGS, as Deputy Commander of the Airborne Army if Browning moved on. It can be argued that men are better judged by those who work for them rather than by their seniors – it is difficult to hide defects from subordinates. Urquhart will be remembered by all who served under him for his rock-like qualities, his cool and clear mind, and for the care he took of his men. He was an inspiring leader.

Montgomery blamed the weather as one of the major factors that denied 'Market Garden' what he termed 'complete success'. But 38 Group, RAF, judged that the weather had not 'unduly hampered operations', and this is the more accurate comment. Certainly mist at take-off airfields, combined with low cloud, did delay the arrival of 4 Parachute Brigade by four hours, and US 82nd Division's glider infantry regiment and a battalion of its artillery were delayed for four days. The Polish infantry battalions were also two days late in entering the battle, but it was possibly fortunate for them that this was so. These delays may have formed one element in the defeat (especially the late arrival of the reinforcements for 82nd Airborne Division), but their effect was small when compared with what would have happened if 30 per cent or more of the first lift had been shot down, something confidently predicted by the air forces. The official historian of the US Army has also blamed the weather for helping to 'deny any really substantial contribution after D-Day from tactical aircraft'. But poor planning and liaison were, in fact, of greater consequence. Adequate close support, something the soldiers had every reason to expect by September 1944, was not available, a significant factor in the outcome of the fighting on the ground. Direct communications between the soldiers fighting the battle and the support aircraft did not function, nor did the arrangement for calling for air support. Equally ineffective was the liaison between First Allied Airborne Army and 83 Group, the RAF formation responsible for providing close support. Consultation between the two headquarters, separated as they were by the Channel, was not easy. In order to avoid confusion between close-support aircraft and the fighter escorts to the transport columns, Brereton's headquarters had prohibited the flying of close-support missions when troop-carrying or supply aircraft were near the battlefield. Given the frequent changes in the timings of the planned programmes for the transport columns, it was impossible more often than not to fly close-support missions even when the airfields in Belgium and France were clear. With time for proper planning, such problems could have been settled before the operation began.

Time, in fact, seemed always to be the missing element: time for clear thought, time for consultation, discussion and argument, time for the detailed and involved planning demanded by such a large-scale operation. 'Market Garden' was the only major airborne operation of the war to be mounted in haste. It was the only one that failed. It was, as the late Ronald Lewin remarked, 'a lash-up and a lash-up between allies' – there is no better recipe for disaster. And luck was lacking. Nearly every error had occurred because of a lack of time for proper preparation. The complexity of airborne operations on such a scale, requiring as they did time to complete the involved planning, had destroyed the speed and flexibility supposedly characteristic of the airborne assault.

'Market Garden' was a gamble for a glittering prize. Given this prize, and the circumstances, the risk was justified. Only with hindsight, with the knowledge denied to those who conceived and planned the operation, does it become clear that, even if it had been successful, the break-through could not have been exploited. The operation had been based all along on the single false premise that German resistance had crumbled and that the resources of the Reich were spent. But spare manpower still existed. The Luftwaffe, the Navy and base units could, and would, be combed; slave labour and women could replace men working on the land and in industry. The German military genius could use these hidden reserves to build the fifty new Volksgrenadier divisions, their men inspired by the dual threat to the Fatherland from both east and west. This Phoenix-like recovery was something few suspected was possible, although

Churchill was among those who counselled caution. What shape the battle might have assumed if Second Army had managed to reach the Ijssel no one can tell, but one thing is near certain – the war would not have been over by Christmas.

AFTERTHOUGHT

In 'Market Garden', a worthwhile use had at last been found for the airborne divisions of First Allied Airborne Army. But how did it happen that, at this critical stage of the war, SHAEF's sole strategic reserve consisted of these élite formations, so difficult to commit to battle?

The American and British airborne forces had grown from minute seeds into vast and complex plants. The early German successes had fertilised the young shoots. The use of gliders and paratroops to help smash the defences of Holland and Belgium in May 1940 startled the military world. On 10 May, the German Blitzkrieg against Western Europe opened with airborne troops seizing the bridges across the Rhine estuary, and then attacking Rotterdam and the Hague. At the same time another force captured two bridges across the Albert Canal in Belgium and the key fort of Eben Emael, the latter seized by less than forty men landing by glider on its roof, who held their positions until relieved the following day. In all, just five battalions of German paratroops, backed up by a single air-transported division, had been used in the Blitzkrieg.

On 6 June 1940, Churchill, struck by the power of this new German weapon, called for the deployment of 5,000 parachute troops. After only fifteen days, parachute training began at Ringway Airport, near Manchester. American reactions were similar, a test platoon being set up in June; three weeks later, orders were issued for a parachute battalion to be activated. Further stimulus was to be provided the following year by the Germans' successful battalion-sized attack on the Corinth Canal, and by the capture of Crete. What was not known until much later, however, was the cost of Crete to the Germans. A division had been dropped and a mountain division landed by air transport, 22,000 troops in all. Of these, 4,000 were to die, most of them paratroops, losses that upset Hitler, who pronounced that 'The day of parachute troops is over'. Thereafter, the Germans were to mount only two airborne operations, both battalion-sized, one at Leros in the Dodecanese, and the other during their Ardennes counter-offensive in December 1944. The Leros operation, in November 1943, in which the battalion disrupted the defences and led the way to the eventual British defeat on the island, was an effective demonstration of how small bodies of airborne troops might be used. As for the Russians, those other pioneers of airborne warfare, they were never to use their parachute troops except in small sabotage parties.

In February 1941, thirty-eight British officers and men were dropped in southern Italy, their ostensible purpose the destruction of the Tragino aqueduct, which provided water for two million people. The aim was a trifle specious, the operation being, in effect, a field trial of equipment and techniques and a training exercise for the new arm. It was intended also to cope with the declining morale of the 1st Parachute Battalion (then known as 11th Special Air Service Regiment), a problem that was to be of ever-recurring concern in airborne forces: after six months of training, with no prospect of action and with their friends fighting in the Western Desert, men were applying to return to their parent units, or taking the law into their own hands and deserting. The Tragino operation achieved nothing except to produce consternation around Italy, and demonstrate to the British public that their nation too could use this new arm. All the party were taken prisoner, except for the unfortunate Italian interpreter, who was shot. The losses had probably been justified. The next parachute operation, Frost's company-sized raid on the Bruneval radar station, was in nearly every respect a brilliant success. In both the official and the public eye, airborne forces were seen as the arm of the future.

As larger bodies of troops became available, both British and American, the scale of airborne operations increased. First came the invasion of North Africa in November 1942. Here the fighting reputation won by 1 Parachute Brigade disguised the fact that the separate battalion parachute drops accomplished little or nothing. It was as ordinary infantry, but infantry short of heavy weapons and transport, that this brigade fought through the mud and rain of those bitter winter months against some of Germany's best troops. It was, therefore, something of a paradox that, by the end of the campaign, the value of airborne troops seemed to have been established.

The invasion of Sicily produced doubts. The disasters that attended the flights of the two regimental combat teams of US 82nd Airborne Division and the two British brigades of 1st Airborne Division were due primarily to lack of proper training of the American aircrew. The absence of adequate planning and control machinery also played a part. Despite the many shortcomings, however, the airborne troops achieved a measure of success. The landings confused the enemy; small parties managed to reach their objectives where they performed tasks which had been allocated to battalions. As Generalfeldmarschall Kesselring, the German commander, was afterwards to admit, the airborne troops had seriously delayed the movement of his reserves. The obvious difficulty, however, in putting large bodies of troops down in the right place, and the heavy casualties likely to be incurred in trying to do so, caused some senior Allied officers to query the value of large formations of airborne troops. The need for airborne battalions, and perhaps even for forces of up to a brigade in size, had clearly been justified, but by then three more airborne divisions, with several independent regiments, were under training in the United States, and a second British division was being formed in England. The expansion went ahead. In September, two successful drops by regimental combat teams of US 82nd Airborne Division to reinforce the Salerno bridgehead did much to restore confidence in the new arm, although some critics felt that this was hardly an economic manner of using airborne troops.

Meanwhile, Wingate's 200-mile-deep raid into Burma had impressed both Churchill and the higher command in Washington, and had demonstrated also how a large force could, for a prolonged period, be supplied from the air. 50 Indian Parachute Brigade had been training in India since October 1941, but by the time Wingate's force went into action the resources needed by the brigade to complete its airborne training were still awaited. It was to be three years from the date of the brigade's formation before it saw action, when it was committed as ordinary infantry into the savage fighting around Kohima and Imphal. Later expanded into 44th Indian Airborne Division, a single battalion was to drop at Rangoon on 1 May 1945, just as the war in Burma was ending.

Elsewhere in the Far East, US 11th Airborne Division was to find plenty to do, but rarely in its airborne role. Only in the concluding stages of the war did elements of this division carry out three small airborne operations on Luzon; two of them met no resistance, the third cost the Americans three casualties. In February 1945, however, 503 Parachute Combat Team was to spearhead the American return to Corregidor. In possibly the most spectacular Allied airborne operation of the war, the troops dropped on to two small open spaces, the larger a golf course about 300 yards by 150 yards, making possible the amphibious landing on the barren rock, which was honeycombed with defensive positions manned by 6,000 Japanese.

The landing of the three airborne divisions, the US 82nd and 101st and the British 6th, on the night before D-Day, to protect the flanks of the seaborne invasion, was not the so-called 'strategic' type of employment for airborne troops favoured by the higher command in Washington. It did, however, make a major contribution towards the success of the Allied landing in Europe. Dropping by night, the troops were scattered, but not so badly as had happened in Sicily. They did what was asked of them, their losses were severe, and the dispersion of the drop helped further to confuse the Germans. Whether the invasion would have succeeded without the help of the airborne divisions is one of the imponderables of war. For all that, it was in Normandy that the Allied airborne troops achieved their most worthwhile results.

The final large-scale airborne operation of the war was to be the landing of the American 17th and the British 6th Airborne Divisions on 24 March 1945, as part of Montgomery's long-planned and set-piece crossing of the Rhine. In the largest airlift of the war, 1,696 transport aircraft carried the whole of two divisions in a single lift – 21,680 soldiers and 700 vehicles. Behind them 240 Liberator bombers delivered 582 tons of supplies. It was another daylight drop, and was technically a complete success, the landing taking place on the high ground west of the river thirteen hours after the ground troops had begun to cross in boats. But casualties were severe, over

2,200 men on the first day of the battle. Fifty-three transport aircraft were destroyed and 440 seriously damaged; IX Troop Carrier Command alone lost 557 aircrew killed, wounded and missing. The amphibious crossing of the river, on the other hand, met comparatively little opposition, and the ground troops advanced quickly against relatively light resistance. The need for the airborne side of the operation has often been queried, and many Americans, in fact, doubted whether such a deliberate river-crossing had been necessary at all. Nearly three weeks earlier, they had 'bounced' a bridge further up the river at Remagen, and they considered that another surprise crossing could have been launched in the north. A single item in the cost of launching this airborne landing had been the construction of the take-off airfields for the transport aircraft; among the stores used were 53,000 cubic yards of hardcore and 13,719 tons of pierced steel planking, with other supplies in comparable quantities.

As we have seen, Eisenhower's sole reserve in September 1944, operationally ready for action, comprised the three airborne divisions used in 'Market Garden', with the 52nd (Lowland) Division standing by to fly in and consolidate a victory. Also in the United Kingdom was the newly arrived US 17th Airborne Division and the British 6th Airborne Division, refitting after Normandy. In the south of France, the equivalent of a weak American airborne division, with British 2 Independent Parachute Brigade Group, had dropped ahead of the 'Dragoon'* invasion force on 15 August, accomplishing little besides further confusing the German defenders; the fighting was negligible. Another American division, 13th Airborne, was to arrive in France in February 1945. Including the troops in the Pacific and the several independent regiments around the world, the two Allies had between them raised some ten airborne divisions. It could well have been more; in April 1943, the Americans alone were planning for twelve such divisions. General Ridgway has described airborne troops at the time as having been a 'brand new toy'. They were also fashionable. It took a bold soldier to query the need to sustain them in such large numbers.

These airborne units were manned by officers and soldiers of a

---

* The code-word for the Allied landings in the south of France between Toulon and Cannes, formerly known as 'Anvil'.

high calibre, hand-picked, most of them volunteers. In the British Army, applications to join parachute units could not be withheld, although they frequently were. Horrocks was among the senior commanders who regretted the loss of many of the best of the actual and potential infantry leaders to what he described as 'private armies'; Slim was another. To the disgust of the commanding officers who were despoiled, recruiting teams in the Middle East were allowed to descend upon infantry units in order to beguile away their best NCOs and men. The enthusiastic volunteers were then often condemned to wait for months, and sometimes for years, before they went into action. So often volunteering from boredom and a desire for excitement, men were to find the unending training around Delhi, the Suez Canal, Salisbury Plain or Fort Bragg equally tedious. To maintain morale in such circumstances was, as we have seen, difficult. When the airborne troops did get into action, the fighting could be hard enough, but the intervening periods were lengthy for all but a limited number of those who had volunteered. Many men, when they heard of the exploits of the units they had left in Burma, Tunisia, Italy or Normandy, felt that they had been 'conned'.

As large as the airborne divisions were, the resources used to carry the troops into action were equally large, although this is hard to quantify because the aircraft had the dual role of transporting men into battle and delivering supplies, both to the airborne formations after they had landed, and to the ground forces as a whole. There is little doubt that had the transport aircraft available to Eisenhower been used solely to supply the ground divisions, they would have played a crucial part in the later stages of the war in North-West Europe. Bradley, never an enthusiast for airborne forces, would have preferred to see the aircraft carrying gasoline to his armoured divisions rather than training for and then taking part in 'Market Garden'. Horrocks's views were similar, judging that the war would have ended in 1944 if Brereton's aircraft had been used during the first half of September to supply Patton and himself. In Europe, however, few had appreciated the potential of air supply, which was widely regarded as being for use only in an emergency.

Air supply in the Far East, however, was a different matter altogether. By 1944, Slim's Fourteenth Army in Burma was supplying by air not just Wingate's force, but also complete ground divisions. By March 1945, only fourteen squadrons were carrying the greater part of the needs of the Fourteenth Army, admittedly by the harsh overworking of both crews and aircraft. Flying two or three sorties daily, they were delivering 1,800 tons each day over distances of about 250 miles. In Europe, divisions required a greater bulk of both ammunition and gasoline, and there were more divisions to supply. The theoretical needs of an American division were for 600 to 700 tons daily, but actual consumption averaged nearer 400 tons, Patton, for instance, receiving some 3,500 tons each day to support his eight divisions attacking in the Moselle valley. In defence, a division would use a far smaller quantity of supplies. During the chase across France, the Allied divisions had existed on about 300 tons daily, much the same amount as a German mobile division consumed when on the offensive in Russia. But this greater demand for supplies in Europe was matched by a greater number of transport aircraft. 1,304 Dakotas flew on 17 September. These aircraft could have landed 4,200 tons of supplies for ground forces, flying only a single sortie in the day, enough to maintain ten divisions in the field for one day. Horrocks's claim rested on firm foundations.

To have diverted the aircraft in this way to supplying the field armies was, however, impossible. The transport fleet had been raised to carry men into battle. There could be no question of leaving the airborne divisions idle in England when the task for which they had been waiting had at last appeared. The alternative would have been to thrust them into the battle as straightforward infantry, an unthinkable course of action in September, although it was to happen in the crisis of the German offensive in the Ardennes in December. Without the airborne divisions, there would have been no IX Troop Carrier Command, USAAF, no 38 or 46 Groups in the Royal Air Force. When the United States committed the vast resources they did to building the aircraft and training the men to fly them, no one had foreseen that large bodies of field troops might be maintained solely from the air.

Small or smallish bodies of airborne troops often produced results out of all proportion to their size. Examples are the German operations in the Low Countries in 1940, the Bruneval raid, the attacks on Leros and Corregidor. The sole successful large-scale 'strategic' use of airborne troops was the German capture of Crete, a

251

success won at prohibitive cost, but one that encouraged the Allies to expand yet further their airborne effort. In 'Market Garden', the one attempt by the Allies to use airborne troops in such a 'strategic' manner, the cost was higher still and the operation failed, primarily because of the lack of time for proper preparation, an ever-present problem in a fluid battle. Never, in fact, did the airborne divisions raised by the United States and Great Britain make a vital contribution to a major battle, except perhaps during the invasion of Normandy. Small operations often succeeded. Some of the larger ones, Sicily among them, might have been better performed by smaller bodies of troops landed or dropped with greater accuracy by better-trained aircrew, and better-trained the aircrew might have been if there had been fewer of them.

It is arguable that Eisenhower would have been better served in the autumn of 1944 by another half-dozen infantry or armoured divisions, backed by adequate logistic resources, than by First Allied Airborne Army. The airborne forces of the United States and Britain were expensive indeed in high quality men and in the special facilities needed to train them, in manufacturing capacity and in base area support, in scientific research and in military planners. Without any doubt, the two Allies had a need for smallish bodies of parachute or glider troops, of battalion or of regimental size. On the other hand it is not easy to justify the scarce resources which the Americans and the British devoted to their fine airborne forces, and to the aircraft which flew them into battle.

NOTES

(Details of works quoted by author's name will be found in the Bibliography)

Page

13   'The trouble with this plan ...'. Exchange of letters Marshall and Eisenhower. Huston 274-6

15   'have as its purpose ...' Brereton 308

15   'He wants imagination and daring ...' Brereton 308-9

15   'Where is the Prince ...' Brereton 330

16   'coins burning holes ...' C.B. MacDonald 119

19   'errs on the side of optimism ...' Churchill 170

23   'I am not so happy ...' Alanbrooke Papers 14/32 6m

24   'Steady Monty ...' Wilmot 489

25   'hope we shall now ...' Alanbrooke Papers 14/32 6m

26   'bicycled along the road ...' Belchem correspondence

26   'I must say that ...' Montgomery, *Memoirs*, 293

30   'two large dining-room ...' Alanbrooke Papers 14/32 6m

30   'with thunderclap surprise ...' First Allied Airborne Army Report

32   'the irritation ...' Circular *Airborne Operations* signed by Browning on 17 August 44

38   'he should seem to be a bit patronising ...' Ridgway 66

38   'General Ridgway ...' Gavin, *On to Berlin*, 82-3

41   'But the Germans ...' Urquhart 17

45   'The enemy is fighting ...' HQ Airborne Corps Op

Instruction No 1, dated 13 September

45 'morsels of information' Urquhart 7

45 'in no fit state ...' HQ Airborne Corps Report, Para 9

45 'no illusions about ...' Urquhart 9

45 'arrogant optimism ...' Sosabowski 146

46 'pepper and salt ...' Hackett interview

47 'Better lose Crete ...' Williams letter

66 'Signal failures ...' Urquhart 37

77 'A bit ambiguous ...' Gavin, *On to Berlin*, 161

77 'The drop was better ...' Gavin, *Airborne Warfare*, 93

77 'It was surprising ...' Gavin, *Airborne Warfare*, 102

79 'a rather conservative ...' C.B. MacDonald 148

82 'The variety of headgear ...' Essame 115

82 'This is a tale ...' Essame 116

84 'I know that you would like ...' Martin 146

84 'It was a classic ...' Horrocks, *A Full Life*, 213

87 'there was a desperate ...' Horrocks, foreword to Bauer, 6

87 'if possible in forty-eight ...' Horrocks, *Corps Commander*, 99

87 Footnote. Several first-hand accounts of the battle contain timings which correlate exactly with those given in Nofi 168

94 'If such a mess ...'. Quoted from the shorthand records of Hitler's conference in Bauer 98

96 'the foremost British ...' Student

98 'Oh, how I wish ...' Student

102 'they proved to be ...' Gavin, *On to Berlin*, 166

110 'it was a grossly ...' Hackett interview

111 'the place for a general ...' Gavin, *On to Berlin*, 252

116 'a movie-thriller ...' C.B. MacDonald 167, quoting war diary

117 'Dutch report Germans ...' C.B. MacDonald 170

118 'the retention of ...' C.B. MacDonald 168, quoting US 82nd Division Chief of Staff Journal reporting conference at 1530 hours, 18 September

118 'Corps Signals in the field ...' HQ Airborne Corps Report, Para 119

127 'It is against text-book ...' Quoted by Bauer 194

128 Such incidents ... Urquhart 88-9

132 The fighting on ... Nicolson 129

133 'Jim, never try ...' Gavin, *On to Berlin*, 170

135	'Dear Boss ...' Brereton 350-1
138	'made little progress' HQ Airborne Corps Report, Para 51
139-40	'I remember talking ...' RE *Journal*, December 1982, 277-8
141	'Touch them ...' Hackett interview
149	'kind, chivalrous ...' Frost 233
149	'the outstanding ...' Gavin, *Airborne Warfare*, 120
150	'handling beautifully ...' Hackett quoted by Hibbert 132
151	'The men were ...' Urquhart 108
156	'For God's sake ...' Horrocks, *Corps Commander*, 112
158	'the most uninhibited ...' Rapport 318
158-9	'Despite their individual ...' Letter from Gavin to Commanding General IX Troop Carrier Command dated 25 September 1944. Quoted in Huston 43
160	'a very American-looking ...' *Saga of the All-American* (no page numbers)
161	'I am proud ...' Gavin, *On to Berlin*, 185
162	'probably the best ...' Gavin, *On to Berlin*, 69
162	'What in the Hell ...' Gavin, *On to Berlin*, 181-2
162	'Essential every effort ...' Ellis 39
162	'Enemy attacking ...' Ellis 39
164	'Thanks for your message ...' Brereton 354. The ambiguous context in which Brereton placed this quotation suggests that the offer was made on the Friday, not the Wednesday. As a consequence some accounts of the incident have dated it to the Friday, thus implicitly and unjustly criticising Browning
170	'Merlin ...' Urquhart 123 and 64th Medium Regiment, RA account
171	'Although I was naturally ...' Urquhart 106
172	As Urquhart ... HQ 1st Airborne Division Report, Para 226
172	'No knowledge ...' Urquhart 132
175	'bogged down ...' Sosabowski 157
176	'extremely difficult ...' Copy in Sikorski Institute archives
180	'without much difficulty ...' HQ Airborne Corps Report, Para 61
183	'By nature ...' Wilmot 518
183	'During the past ten days ...' Alanbrooke Papers 14/36 6p
184	he commanded his armies ... Williams interview

238   'We shall soon ...' Ellis 77

239   'the weight of responsibility ...' Slim 261

239   'a lack of grip ...' Williams letter

239   'it is possible that ...' Urquhart 203

240   'The long ordeal ...' Martin 147

240   Between 13 and 21 ... Martin 350

240   informing the CIGS ... Alanbrooke Papers 14/32 6m

241   recommended by Montgomery ... Alanbrooke Papers 14/32 6m

242   'deny any really substantial ...' C.B. MacDonald 200

243   'a lash-up ...' Lewin, RUSI seminar

246   'The day of ...' Liddell Hart 168

249   'brand new toy' Ridgway 93

SOURCES

Unpublished Sources – Reports and War Diaries, Orders and Plans in the Public Record Office, Kew

Twenty-First Army Group – Operation 'Market Garden'	AIR 37/1249
I British Airborne Corps – Allied Airborne Operations in Holland September – October 1944	AIR 37/1214
US XVIII Airborne Corps – Operation 'Market'	AIR 16/1026
VIII Corps War Diary	WO 171/287
XII Corps War Diary	WO 171/310
XXX Corps – Operation 'Market Garden' 17-26 September 1944	WO 205/1126
US 82nd Airborne Division – Lessons and Operational Report on Operation 'Market'	AIR 16/1026
US 101st Airborne Division – Participation in Operation 'Market' for period D-D+10	AIR 16/1026
11th Armoured Division War Diary	WO 171/456
8 Armoured Brigade War Diary	WO 171/613
4th Battalion, The Dorsetshire Regiment War Diary	WO 171/1286
156th Battalion, The Parachute Regiment War Diary	WO 171/1247
Glider Pilot Regiment War Diary	WO 205/1123
Allied Expeditionary Air Force report – Operation 'Market Garden'	AIR 24/43
2nd Tactical Air Force – Operations file	AIR 37/615

38 and 46 Groups Royal Air Force–Report on the
    British Airborne effort in Operation 'Market'   AIR 37/418
First Allied Airborne Army – Report on German
    Airforce reaction to airborne landings in Holland   WO 205/693
Twenty-First Army Group – Operation 'Market'
    outline plans   WO 205/313-4
XXX Corps – Operation order for 'Garden'   WO 171/341
Headquarters Airborne Troops Instruction No 1
    'Comet'   WO 205/850
38 Group Royal Air Force – Operation Order
    'Market'   AIR 37/981
General Sir Miles Dempsey, KCB, KBE, DSO, MC
    – War Diaries   WO 285/10-15
SS Panzer Grenadier and Reserve Battalion 16 report   AIR 20/2333

Unpublished Sources – Reports and War Diaries
(Privately loaned to the author)
Account by 64th Medium Regiment, Royal Artillery, of their
    support for 1st Airborne Division
1st Battalion, The Border Regiment, War Diary
Anonymous account of 2nd Parachute Battalion's operations at
    Arnhem
21st Independent Parachute Company War Diary
Report by Belgian Special Air Service Squadron – Operation
    'Regan' (later renamed 'Fabian')
38 Group, Royal Air Force, Operation Order 'Comet'
1st Airborne Division – Report on Operation 'Market' 17-26
    September 1944, which includes:
    Directive received from Commander, British Airborne Corps
        (Lt-Gen Browning)
    Operation Instructions – 1st Airborne Division
                       1 Parachute Brigade
                       4 Parachute Brigade
                       1 Airlanding Brigade
                       1 Polish Independent Parachute Brigade
                       Group
    Divisional and brigade war diaries, and reports by arms other
    than infantry
1st Airborne Division Planning Intelligence Summary No. 2,

Operation 'Comet'   The Sikorski Institute,
                                          AV/20/31-13

Unpublished Sources – Personal Papers and Correspondence
Alanbrooke Papers   King's College,
                                          University of London
Liddell Hart Papers   King's College,
                                          University of London
Sosabowski papers, and papers referring to
   1 Polish Independent Parachute Brigade
   Group   The Sikorski Institute
Urquhart papers   Major-General R.E. Urquhart
Correspondence of the late Major-General   Mrs Ellen Belchem
   R.F.K. Belchem

Unpublished Sources – Personal Diaries and Accounts
Brigadier J.W. Hackett
Captain A.G.C. Jones
Brigadier G.W. Lathbury
Colonel G.M. Warrack
Major J.L. Waddy

Unpublished Sources – German Reports
Generaloberst Student
Obersturmfeurher Labahn
Report on 'Battle with and defeat of 1st Airborne Division in the
   western sector of Arnhem' (attached to 38 and 46 Group RAF
   Report, PRO, Kew)

Unpublished Sources – Miscellaneous
RAF Narrative, *The Liberation of N.W. Europe Vol. 4: The Break
   Out and the Advance to the Lower Rhine.*
Second World War 1939-45: Airborne Forces, Air Publication 3231
Current Reports from Overseas No. 69, War Office Publication
*USAAF Historical Studies No. 97, Airborne Operations in World
   War II, European Theatre* USAAF Historical Division,
   Research Studies Institute, Air University, September 1956
   (written by Dr John C. Warren)
Proceedings of seminar on the Battle of Arnhem held on 8 March
   1978 at the Royal United Services Institute for Defence Studies,
   London

Published sources – Books

Aalbers, P.G., *Slag om Arnhem: bibliografie van gedrukte werken*, Bibliotheek Arnhem, 1975

——, *Supplement* to above, 1978

Angus, Tom, *Men at Arnhem*, Leo Cooper, 1976

Anon., *Arnhem Lift: Diary of a Glider Pilot*, Pilot Press, 1945

——, *Arnhem September 1944*, Arnhem, Gemeentearchief, 1969

——, *By Air to Battle*, HMSO, 1945

——, *Saga of the All-American: 82nd Airborne Division in World War II*, Battery Press, Nashville, reprint of 1945 edition

Bauer, Cornelis (information supplied by Lieutenant-Colonel Theodoor A. Boeree), *The Battle of Arnhem*, Hodder & Stoughton, 1966

Bennett, Ralph, *Ultra in the West*, Hutchinson, 1979

Bradley, Omar N., *A General's Life*, Sidwick & Jackson, 1983

Brereton, Lewis H., *The Brereton Diaries*, William Morrow, New York, 1946

Chalfont, Alun, *Montgomery of Alamein*, Weidenfeld & Nicolson, 1976

Chatterton, George, *Wings of Pegasus*, Macdonald, 1962

Churchill, Winston S., *The Second World War*, Volume VI, Cassell, 1954

Clay, Major Ewart W., *The Path of the 50th*, Gale & Polden, 1950

Cole, Lieutenant-Colonel Howard N., *On Wings of Healing*, William Blackwood, 1963

Courage, Major G., *The History of the 15/19 The King's Royal Hussars 1939-1945*, Gale & Polden, 1949

Craven, Wesley Frank, and Gale, James Lea (eds), *Army Air Forces in WW II*, Volume 3: *Europe: Argument to V-E Day*, University of Chicago Press, Chicago, n.d.

Deane-Drummond, Anthony, *Return Ticket*, Collins, 1953

de Groot, Norbert A., *Als Sterren van de Hemel*, Van Holkema & Warendorf, Bussum, 1977

de Guingand, Major-General Sir Francis, *Operation Victory*, Hodder & Stoughton, 1947

Dixon, Norman, *On the Psychology of Military Incompetence*, Cape, 1976

Dover, Major Victor, *The Sky Generals*, Cassell, 1981

Ehrman, John, *Grand Strategy*, Volume 5: *August 1943-September*

1944, HMSO, 1956

Eisenhower, Dwight D., *Crusade in Europe,* Heinemann, 1948

Ellis, Major L.F., *Victory in the West,* Volume II, HMSO, 1968

Essame, Major-General H. *The 43rd Wessex Division at War: 1944-1945,* William Clowes, 1952

Fairley, John, *Remember Arnhem,* Pegasus Journal, 1978

Farrar-Hockley, Brigadier Anthony, *Airborne Carpet: Operation Market Garden,* Macdonald, 1970

Firbank, Thomas, *I Bought a Star,* Sidwick & Jackson, 1951

Foot, M.R.D., *SOE in France,* HMSO, 1966

———, and Langley, J.M., *MI9,* Bodley Head, 1979

Fraser, David, *And We Shall Shock Them,* Hodder & Stoughton, 1983

Frost, Major-General John, *A Drop Too Many,* Buchan & Enright, 1982

Gavin, James M., *Airborne Warfare,* Infantry Press Journal, Washington, 1947

———, *On to Berlin,* Leo Cooper, 1979

Gill, Ronald, and Groves, John, *Club Route in Europe,* privately printed, Hannover, 1946

Giskes, H.J., *London Calling the North Pole,* Kimber, 1953

Gorlitz, Walter, *The German General Staff 1657-1945,* Hollis & Carter, 1953

Gregory, Barry, *British Airborne Troops,* Macdonald & Janes, 1974

Hackett, General Sir John, *I Was a Stranger,* Chatto & Windus, 1977

Hamilton, Nigel, *Monty: Master of the Battlefield 1942-44,* Hamish Hamilton, 1983

Heaps, Leo, *The Grey Goose of Arnhem,* Weidenfeld & Nicholson, 1976

Hibbert, Christopher, *The Battle of Arnhem,* Batsford, 1962

Horrocks, Lieutenant-General Sir Brian, *A Full Life,* Leo Cooper, 1974

———, with Eversley Belfield and Major-General H. Essame, *Corps Commander,* Sidgwick & Jackson, 1977

Howard, Michael and Sparrow, John, *The Coldstream Guards 1920-46,* Oxford University Press, 1951

Huston, James A., *Out of the Blue: U.S. Airborne Operations in World War II,* Battery Press, Nashville

Irving, David, *The War Between the Generals*, Allen Lane, 1981

Kessel, Lipmann, *Surgeon at Arms*, Leo Cooper, 1976

Lamb, Richard, *Montgomery in Europe 1943-1945: Success or Failure?*, Buchan & Enright, 1983

Lewin, Ronald, *Montgomery as Military Commander*, Batsford, 1971

——, *Ultra Goes to War*, Hutchinson, 1978

Liddell Hart, B.H., *The Other Side of the Hill*, Cassell, 1948

Maalderink, P.G.H., C.M. Schulten and B.J. Kasperink-Taekema, *Korps Commandotroepen*, Roosendaal, Netherlands, 1982

Maassen, G.H. *Oosterbeek Destroyed 1944-1945*, Meyer & Siegers, Oosterbeek, 1981

MacDonald, Charles B., *The Siegfried Line Campaign*, Department of the Army, Washington, DC, 1963

Macdonald, George, *The Somerset Light Infantry 1919-45*, privately printed, n.d.

Mackenzie, Brigadier C.B., *It Was Like This*, Adremo, Oosterbeek, 1967

Martin, Lieutenant-General H.G., *The History of the Fifteenth Scottish Division 1939-1945*, William Blackwood, 1948

Mawson, Stuart, *Airborne Doctor*, Orbis, 1981

Montgomery of Alamein, Field-Marshal the Viscount, *Memoirs*, Collins, 1958

Montgomery, Brian, *A Field-Marshal in the Family*, Hutchinson, 1973

Nicolson, Captain Nigel, and Forbes, Patrick, *The Grenadier Guards in the War of 1939-1945*, Volume I, Gale & Polden, 1949

Nofi, Albert A. (ed.), *The War Against Hitler: Military Strategy in the West*, Hippocrene Books, New York, 1982

Norton, G.G., *The Red Devils: The Story of the British Airborne Forces*, Leo Cooper, 1971

Pogue, Forrest C., *The Supreme Command*, Department of the Army, Washington, DC, 1954

Rapport, Leonard, and Northwood, Arthur, Jr, *Rendezvous with Destiny: A History of 101st Airborne Division*, 101st Airborne Division Association, Parchment, MI, 1948

Ridgway, General Matthew B., *Soldier*, Harper Bros, New York 1956

Ruppenthal, Roland G., *Logistical Support of the Armies*, Volume 2,

1944-May 1945, Department of the Army, Washington, DC, 1959
Ryan, Cornelius, *A Bridge Too Far*, Hamish Hamilton, 1974
St George Saunders, Hilary, *The Red Beret*, Michael Joseph, 1950
Sims, James, *Arnhem Spearhead*, Imperial War Museum, 1978
Slim, Field-Marshal Sir William, *Defeat into Victory*, Cassell, 1956
Sosabowski, Major-General Stanislaw, *Freely I Served*, Kimber, 1960
Tedder, Lord, *With Prejudice*, Cassell, 1966
ter Horst, Kate A., *Cloud over Arnhem*, Allan Wingate, 1959
Thompson, R.W., *The Eighty-Five Days: The Story of the Battle of the Scheldt*, Hutchinson, 1957
Tugwell, Maurice, *Arnhem: A Case Study*, Thornton Cox, 1975
Urquhart, Major-General R.E., *Arnhem*, Cassell, 1958
van der Zee, Henri, *The Hunger Winter: Occupied Holland 1944-5*, Jill Norman & Hobhouse, 1981
Verney, Major-General G.L., *The Guards Armoured Division*, Hutchinson, 1955
Wilmot, Chester, *The Struggle for Europe*, Collins, 1952
Warrack, Graeme, *Travel by Dark*, Harvill Press, 1963
Weigley, Russell F., *Eisenhower's Lieutenants*, Sidwick & Jackson, London, 1981
Woodburn Kirby, Major-General S., *The War Against Japan*, Volume 3, HMSO, 1962

Published Sourches – Articles
Anon, 'Pegasus and the Wyvern: The Evacuation of the 1st Airborne Division from Arnhem', *Royal Engineers Journal*, March 1946
Anon, 'Arnhem', *After the Battle*, May 1973
Breeze, Major C.F.O., 'The Airborne Operations in Holland September 1944', *The Border Magazine*, September 1948
Hackett, General Sir John, 'Arnhem: The Missing Orders', *Sunday Times*, September 15, 1974
Haslam, E.B., 'A Bridge Too Far', *Royal Air Force Quarterly*, Spring 1978
Lamb, Richard, 'Arnhem', *War Monthly*, March 1979
Myers, Brigadier E.C.W., 'At Arnhem – September 1944', *Royal Engineers Journal*, September 1982
(Letters on Brigadier's Myers's articles from General Sir Victor FitzGeorge-Balfour and Major-General A.G.C. Jones can be

found in the December 1982 number of the Journal).

'Parachute Sapper', 'The Battle of Arnhem Bridge', *Blackwood's Magazine*, October 1945

St. Aubyn, Lieutenant the Hon. Piers, 'Arnhem', *King's Royal Rifle Corps Chronicle*, 1946

Society of Friends of Arnhem Museum, Oosterbeek, various articles in Newsletters 1–10, September 1980–September 1983

Taylor, George, 'With 30 Corps to Arnhem', *Ca Ira*, Volume XIII, No. 2, 1949

Interviews and Correspondence
Colonel R.G. Collins
Lieutenant-Colonel D.E. Crawley
Major-General J.D. Frost
General James M. Gavin
Major-General R.F.K. Goldsmith
General Sir John Hackett
Major J.J. Lorys
Brigadier C.B. Mackenzie
Mr James H. Money
General Sir Charles Richardson
Brigadier E.C.W. Myers
Brigadier G. Taylor
Mevrouw K.A. ter Horst
Major-General R.E. Urquhart
Brigadier J.O.E. Vandeleur
Colonel J.L. Waddy
Brigadier A.G. Walch
Colonel G.M. Warrack
Sir Edgar Williams
Colonel Carel Wilhelm

GLOSSARY

AA	Anti-aircraft
Abwehr	The German High Command's espionage, counter-espionage and sabotage service (lit. 'defence', 'resistance')
ADGB	Air Defence of Great Britain; the RAF's unified air defence command
ADMS	Assistant Director of Medical Services
AFDAG	Airborne Forward Delivery Airfield Group
AT	Anti-tank
Bazooka	US hand-held infantry anti-tank weapon
Betuwe	The area between Nijmegen and Arnhem, from an Old Dutch word meaning 'fertile land'
Bocage	French word meaning grove, coppice or copse; applied particularly to an area of Normandy where the fields are enclosed by raised banks surmounted by hedges or copses, and where much of the break-out fighting took place after the Allied invasion
Bund	Embankment or causeway, raised bank
CIGS	Chief of the Imperial General Staff
DCLI	Duke of Cornwall's Light Infantry
DUKW	American-built 2.5 ton 6 × 6 amphibious vehicle used by the Allies. The letters stand for year of design (D = 1942), type of vehicle (U = amphibian), type of transmission (K = all-wheel drive), and axle configuration (W = dual rear axles)
DZ	Drop-zone; area designated for paratroop landings
'Eureka'	Homing beacon used to guide in gliders by means of a transmitted signal
FAAA	First Allied Airborne Army
Flak	Universally used German word for anti-aircraft fire
Gammon bomb	British anti-tank device, exploding when thrown against armoured vehicles
'Garden'	Code-word for British Second Army operations in support of the airborne forces

266

Gestapo	Nazi secret police, from *Geheime Staats Polizei* (Secret State Police)
GHQ	General Headquarters
'Jedburgh'	SOE teams parachuted in to make contact with the Dutch resistance
JIC	Joint Intelligence Committee
KOSB	King's Own Scottish Borderers
LZ	Landing-zone; area designated for glider landings
'Market'	Code-word for the operations by the three airborne divisions
MDS	Medical Dressing Station
Moffen	Old German word meaning 'boorish' – a term of contempt applied by the Dutch to the Germans
NCO	Non-commissioned officer
Panzer	German word for armour
Panzerfaust	German hand-held infantry anti-tank weapon, a rocket-propelled hollow-charge bomb fired from a tube
PFC	Private First Class (US)
'Phantom'	Code-word for the GHQ Liaison Regiments, special units sent forward of Allied forces
PIAT	Projector Infantry Anti-Tank; British hand-held infantry anti-tank weapon
Polder	Dutch word for land reclaimed from the sea or rivers, usually flat, silty and fertile
PRO	Public Relations Officer (also Public Record Office)
PRU	Photographic Reconnaissance Unit
RA	Royal Regiment of Artillery
RASC	Royal Army Service Corps
RE	Corps of Royal Engineers
RTR	Royal Tank Regiment
SAS	Special Air Service Regiment
SHAEF	Supreme Headquarters, Allied Expeditionary Forces
SLI	Somerset Light Infantry
SOE	Special Operations Executive; British clandestine organisation concerned with resistance and sabotage in German occupied countries
SP	Self-propelled gun; heavy calibre artillery/anti-tank weapon mounted on tracked armoured chassis. Not having a turret, the gun's elevation, depression and traverse were limited
SS	*Schutz Staffeln* ('Protection Detachments'). The Waffen-SS were élite Nazi corps, separate from the Wehrmacht and under the overall control of Himmler, as was the rest of the SS
TAF	Tactical Air Force
USAAF	United States Army Air Force. The American air forces during the war were part of the army or the navy, and not separate services
Wehrmacht	The German armed forces, excluding the SS

INDEX

(Ranks shown are those held on 17 September 1944)

269

withdrawal of, 138-141, 126-8;
destruction of, 165-168, 149-51;
remnants in perimeter defence, 151-2,
168-9;
casualties, 205
1 Airlanding Brigade, 61, 62, 65-6, 107, 109,
126, 128, 170, 192, 222
50 (Indian) Parachute Brigade, 247
Household Cavalry, 114, 131, 190-91, 193
4th/7th Dragoon Guards, 191, 193-4, 203
15th/19th Hussars, 136, 154
Sherwood Rangers Yeomanry, 136
44th Royal Tank Regiment, 154, 197, 212, 216
1st Airborne Recce Squadron, 61, 64-5, 66, 68,
96, 122, 123, 147, 151, 168, 205
1st Airborne Divisional Artillery, 62
1st Light Regiment, RA, 121, 123, 129, 166, 188
64th Medium Regiment, RA, 170, 172, 209, 220
Royal Engineers, 69, 84, 105, 121, 131, 148,
169, 177, 191, 220
Grenadier Guards Group, 87, 139-10, 144, 182,
215;
attempts reach Nijmegen bridges, 144-146;
131-2;
captures road bridge, 154-62;
turned back, 198-9, 201
Coldstream Guards Group, 132, 157, 162-3,
198-9, 201, 215
Irish Guards Group, 82, 140, 156, 159-60, 162;
takes de Groot bridge, 20;
breaks out bridgehead, 86-7;
advances to Son, 113-14;
advances from Nijmegen, 179-80
Welsh Guards Group, 87, 180
7th Somerset Light Infantry, 193-4
7th King's Own Scottish Borderers, 65, 96, 108,
109, 124, 127, 129, 165, 168, 189, 205
1st Worcestershire Regiment, 195
5th Duke of Cornwall's Light Infantry, 191,
193-5, 240
1st Border Regiment, 65, 128, 129, 151, 152,
166, 168, 169, 192, 204, 205
2nd South Staffordshire Regiment, 213, 214-15,
220, 221
Durham Light Infantry, 218
1st Parachute Battalion, 64, 96, 105, 106, 122,
143, 186, 246
2nd Parachute Battalion, 64, 143;
captures Arnhem bridge, 64-71;
defends bridge, 104-6, 120-22, 143, 147-9;
resistance ends, 165
3rd Parachute Battalion, 64, 65, 66, 67, 68, 96,
106, 122, 143, 186
156th Parachute Battalion, 107, 109, 124-5, 127,
143, 149, 150, 151-2, 166, 205, 219
10th Parachute Battalion, 107, 124, 126, 127,
130, 150, 151, 152, 166, 168
11th Parachute Battalion, 107, 110, 122

21st Independent Parachute Company, 62, 108,
129, 165, 189, 205
Glider Pilot Regiment, 8, 129, 151, 158-9, 205,
221
Royal Army Service Corps, 68
Royal Army Medical Corps, 151, 186-8, 210-11,
221, 226
GHQ Liaison Regiment (Phantom), 112, 170
Airborne Forward Delivery Airfield Group, 202
16th Field Ambulance, 186-7
133rd Field Ambulance, 187
181st Field Ambulance, 186-7
Brooke, F-M Sir Alan, 25, 183, 184, 218, 241,
242
Browning, Lt-Gen F.A.M. 15, 56, 72, 82, 93,
110, 128, 129, 131, 132, 133, 134, 141, 158,
159, 172, 176, 190, 192, 201, 202, 214,
217-18, 236;
planning for 'Market Garden', 29-39;
lifts tactical HQ on first day, 36, 118-19,
140-41;
his background, 37-9, 46-7;
and 'Market Garden' intelligence, 44-8;
and orders to Gavin, 75-6, 117-19, 133;
his limited role, 118-19, 140-41;
rejects offer from 52nd Division, 163-4,
206-7;
criticises Sosabowski, 176;
frustration, 206;
writes Urquhart, 217;
addresses troops, 223-4;
Montgomery's confidence in, 241
Bruneval, raid on, 67, 246, 251
Brussels, 18, 20, 25, 27, 85, 90
Burma, 13, 14, 238-9, 247-8

Caen, 38
Cain, Maj Robert, VC, 169
Canadian:
First Army, 18, 20, 22;
I Corps, 231;
Engineers, 220-21
Carrington, Capt the Lord, 162
Casualties:
Second Army, 85, 139, 163, 215, 240;
1st Airborne Division, 10, 124, 130, 186-8,
205;
US 82nd and 101st Airborne Divisions, 32,
133, 224, 233;
1 Polish Parachute Brigade, 177, 224;
German, 136, 160, 169, 198. *See also* under
units
'Cauldron' (*see 'Der Kessel'*)
Channel Ports, 17, 20, 90
Chatterton, Col. G.J.S., 36
Cherbourg, 16n;
peninsula, 24
Chill, Generalleutnant Kurt, 90-91, 98

Index

complains about lack of intelligence, 45;
and views of possible German resistance,
46;
cut off from headquarters, 106-7, 111;
returns to headquarters, 126;
plans defence of perimeter, 165-6;
and air support, 170-71;
adjusts perimeter defences, 189;
sends messengers out, 190;
abandons plan to retake Westerbouwing,
204;
withdraws division, 217-22;
communications of, 241;
errors, 241-2;
character of, 242
Utrecht, 59, 64, 100
Utrechtseweg, 149, 151, 211, 219
V2 rockets, 26, 101
Valburg, 194, 195, 202, 214
Valkenberglaan, 150
Valkenswaard, 86, 113, 153, 183, 239
Valkhof, 115, 132, 156
van der Krap, Charles L.J.J. Douw, 122
Vanderleur, Lt-Col G., 86
Vanderleur, Lt-Col J.O.E., 82, 86-7, 180
van Hoof, Jan, 161
Veghel, 31, 81, 87, 97, 114, 137, 144, 154, 196-8,
199, 200, 201, 212
Velp, 227
Venlo, 42, 117
Verney, Maj-Gen G.L., 87
Volkel, 201

von Rundstedt, Generalfeldmarschall Gerd,
89-90, 219
von Tettau, Generalleutenant, 95, 96, 143
Vreewijk Hotel, 187, 210

Waal river, 24, 30, 41, 74, 75, 76, 94, 141, 142,
145, 154, 159-60, 179, 184, 215, 235, 239
Walcheren Island, 16, 51, 176
Walther, Oberst, 97, 196, 197, 200
War Office, 23, 25-6, 241
Warrack, Col G.M., 210-11, 221, 226-7, 228
Warsaw, 17, 175; 224
Weert, 138
Weigley, Russell, 234
Wesel, 20, 25, 26, 52
West Wall, *see* Siegfried Line
Westerbouwing, 62, 111, 123, 128, 169, 204, 215
Wilhelmina Canal, 74, 80, 81, 97, 113, 114, 131,
136, 145, 163
Willems Canal, 74, 80, 197, 200
Williams, Brig E.T., 43, 47, 184, 239
Williams, Maj-Gen Paul L., 34, 74, 236
Wilmot, Chester, 182-3
Wingate, Maj-Gen O.C., 12-13, 238, 247, 250
Wolfheze, 65, 96, 126-7, 149
Wolfhezerweg, 149
Wolters, Lt-Cdr Arnoldus, 210-11
Wyler, 78, 116, 133, 144, 155

Zuid Willems Canal, 212
Zutphen, 42, 85, 95